D0742282

In Darwin's Wake

REVISITING *BEAGLE*'S SOUTH AMERICAN ANCHORAGES

In Darwin's Wake

REVISITING *BEAGLE*'S SOUTH AMERICAN ANCHORAGES

JOHN CAMPBELL

WATERLINE

For Lana, who happens to be my best friend as well as my wife.

Acknowledgments

I would like to thank the crew, Nick, Chris and Tony the Doc., for their mostly cheerful compatibility, and especially Jeff, who against all odds, managed to keep all the machinery running. I, and all the crew, owe a big thanks to Lana, who had the most difficult job on board, keeping us all fed, which she did admirably.

Also I would like to thank Dennis O'Sullivan, whose timely encouragement stopped the writing project foundering, and to Denny Desoutter, who has helped greatly with all my various writing endeavours.

Last but not least, I would like to thank *The Owner.* After all, he paid for the voyage!

Copyright © 1997 John Campbell

First published in the UK in 1997
by Waterline Books, an imprint of Airlife Publishing Ltd

British Library Cataloguing in Publication Data
A catalogue record for this book
is available from the British Library

ISBN 1 85310 755 7

All rights reserved. No part of this book may be reproduced or transmitted in any form or by any means, electronic or mechanical including photocopying, recording or by any information storage and retrieval system, without permission from the Publisher in writing.

Typeset by Service Filmsetting Ltd, Manchester
Printed and bound in Great Britain by
Biddles Ltd, Guildford and King's Lynn

Waterline Books

an imprint of Airlife Publishing Ltd
101 Longden Road, Shrewsbury SY3 9EB England

Contents

Chapter 1

Because It Is There

I looked out of the hatch. The horizon to the east was beginning to lighten. Dawn would soon be here. Just 9 miles away was the unmistakable shape of Cape Horn, silhouetted against the pre-dawn sky.

It had been a long night. I suppose I had dozed, but every little puff of wind, each whisper of breeze in the rigging, even the noise of the crew changing watch on the even hour had brought me wide awake. I was as nervous as a cat, being anchored for the night within sight of Cape Horn.

The barometer was still high, but as I reached over and gave it a tentative tap on the glass, the pointer edged down towards its more usual position. This spell of good weather would not last much longer. We should not be sitting here waiting to get thrashed, we should be heading up into more sheltered waters before the next gale arrived. In fact, if I had had my way we would not even have stopped for the night. We would have dashed north as soon as we had rounded the Cape, and spent the night in the comparative shelter of Puerto Williams.

But we had not done that. We had stayed the night at Hermite Island for the simple reason that the owner of the boat was snoring away in the after cabin. It is hard to argue with the man who writes the cheques! He had wanted to round the Horn from east to west, which we had done the previous afternoon. Now, after spending the night at Hermite Island, he felt that by sailing back, he could claim a rounding from west to east. Who was I to argue? I was only the captain, he was the owner.

I felt that by lingering there we were thumbing our collective nose at Cape Horn. The longer we stayed, the more likely it became that Cape Horn would flex its metaphorical muscles, and perhaps blow us to eternity.

I went out into the cockpit. Nick, who was on watch, grinned at me with a cheery 'G'day mate'. There was no hiding his Australian origins.

He seemed oblivious to the enormity of the whole thing. He was

7

sheltering from the cool pre-dawn breeze, lurking under the spray dodger, his red woolly hat clamped firmly in place by the earphones of his Walkman, from which he was seldom parted. He was beating a tattoo on his knees in accompaniment to the music I could faintly hear coming from his earphones.

I prised one earphone out far enough for him to hear me. 'Why don't you go and roust the others out. I'd like to head out as soon as it's light.' Let the Boss have his second rounding of Cape Horn, and then we could get north, into sheltered waters sooner rather than later.

As the sky began to get lighter, the clouds took on a more ominous look. The weather was definitely changing, and in that part of the world, it can do that all too quickly.

Too nervous to bother about breakfast, I sat in the cockpit, waiting for the others to get woken up, dressed and fed. Then we could recover our anchors and move out. I could hardly take my eyes off Cape Horn. It was hard to believe that we were really there, anchored barely 9 miles from the most famous, most treacherous headland in the sailors' world.

Lana and I had been working on the boat, *Thalassi*, for almost a year. We had joined it in Spain, and now we had achieved a long-held ambition of mine – we had sailed to Patagonia.

Jeff came into the cockpit for his pre-breakfast cigarette. He was almost a chain-smoker, but was good about not smoking below. He sniffed the breeze, peered at the gathering clouds, and rather unnecessarily said, 'It's going to come on to blow.' Then he huddled down under the spray dodger to light up.

Despite his sometimes pessimistic outlook on life, I thought again how lucky we had been to find him. Jeff was our engineer, and not only had he managed to keep all the mechanical bits and pieces running relatively smoothly, but he had also turned out to be a good shipmate.

The only job more demanding than Jeff's was Lana's. She had to keep the crew fed, and especially in the case of Nick and Chris, the two young deckhands, this was a daunting task. They say that growing gannet chicks eat their own bodyweight in food each day; Nick and Chris seemed to come close to that at times.

The five of us had sailed *Thalassi* down from Spain. We had recently signed on Tony, a young Irish doctor, whom we had found in the Falklands. He had spent the winter in the Antarctic, and joined us to replace Chris, who was scheduled to fly back to reality, from Punta Arenas, in a few days.

Then there was the owner. He has requested anonymity – from

whom, one can only guess. So for the purpose of this narrative, he shall appear as 'the Boss'. Suffice it to say, he is a Spanish hotel owner, made rich by the package tourists who flock to Mallorca. He would join us from time to time, in various places, occasionally with guests. The rest of the time he would be busy at home, taking care of his many business interests, while we moved the boat to the next area that he wanted to visit. Meanwhile there he was, tucked up in his bunk, still snoring.

The Boss's plan was to circumnavigate South America. Lana and I soon realised that we would more or less be following the route that Darwin had taken on the survey ship *Beagle*, 150 years earlier. For us, cruising is more interesting if we have a project or a theme, so we decided to try and share as many anchorages as we could with the ghost of the *Beagle*. Wigwam Cove, in the shadow of Cape Horn, was just one of them. We were following in Darwin's wake.

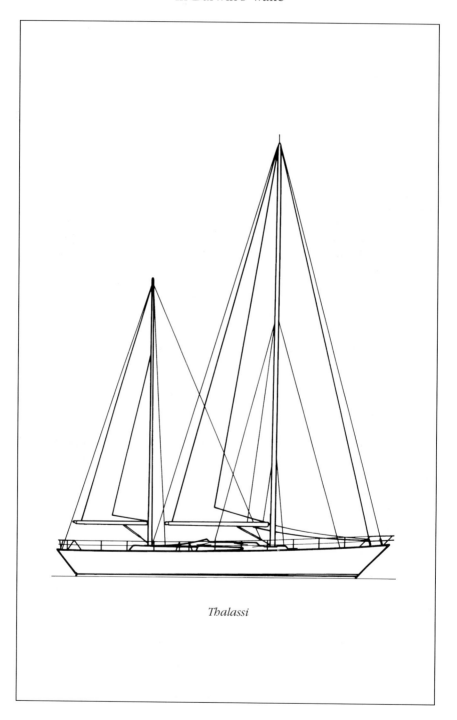

Thalassi

Chapter 2

Preparations

After *Thalassi* had been built in Spain, she had done a double Atlantic crossing, partly as a shakedown and partly so that she could be shown in a couple of American boatshows to advertise the builders. The trip gave her a good shakedown alright, and the crew had arrived back at the builders with a long list of problems. They gave the list to the yard and then promptly left the boat, to go sailing elsewhere.

When Lana and I took over the running of *Thalassi*, we found her in the little Spanish harbour of Calpe. Her 83ft length seemed enormous in the tiny, congested harbour, and her 100ft mainmast towered above every other boat there.

We took over the work list from the previous skipper, and before we had been there a month, we had added almost as many items of our own.

In addition to the work list, we inherited two crew. It is extremely difficult to find five or six people who can live and work together, in close quarters, twenty-four hours a day, seven days a week. Many people see only the glamorous side of the job, and overlook the difficult, strenuous and tedious aspects. The choice of crew can make the difference between a successful, happy voyage, and one that is a chore, when everybody is thankful that it is over.

We were faced now with two crew – Nick, a deckhand, and Tim, the engineer – who had been on board for several months, and had become established in their own routines. They were both late-night people, and it was their habit to disco the night away, and get back to the boat at 4 or 5 a.m. Trying to get them to turn to at 7.30, when the yard started work, was impossible. Yet a lot of the work that needed to be done was in the engine room, and Tim should certainly have been supervising that.

As the days passed, Lana and I realised that Tim thought he could run the boat, and felt he should have been given the skipper's job. Tensions rose. I was determined to do things my way, which basically is to get the work done first, then we can all play.

I tried explaining my views to Nick and Tim, but it had little or no effect. I appealed to the Boss to let me hire my own crew, but he felt that Tim was vital to the whole operation. Finally Lana and I became so frustrated that we went to him with an ultimatum: it was to be Tim or us. We were not going to start a voyage with tensions so high and morale so low. If *Thalassi* could not become a happy ship, then we would rather not sail on her.

Finally the Boss relented. We could fire Tim and hire our own crew. We told Nick he was on a month's probation, and he had to prove himself an asset in that time, or follow in Tim's footsteps.

Nick seemed almost relieved that he no longer had to try to keep up with Tim's drinking and partying, and he enjoyed having a full night's sleep; an average of two or three hours a night had just about worn him out. He began to put in a full day's work, and was cheerful about it.

The day we fired Tim, there was a knock on the hull. It was a young Englishman called Chris. He told us that Tim had said he could come as crew, and he had flown out from England on the strength of that promise. My every instinct told me that we should not take on a legacy from Tim, but poor Chris looked so woebegone when I told him the situation that I took pity on him. He too was hired on a month's probation, and turned out to be quite a good crew.

At last we could concentrate on getting items crossed off the job list. The sooner the list was finished, the sooner we could leave.

To be fair to the builders, many of the items were minor, but we were heading for remote areas where repairs would be difficult, so it was in our interest to ensure that the boat was in the best possible condition. Sometimes it was hard to convince the yard that a particular job was important. All too often, we had to go through a time-consuming process of repeated and complicated explanations through the various bureaucratic layers of the boatyard management. For the most part these were concluded in fractured Spanish. At least, I thought it was Spanish I was learning from the workers, but it turned out that it was Catalan, which is not even as close to Spanish as Dutch is to German.

Nick was becoming as anxious to sail as we were, and began to show a spark of initiative by taking things into his own hands. The yard, in its infinite wisdom, perhaps to save $50 on the $2 million project, had decided to drain the two forward showers using a single pump. One shower served Nick and Chris, while the other was for Lana and myself. Not a major problem, one might suppose. However, whenever Nick or Chris pumped out their shower, such an evil smell came out of ours, that Lana and I had to evacuate our cabin.

We explained the problem to José, our beleaguered project

manager, and requested that they install a second pump, so that each shower could be pumped independently of the other. Instead of just taking our word for it and asking somebody to fit the extra pump, José had to satisfy himself that there was indeed a problem with the system, which it turned out he had designed. He went down on his hands and knees and sniffed our shower drain while the other was pumped out. He must have had some kind of nasal problem, because he swore that he could not smell anything untoward.

Nick was feeling as frustrated as I was, and finally solved the problem as only an Australian could. 'Try one more time, mate,' he said, running water into the other shower. José got back on his knees and Nick crept up close behind him. Drowning the noise with a discrete cough, Nick, who seemed able to do these things to order, made a smell that registered even with José's insensitive nose. The second pump was fitted the next day, but the explanations had already wasted half a day.

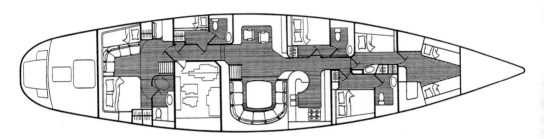

Thalassi – *accommodation plan.*

A much more serious problem occurred with the mast. It just did not seem strong enough. The previous skipper had said they had had trouble with it bending too much. We kept taking the boat out sailing, and tuning and retuning the rig, but to no avail. In the slightest breeze the mast would bend alarmingly. 'Put more tension on,' said the racing pundits. We cranked up on the hydraulic mast jack until there was 60 tons of compression on the mast at rest and went out for a sail; the mast bent worse than ever.

'Too much compression.' said the cruising men, scratching their collective beards. We slackened everything off, but if anything the mast bent more than before. Finally we did what we should have done at the start: we got somebody down from the mast-maker in Holland. Their chief rigger, Hans, arrived, brimming with confidence, expecting to be finished in an hour or two.

He spent four days with us, tweaking the rigging and testing. He fitted two additional stays about two-thirds of the way up the mast and said that was the best he could do. It did not look very much better than before he came. Off the record, he suggested that what was needed was a stronger mast. We all agreed, but we were unable to convince the owner. The mast was to prove a constant source of worry for the next 30,000 miles.

Between these various trials and tribulations, we sailed over to the island of Mallorca for a bit of a shakedown, and to let the Boss show the boat off to his friends. Although we had not missed Tim's presence in the engine room, I knew that we had to find ourselves an engineer as soon as possible. There was a lot of machinery to take care of, and I did not want to have to look after it all myself. There was the main diesel engine of course, and two generators. Then we had a machine for making fresh water from sea water, the refrigeration compressors, the air-conditioning system and the hydraulics. The hydraulic system in itself was very complicated. The sails were hoisted, furled, reefed and trimmed by hydraulic power. The centreboard was raised and lowered by hydraulics. The bow thruster, (a propeller mounted in the bows to help manoeuvre the boat) was also hydraulically operated. All this mechanical help let one or two people sail the boat efficiently, provided it all worked. We needed a good engineer to keep it all in order.

Palma, Mallorca, is a good place to look for crew. There are always people changing boats or looking for something better. We put the word out and were soon inundated with literally dozens of people claiming to be 'qualified marine engineers', whatever that might mean.

What Lana and I were most anxious to avoid was some prima donna who thought he was indispensable. The crew were finally starting to work together so I wanted to find somebody who could fit in and not upset the system. Hopefully they would also be good at maintaining and mending things.

We waded through the list of 'qualified marine engineers' and interviewed at least a dozen candidates without finding anybody Lana and I felt comfortable with. At all costs we wanted to avoid signing on another Tim. We were beginning to feel a bit despondent when we heard about Jeff.

He had not applied for the job, but a friend told us about him and said he was good at fixing things. I tracked him down at the bar which was his contact address and second home. About the first thing he said was, 'I'm not exactly a qualified marine engineer, but I can fix things'. Maybe he was what we were looking for.

He came down to the boat, and Lana and I had a long talk with him. He had an engineering background, and had done a lot of sailing, skippering a boat only a little smaller than *Thalassi* for a number of years. We hired him that afternoon, and never regretted it.

Now that the crew was complete, we decided to declare the boat to be as ready as she was going to get. September, and the beginning of the Austral summer, was upon us. It was time to get down to Patagonia. The Boss was now becoming as anxious as we were for the boat to leave. If we did not go soon, we would have to wait until the following season; we did not want to be poking around Cape Horn in the winter. So we said *adios* to Spain and headed west, towards Gibraltar. The voyage had begun.

*B*eagle's refit did not go any quicker than ours. In fact they were even further behind schedule than we were. It was to be December before they got away, and nobody wants to sail down channel that late in the year if they can help it.

Late or not, the fact that she was going at all was almost entirely due to her captain, a gentleman by the name of Robert Fitzroy.

Some five years previously, in 1826, the Admiralty had sent *Beagle* to South America under the command of Captain Pringle Stokes. They were sent to survey the coast from Rio de Janiero to Cape Horn, then up the Chilean coast to Chiloe. While they were in the deep south, in the Straits of Magellan, Captain Stokes was overcome with 'a fit of melancholy', and committed suicide. The mate sailed the ship back up to their base in Montevideo. The powers that be chose Lieutenant Fitzroy, who was serving on HMS *Ganges*, to take over. They promoted him, and gave him command of the *Beagle*. He was just twenty-three years old, more or less the same age as 'our' Nick and Chris! Hard to imagine.

Had it not been for the demise of Captain Stokes, Fitzroy might never have got command of the ship, and as we shall see, Darwin would probably not have had the chance to make his voyage, and so to propound his theory of evolution.

As soon as Fitzroy took command of the ship, he proved himself to be enthusiastic about the job, as well as very capable. He quickly realised that although the survey work was undoubtedly important, they were missing a huge opportunity to take other scientific observations, just because they had nobody on board who was capable of doing so. He made a vow that if he ever got the chance to command a similar voyage, he would ask the Admiralty to add geological and zoological studies to the ship's task, and to put a scientist on board.

Until such time as he could sail with a scientist on board, Fitzroy was doing his best to record his own, layman's observations. In an attempt to understand the local Fuegans better, he decided to try and educate one. To this end, he bought a teenage boy from his parents, for the princely sum of one pearl button, with the idea of taking him back to England.

While Fitzroy was mulling over his scientific thoughts, the *Beagle* was anchored back down in the Straits of Magellan, off Tierra del Fuego, close to where his predecessor had caught the 'melancholies'. Another series of incidents occurred that was going to affect future events and ensure that Darwin would make his voyage.

Theft by the natives was a continuous problem, and when a whale-boat was stolen from the ship, Fitzroy ordered the crew to capture three Fuegans as hostages, against the return of the boat. So, temporarily at least, they now had four Fuegans aboard. Suddenly a gale blew up. Their anchorage quickly became untenable, and Fitzroy had no choice but to slip his anchor and run before the rising wind.

The plan had been to return at least the three hostages, but the gale drove them out of the Straits, far out to sea. Perhaps it was nearly time to head for home anyway, because Fitzroy decided not to try and beat back into the Straits, but to head for England, taking the four Indians with him. He thought he might try and educate all four of them, in the hope that if he could teach them some English, he might be able to learn a little of their ways. He promised them that he would return them on the next voyage, which he felt certain would be ordered by the Admiralty.

Sadly, one of the Fuegans died from smallpox within days of reaching England, but the others survived, were treated well, and even had tea with the King and Queen. The only fly in the ointment was that Britain was suffering a recession, and cutbacks had been ordered in the Admiralty. All future surveys of South America were cancelled, or at least postponed for the forseeable future.

Now Captain Fitzroy was a gentleman, and in those days a gentleman's word was his bond. He had said he would take the Fuegans back, and take them back he would. He had some money put by, and started to fit out a small ship at his own expense, with the sole purpose of sailing the Indians back home.

Then he had a stroke of luck. A distant uncle, who was in the Admiralty, heard what his nephew was trying to do, and started to pull some strings. Decisions were reversed, and once more Captain

Fitzroy was given command of the *Beagle*, ostensibly to continue the survey of Patagonia, but in fact to let him take the Fuegans home at the taxpayers' expense.

Fitzroy's enthusiasm was not to be underestimated. He took the appointment seriously, and pretty soon *Beagle*'s voyage was becoming a full-blown expedition. True to the promise he had made to himself in the Straits of Magellan, he approached the Hydrographer to authorise the signing on of a civilian scientist.

The Hydrographer was Captain Beaufort, who shortly afterwards became an admiral. We remember him today by his Beaufort Scale, which is still used to describe wind strengths. He listened to Fitzroy's arguments, and eventually agreed; *Beagle* would take a scientist on the voyage.

The fates that brought Charles Darwin to the ship are even stranger than those which put Captain Fitzroy in command. Darwin was only twenty-two years old, and far from qualified technically for such an onerous post as scientific observer to an Admiralty expedition. His grandfather, Erasmus Darwin, would have been more suited, had he still been alive. He had been a well-respected doctor, and had published a number of medical treatises, although his favourite writings were, believe it or not, botanical poems! He not only became wealthy, but also well connected. One of his friends was James Watt, of steam engine fame, but the friend who was to influence the aspect of history in which we are interested was Josiah Wedgwood, the pottery man. The ensuing generations of Darwins and Wedgwoods were to remain fast friends and become connected through marriage.

Erasmus had three children. Charles (our Charles's uncle), Erasmus junior and Robert. Charles was chosen to follow in his father's footsteps and take over the still lucrative medical practice. Unfortunately he died before he even qualified, of blood poisoning contracted when he cut himself while doing a dissection.

Erasmus now turned his attention to Robert, the youngest, and decided that he should become the doctor, even though the sight of blood upset him. Meanwhile Erasmus junior became depressed, perhaps because his father's attention was being lavished on his younger brother, and drowned himself. So Robert became a slightly reluctant doctor, and sole heir to the family fortune and the medical practice.

Robert, whose financial well-being was already assured, married Susannah Wedgwood, who stood to inherit a substantial fortune from her father, Josiah. So young Charles was born to wealthy parents, on 12 February 1809. He had four sisters and a brother.

From a very early age Charles became a collector of things,

especially small animals. The habit was encouraged by his mother, who had known and admired his grandfather. Unfortunately she died when Charles was only eight, and he grew up rather in awe, and perhaps somewhat in fear, of his father. The latter tended to be a little distant with the children, but did sometimes take young Charles on his medical rounds with him, and would often take the trouble to identify animals that they spotted along the way.

Robert assumed that Charles would become the third generation to run the practice, but Charles was not so sure. His aversion to blood was even stronger than his father's. Despite this, he was sent to study medicine at Edinburgh University, but it soon became obvious that he was not applying himself. The realisation that his father would leave him well off and without the need to earn a living, was probably no help to his motivation.

This is where fate once again changed the course of history. Robert finally realised that his son was not going to be the one to continue the family tradition, and decided that the only other respectable occupation for him would be the Church. Charles was sent off to Cambridge University to read theology.

Through friends he made there, he became interested in entomology, or bug hunting as he preferred to call it. Despite the bugs and other distractions, he got his divinity degree, and only needed two years of residence to be ordained. Fortunately for history, he had attracted the attention of two professors, one his maths tutor and the other a teacher of mineralogy. They were friends of Captain Beaufort, who had asked them to suggest a scientist for the *Beagle*. They must have recognised some spark of genius in Darwin because, despite the lack of any technical qualifications, they recommended him for the job.

At first Darwin's father was against his going on the expedition. It took his uncle, Josiah Wedgwood, to help him persuade his father to agree, but eventually Robert gave his somewhat reluctant consent for him to apply for the position.

Darwin travelled to London to be interviewed by Captain Fitzroy, and took an immediate liking to him. But Fitzroy, who studied physiognomy, decided that he did not like the shape of the prominent nose, which for generations had been a Darwin trademark. He and the naturalist would be living in close quarters, and as we had found, Fitzroy knew it would be impossible to live in harmony on a small ship with somebody who did not fit in. His study of physiognomy told him plainly that somebody with such a big nose would be a misfit. He started making excuses, and might have put Darwin off the venture if it had not been for the young man's mounting enthusiasm.

Finally Fitzroy relented. He decided to ignore the nose and hire him for the voyage.

Once the Admiralty had decided that the voyage was to go ahead, they spared little expense to refit the ship. She had a complete new deck laid, and while they were at it Fitzroy had them raise the after deck some 12in. This gave more room below, and increased the freeboard aft to make her drier in a following sea. The bottom of the ship was sheathed with 2in fir planks, which were then covered with copper sheets bedded in felt. This added 15 tons to her displacement, but reduced leaks to a minimum, and the copper sheathing would keep her bottom relatively free from seaweed and barnacles.

Fitzroy knew that much of the survey work would be done from small boats. He asked for seven new ones to be built, and when the Admiralty balked at the cost, he had two of them built at his own expense. Getting them built was not the only problem; it required some ingenuity to stow them all on board the *Beagle*.

The smallest, the Captain's jolly-boat, was carried astern in davits. It became known as the dinghy, and it is thought that this term was

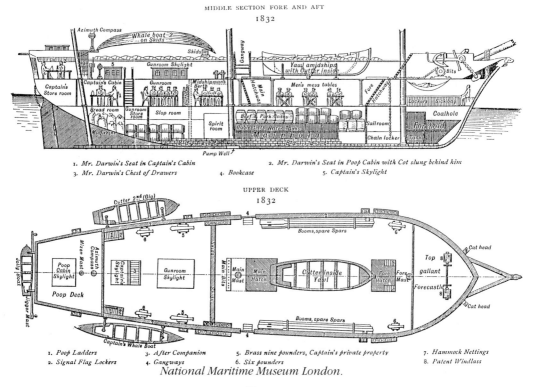

H.M.S. BEAGLE

MIDDLE SECTION FORE AND AFT

1832

1. *Mr. Darwin's Seat in Captain's Cabin*   2. *Mr. Darwin's Seat in Poop Cabin with Cot slung behind him*
3. *Mr. Darwin's Chest of Drawers*   4. *Bookcase*   5. *Captain's Skylight*

UPPER DECK

1832

1. *Poop Ladders*   3. *After Companion*   5. *Brass nine pounders, Captain's private property*   7. *Hammock Nettings*
2. *Signal Flag Lockers*   4. *Gangways*   6. *Six pounders*   8. *Patent Windlass*

National Maritime Museum London.

in fact coined aboard the *Beagle*. The biggest boat was the yawl. It was 28ft long, and it stowed on deck between the fore and main-masts. Stowed inside that was the cutter which, at 25ft, was only a little smaller. Both of these boats were built by the new method of double diagonal planking. The foreman of the Plymouth dockyard, where they were built, was given £300 in recognition of his invention of this building method.

Captain Fitzroy's own two 25ft whale-boats were stowed in skids over the quarterdeck, with a third, similar whale-boat hung in iron davits on the starboard quarter. The last boat was a smaller, lighter cutter, which became known as the gig. It was hung in davits on the port quarter.

Beagle's refit began in July, and it was early September when Darwin saw her for the first time. She was in the Royal Naval Dockyard in Devonport, and he was appalled at what he saw. There were no masts stepped, and she looked more like an old hulk destined for the scrapyard than a Royal Navy ship getting ready for a voyage round the world. Not only did the apparent chaos concern him, but the ship was much smaller than he expected. Indeed at 98ft overall she was only about 15ft longer than *Thalassi*, yet she was going to sail with seventy-four crew. I think she would have seemed small to me too, if we had had a crew of that size.

The crew consisted of thirty-four seamen who, together with six apprentices, would take care of the physical aspects of sailing the ship. Captain Fitzroy and his twenty-four officers would do the organising, and undertake the survey work. Then there were nine supernumeraries, of which Darwin was one. He took along his own servant, as did the Captain. In addition to medical men and a chaplain, they took a ship's artist, whose job it was to record the places they visited. Then there were the three Fuegans whom they were taking home.

Finally there was George Stebbing who was to tend the chronometers. One of the tasks given to the ship was to fix the longitude of the various places they visited accurately. When taking a sun sight with a sextant, it is easy enough to fix one's latitude very accurately, without having to know the time. To measure the longitude, however, one must know the time very accurately. Any small error in time can result in large inaccuracies in the longitude. *Beagle* was to carry twenty-two chronometers, whose rates could be compared. Any obviously inaccurate readings would be discounted. The chronometers were suspended in gimbals in wooden boxes, which in turn were cushioned in 3in of sawdust. Part of Fitzroy's cabin was cleared for the chronometers, which were placed on the centre-line of the ship, and as low down as possible, to reduce the motion to a minimum. Stebbing, who was the son of the watchmaker who had made several of the chronometers, wound them daily at 9 a.m. Once again, Fitzroy took the task very seriously. He was not satisfied with the seventeen chronometers that the Admiralty supplied, so he bought five more with his own money.

Even the best of the chronometers ran at different speeds as the temperature changed, so whenever the ship was in a port whose position was accurately known, the officers took a series of sights. Any discrepancy between their calculated position and the known one had to be due to an error in time, and it was then a simple matter to correct the chronometers for the error. By repeating the exercise over a six-day period, they could see at what rate the chronometers were gaining or losing time at that particular temperature. That correction would be applied each day for the next leg of the voyage.

When they arrived at a port whose position was not known, they repeated the same procedure of daily sights for six days. By comparing the daily differences, they could again calculate the daily error and re-rate the chronometers. By the end of the voyage, after five years, eleven of the chronometers were still running reasonably accurately.

Beagle displaced 240 tons, which is about three times the displacement of *Thalassi*, so *Beagle* obviously had quite a lot more volume than we did. She did not have the benefit of all the hydraulic winches which we had on *Thalassi* (provided Jeff could keep them all running), so she needed the muscle provided by the extra crew. A patent anchor winch was fitted during the refit, and although it was still manually operated, it was much more efficient than the capstan it replaced.

Beagle's sails, all twenty-one of them, were hoisted and trimmed by the 'Armstrong method' – lots of people pulling on ropes. The crew had to go aloft to reef or stow the heavy flax square sails, whereas we could do everything from the deck, mostly with a push of a button.

It was bad enough for us trying to provision *Thalassi*, but for them, trying to stow provisions for seventy-four people for a five-year voyage must have been a nightmare. They did not have the benefit of either refrigeration or canned food as we know it. They did, however, ship some of the newly available preserved food from Kilner and Moorson, a company which was pioneering the preservation of food in sealed glass jars, and which supplied the ship with preserved vegetables, soup and a small amount of meat.

Fresh vegetables such as potatoes, cabbages and onions will keep

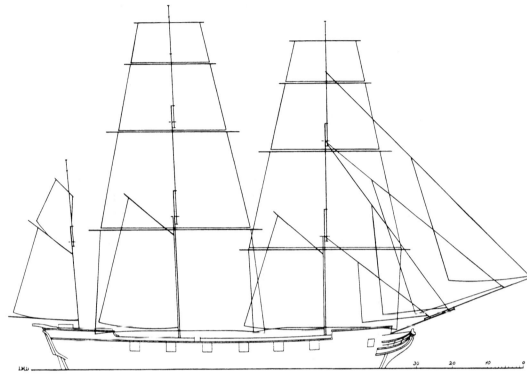

This sailplan of the Beagle *as she was fitted for surveying is based partly on the tables and drawing found in John Edye's* Naval Calculations *of 1832 and partly on contemporary sketches of the* Beagle.

for a month or two. They would therefore be replaced whenever possible, but when they were gone the carbohydrate content of the diet would consist of ship's biscuits. Towards the end of the voyage, these biscuits would have been adding to the protein in their diet – the biscuits always became infested with weevils.

The effects of scurvy were well known at this time, and as antiscorbutics they took along dried apples, pickles and lemon juice. They carried other dried fruit such as raisins and sultanas, but at least for the crew forward of the mast, these would be limited to the weekly 'duff', a kind of suet pudding usually served as a Sunday treat.

Meat was not much easier to store. Salt pork, and to a lesser extent salt beef, stowed in barrels of brine, were the mainstay. The sailors often disparagingly referred to it as 'Salt horse', and they were perhaps nearer the mark more often than they realised. The chandlers who supplied the ship knew that their products would often not be eaten for a year or more, and that it could be as much as three or

four years before a ship would be back. They could be sure, therefore, that the chance of ever receiving a complaint was small.

On such a diet, our crew would have lasted about a day. With
Lana's careful planning, and *Thalassi*'s large coolers and freezers, we
ate a 'normal' diet for the whole trip.

As big a problem as food storage was for the *Beagle*, the supply
of fresh water was even more important. The ship's tanks held 15
tons of water, and although the crew would never miss a chance
to top them up whenever good water was available, fresh water
was on permanent ration. Indeed, water was usually the deciding
factor in how long a vessel could stay at sea, or in a remote location. Even now, on the older charts for many of the remoter areas
of the world which have not yet been superseded by modern
insipid metric charts, we can still see notes saying, 'Good water
here', 'Watering place', 'Sweet spring water' and similar helpful comments. Finding a supply of fresh water was often literally a matter
of life and death.

On *Beagle*, the afterguard, as the officers were termed, had jugs of
water brought to their cabins regularly throughout the day, but the
crew would draw it by the mugful from the 'Scuttlebut', a barrel on
deck. This was filled each day, so consumption could be closely mon-
itored. Sailors would often linger at the scuttlebut and swap news
with other crew members. Even now, we refer to nautical gossip as
scuttlebut.

Little if any fresh water would be wasted on washing. Clothes,
dishes and bodies would all be washed in sea water, unless a timely
rain squall served. This was not too much of a problem in the tropics,
but in Patagonia, with a sea temperature close to freezing, it was a
different matter altogether.

On *Thalassi*, we carried about 3 tons of water, and what with daily
showers, the washing machine and the dishwasher, the five of us
used as much water each day as the seventy-four men on the *Beagle*
did. Despite this profligate use, we never had to carry buckets of
water from nearby streams to top up the tanks, as *Beagle*'s crew did.
All we had to do was hope that Jeff could keep the water maker
running. This machine turns sea water into drinking water at the rate
of about 50 gallons an hour, so we could top up the tanks more or
less at will. Provided we had fuel enough for the generator to run the
water maker, we effectively had an infinite supply of water.

When all the stores and water were finally aboard the *Beagle*, and
Captain Fitzroy deemed the ship ready to go to sea, the supernumer-
aries joined the ship. Darwin moved his gear aboard on 21 November.
They were already more than a month late, yet still more delays held

them up for another three weeks before they finally hoisted the anchor and stood out to sea.

It was by now winter, and they sailed straight into a strong south-westerly gale. Darwin took to his hammock, sicker than he thought it possible to be. *Beagle*, like all square-riggers, could not sail very close to the wind. The best she could manage was about 65 or 70 degrees. *Thalassi* can do some 30 degrees better than that, and because of her efficient keel, she does not make as much leeway (slipping sideways) as the *Beagle* did. The gale blowing up the English Channel effectively stopped the *Beagle* in her tracks.

After a fruitless thirty-six hours, they gave up and ran back into the shelter of Plymouth harbour to wait for the gale to abate.

It finally blew itself out ten days later. A day or two ashore had quickly renewed young Darwin's adventurous spirit, and he was excited when they set sail once more, on 21 December. Unfortunately the excitement was short-lived. An awkward gust caught them aback, and they ran hard aground off Drake's Island, still within the confines of the harbour. By the time she was refloated, the wind was back in the south-west, so Captain Fitzroy elected to spend Christmas at anchor.

The morning of 27 December dawned dull but calm. Indeed, there was no wind at all. While that would have suited us quite nicely, *Thalassi*'s Mercedes diesel being able to push her along at 10 knots if needed, *Beagle* had no engine and could only wait for the wind.

While waiting, Darwin, the Captain and some of the officers lunched ashore on mutton chops and champagne. With a meal like that inside him, it was no wonder that Darwin was again sick when they set off, even though they had a fair wind from the east. The favourable breeze sent them bowling down channel.

Darwin's outlook was not improved the next day when Captain Fitzroy ordered the flogging of the worst of the Christmas drunkards. It was a salutary reminder that they were on a naval vessel and naval discipline would rule.

Despite the inauspicious start, Darwin was excited. They were off to the Canary Islands, and around the world – much more interesting than learning to be a vicar.

Chapter 3

The Voyage Begins

*B*eagle's passage across Biscay was not an easy one. The weather was cold, the skies grey. The wind had dropped a little, but was still quite strong. The ship was very heavily laden, and she rolled and rolled on the big swell left over from the winter gales. It is very tiring just trying to live under these conditions. In a big swell the boat can be rolling 30 or 40 degrees one way then the other, the whole cycle being repeated several times a minute. It is hard to sleep, and difficult to prepare or even eat food. Nothing can be put down without wedging it firmly in place.

Darwin was sick. He mostly stayed in his hammock, but occasionally lay on the sofa in Fitzroy's cabin. If Fitzroy was having second thoughts about the suitability of his naturalist, he did not show it. He was sympathetic, and saw to it that Darwin was always looked after.

Darwin ate little. He found he could not face the shipboard meals at all, and for almost the whole of the first week, all he ate was a few raisins. Not even the sighting of the island of Madeira could entice him from his bunk.

Even though Darwin could not be bothered to get up to see it, the passing of Madeira marked a turning point in the voyage. The bad weather ended, the clouds parted, and the grey skies and seas turned blue. It was *Beagle's* eighth day out from England. Darwin finally ventured out on deck, and found life was not so bad after all. He managed a bite or two of food, and made the first entry in his journal.

Just twenty-four hours later they sighted Tenerife, the biggest of the Canary Islands. As a child, Darwin had read an account of a visit to Tenerife written by the German explorer Baron Alexander von Humboldt (after whom the current in the Pacific is named). Something in the account caught his imagination, and it became his strong ambition to visit the island. Indeed, it was perhaps the promise of that particular landfall that had made him determined to go on the voyage in the first place. *Beagle* sailed south, between Tenerife and Gran Canaria. As the sun rose, and the clouds cleared, Darwin saw the snow-tipped peak of Tenerife's volcano. He was about to live one of his earliest dreams, or so he thought.

Unfortunately, it was not to be. As they anchored off the town of Santa Cruz, they were met by the British Consul. They always say that bad news travels fastest. The Consul told them that reports had been received of an outbreak of cholera in England. The island's officials had therefore decided that all ships arriving from England were to be quarantined for twelve days. Nobody would be allowed ashore during this period, so that they could be sure that none of the crew had cholera.

Despite Darwin's pleas, Fitzroy refused to wait for the twelve days. They were already behind schedule and he was determined to press on south. They were allowed to buy fresh fruit and vegetables, but by nightfall *Beagle* was once more underway, headed south.

As if to tantalise Darwin further, the wind went light, and they were becalmed in sight of the island for the whole of the next day. Darwin could hardly bear to take his eyes off the volcanic peak, until darkness finally blotted it out.

The wind gradually returned that night, and by the following morning, Tenerife was no more than a memory.

By starting from southern Spain, we avoided the cold, ugly thrash down channel that *Beagle* had had to endure. Our first passage was a nice gentle reach westwards to Gibraltar, which let us all find our sea legs in the easiest possible way.

In Gibraltar, our main task was to collect a big box of spare parts which had been sent down from England for us. The easy part was unpacking the extra anchors, rope and various odds and ends. The hard part was finding places to stow them all.

Lana co-opted Nick and Chris to bring back what appeared to be about half the stock of the Safeway supermarket. *Thalassi* was beginning to bulge at the seams.

Jeff showed the same interest in *Thalassi's* fuel tanks that Captain Fitzroy had shown in the *Beagle's* water tanks. Neither of them ever missed an opportunity to fill up. *Thalassi* carries 3 tons of diesel fuel, which of course supplies the main engine, but also runs the generators. The electricity from the generators not only makes the fresh water, but also charges the batteries for lighting and keeps the freezers frozen. Without an ample supply of diesel fuel, life would quickly become almost as basic as aboard the *Beagle*, and nobody wanted that. We were all becoming thoroughly spoilt by *Thalassi's* luxuries!

Once Jeff had topped up the fuel tanks, and Lana had organised the stowing of the last of the provisions, we were ready to head westwards once more.

For a sailing vessel trying to leave the Mediterranean, the Straits of Gibraltar can be a difficult passage. Because of the evaporation from the surface of the enclosed sea, there is almost always a current flowing into the Mediterranean. Moreover, the prevailing wind is from the west. Indeed, the only time it ever seems to blow from the east is when one is trying to sail into the Med!

Fortunately, the west wind was fairly light, so we were able to motorsail against it quite easily. Picking a gap in the endless stream of ships, we dashed across to the African side. We passed a few miles north of Tangier, and before dusk we were clear of the narrow section and the almost constant procession of ships. We were able to set our course towards the Canaries, 600 miles to the south-west. At last we felt that the voyage had begun. The Atlantic Ocean lay ahead.

The Boss was not with us, at least not in the flesh. Sometimes, however, it seemed as if he was there in spirit. Lurking next to the chart table, in a shiny brown plastic case, was a telex machine. Aboard the *Beagle*, they might literally go for years without news from home or fresh orders. On *Thalassi*, we were never out of range of the long arm of the Boss. Via the telex, he could reach us any time he wanted, which was not always an advantage.

Via the ham radio, we were able to speak to our neighbour in Ireland, and to George, who was the Boss's Agent in Britain. Sometimes the miracles of modern communication work to our advantage, but on other occasions it would have been nice to sail in blissful ignorance.

As we cleared the straits, the telex started chattering away. There was a change of plans already. Instead of Tenerife, we were to make Lanzarote our Canary Island landfall. Although Tenerife was the *Beagle*'s first destination, and our usual stopping place in the Canaries, we were happy enough to divert and visit Lanzarote instead. Tenerife has suffered greatly at the hands of the developers, and is perhaps the most commercialised of the islands. Besides, none of us had been to Lanzarote before.

Although he would not be meeting us there, the Boss told us to go to a little bay at the south end of the island called Playa Blanca. He was planning to build a hotel or two there, and he wanted us to show off his boat to his partner, who also happened to be Mayor of the nearby town.

The harbour was tiny; I was sure there would not be room for *Thalassi*'s 83ft, and was all set to anchor out in the bay, when Lana spotted somebody on the quay waving for us to come in. We crept in, and turned round to facilitate our eventual escape. There was not much room to manoeuvre, but *Thalassi*'s bow thruster, known familiarly as the thrutcher, made the turn possible. The thrutcher is close to the bows of the boat, and consists of a propeller on the end of a retractable leg. When the leg is lowered, the propeller is used to push the bows from side to side. It certainly makes life easier when trying to manoeuvre the boat in tight spaces.

There was a group of yachties watching us, with uniformly open mouths, as we wriggled into a space about a foot longer than the boat. Not one of them came to catch our lines; they just stood and watched – not a very friendly reception.

Thalassi *laying alongside in the harbour at Playa Blanca, in Lanzarote.*

All was made clear the next day. We discovered that the Harbour-master, on the instruction of the Mayor, who had got word from the Boss, had moved six yachts to make space for us. They had all thought they were settled in that particular corner of the harbour for the winter and none of them was happy at having to move for our short visit.

Feeling a bit like the Royal Yacht, we duly entertained the Harbour-master, the Mayor and the editor of the local newspaper.

Once we had done our duty, we felt that we had better make the expedition that Darwin might have made had he been there. Lana and I drove up into the interior of the island in a rented car. Even knowing little or nothing about geology, we could see that Lanzarotte is volcanic. The whole island looks pretty much like a great big heap of cinders.

As we drove up into the centre, to the National Park, the cliché of a 'lunar landscape' kept springing to mind. There was mile after mile of black sand and heaps of jagged cinder-like lava, with absolutely nothing growing, for as far as the eye could see.

In the main part of the park, there is a restaurant, built beside a series of hot volcanic vents. One such vent comes to the surface strategically close to the kitchen door. A heavy steel grille has been built over the vent, and an endless supply of steaks and chicken are barbecued on it, courtesy of the hidden volcano.

After the visit to the restaurant, we decided to take a camel ride up the side of one of the volcanos. Perhaps because Lanzarote is so close to Africa, camels have become the accepted beasts of burden on the island. Camels walk differently from horses, and indeed from most other animals. Rather than moving diagonally opposite legs at the same time, they move both legs on one side, then both on the other. We had heard them called 'ships of the desert' before, and I had thought the name just referred to the fact that they could cross ocean-sized tracts of desert. Lana and I rode double on one camel, and as soon as it lurched to its feet, we realised that the name had probably been given for other reasons. The curious lurching gait gave a motion similar to a less than sea-kindly vessel in a rolling swell. By the time we reached the top of the volcano, we were both a little green around the gills, and feeling decidedly camel-sick.

Perhaps of more interest to Darwin would have been the vineyards a little further north. Grapes are grown, under seemingly impossible conditions, for a locally produced wine. No ordinary grapevine could survive for long on the dry, windswept slopes of the mountains, but over the years the islanders have developed a special plant, and a unique technique for growing the grapes.

The grape vines which are grafted onto cactus roots to enable them to grow in the very dry climate. In this instance, man has modified Darwin's Law of Evolution, to allow a plant to survive where it could not do naturally. The stone walls shelter the plants from the incessant wind.

For each plant, a hollow is dug into the volcanic ash, and any stones or lava are heaped up in a horseshoe shape on the windward side. This gives the growing plant a little shelter from the almost perpetual wind. In the centre of each hollow, they then plant a cactus, which is allowed to grow until it is well established. Once it is well rooted, they cut it off just above ground level, and graft on the grapevine. The vine is not supported in any way, but allowed to grow on the ground, up the sides of the hollow. Rain is rare on Lanzarote, but this hybrid plant is able to absorb enough moisture from the dew not only to survive, but to flourish and produce grapes.

It was of course later in his voyage that Darwin first developed his theories of natural selection, whereby plants and animals change to adapt to certain conditions, but here was a case where man was helping nature develop a unique plant for a specific environment.

By chance we stumbled across another curious crop that the people of Lanzarote cultivate. We saw several small fields of cacti growing, and assumed that they were there to provide root stock for further generations of vines. We were wrong. It turned out that they were prickly pear cacti being grown because they were the favourite food of the cochineal beatle.

Somewhere in the dim recesses of my mind, I knew that the food colouring cochineal came from squashed beetles, but I had never stopped to wonder where those beetles came from. Now we knew. Cochineal beetles are an important export from Lanzarote, even in this day of artificial colourings and 'E' numbers'.

As usual, before we left, Lana visited the local market to load up with fresh fruit and vegetables, and Jeff had managed to persuade the driver of a little fuel truck to come down to the dock to top up the fuel tanks. We had entertained the Boss's friends, done a little exploring, and now we were ready to follow the *Beagle* south. The Cape Verde Islands lay ahead.

Chapter 4

To the Cape Verdes

As we left the Canaries behind us, the wind was fair and the weather became warmer by the day. Chris began to work seriously on his suntan, and despite his shipmates casting doubts on his masculinity, he tried to bleach his hair in the sun, using the juice of lemons filched from Lana's galley.

The days passed easily enough for all of us except Nick, who was getting low on cigarettes. He and Jeff were the only smokers. Jeff was a fifty-a-day man, and in Gibraltar he had filled every spare inch of his cabin with cartons of duty-free cigarettes. He reckoned he had enough to last him as far as Brazil, and was quite rightly reluctant to give any to Nick, just because Nick had not bothered to stock up. At first Nick was philosophical about it, saying that he wanted to give up smoking anyway. But as the days passed, he became more and more fidgety and less the happy-go-lucky, easy-going Nick that we knew.

As we approached the Cape Verde Islands, the visibility steadily became worse. Eventually it was down to a couple of miles. It was not foggy or misty; the air was very dry. What was reducing the visibility was dust in the air, and indeed a fine red dust was beginning to settle all over the boat.

The poor visibility was no real problem for us, as the satellite navigator was ticking away, updating our position regularly, and the radar did not even know that there was a haze; it could still see everything around us for 30 miles or more. But there was not much for us to see from on deck.

We closed the north eastern-most island, Sal, in the late afternoon, and sailed gently down the west coast as the sun set. A developer's potential paradise, the island looks to be composed of a series of sand dunes fringed with virgin white sand beaches.

There was just the occasional house and one small village, but we did not see any particularly inviting anchorages, so I decided to sail on through the night and go to Brava, which I knew has a well protected bay on its south side.

We sailed gently through the night, passing to the north of Santiago, to make a picture-book landfall at dawn, off the island of Fogo. This island is an almost perfectly conical volcano, rising straight out of the sea. At dawn, the whole island was visible, but as soon as the sun began to rise, clouds formed at the peak. As the sun got higher, the clouds worked their way steadily down the mountain. By breakfast time they had enshrouded at least half the island.

The last of the breeze vanished with the dawn, so we motored the remaining few miles towards Brava, the south western-most island in the group. Lana spotted a small boat, perhaps half a mile off the shore. Through the binoculars we could see that the three crew members were all waving furiously. Thinking that they might have broken down and be in danger of drifting out to sea, we motored over to them. It transpired that they were fishermen with a large catch of lobsters, and they were hoping for a bit of early-morning business.

Communication presented a bit of a problem. While it was obvious that they were trying to sell lobsters to us, we had difficulty explaining that we did not even know what their local currency was, nor did we have any of it. We showed them the bundle of pesetas that we had left over from the Canaries. They realised it was money, but had never seen anything like it before. They seemed happy enough to give us two buckets of lobsters in exchange for a bundle of the mysterious notes, and were all set to pass up a third bucketful before the cook called a halt. I hope they were not disappointed when they managed to change the pesetas.

As we motored round the corner into Blacksmith's Bay, we were met by a flotilla of six more fishing boats. They did not try to sell us anything, they were just curious. It must be rare enough for a yacht to come into their bay. Even after the anchor was down, the boats continued to circle around us, just looking, for the most part smiling, and occasionally waving.

Perched up on the cliff, high above the bay, was a small village of about half a dozen houses. Perhaps this was how Darwin saw Praia. Certainly few changes can have occurred here, in this little bay, in the last 150 years. There was still no electricity nor running water, and little contact with the rest of the island, let alone the outside world.

The Boss had already informed us of his anticipated arrival date in Brazil, still some 1400 miles away. Since we were supposed to be there for his arrival, we did not have much time to spare. We would only be able to spend the day in Brava, and then we would have to leave that night to stay on schedule.

By anchoring in such a secluded bay, I must confess, we had hoped to avoid any contact with officialdom. Normally we play strictly by the rules, but on this occasion, with our stop being only for eight or nine hours, I had decided, mainly to save time, to take a chance and not clear with the authorities in the main town of Faja, on the north side of the island.

We were just getting ready to put our dinghy over the side when we saw one of the small boats heading our way rather purposefully. An older man was sitting in the stern sheets, and two youths were rowing him directly towards us. Sure enough, they came alongside.

My heart sank when I realised that he was telling us that he represented officialdom. I could do nothing but invite him aboard. They seemed to understand our Spanish without difficulty, but there was little in their Portuguese reply that was intelligible to us. However, we did understand that he wanted to make a note of the ship's particulars, although it turned out that he had neither pen nor paper.

Lana presented him with a notebook and ballpoint pen, and told him that he could keep them both. He was so pleased with them that he forgot to write anything down. We gave him and each of his muscular rowers a can of Coke to drink. None of them knew how to open the cans. Perhaps it was the first time they had seen drinks in cans, although they all recognised the Coca Cola symbol, so knew what was in the can.

Formalities completed, cans of drink safely opened, there were smiles all round. We felt it was safe enough to go ashore. Jeff offered to stay aboard to keep an eye on the boat; he wanted to check over everything in the engine room ready for the crossing to Brazil. It was much easier for him to work in the engine room while we were anchored in the shelter of the bay, rather than rolling about in mid-Atlantic. Lana said she would stay as well. The lobsters were taking it in turns to climb out of the buckets, so she decided to quieten them down by cooking them.

So it was the three of us, Nick, Chris and I, who set off ashore. We decided to walk up to the village overlooking the bay, with Nick hoping to find a village shop that stocked his brand of cigarettes.

As soon as we got ashore, it seemed as if every child for miles around came to follow us up the track. There were dozens of them – far more, we thought, than the few houses in the village could possibly accommodate. So, feeling more like the Pied Piper than Charles Darwin, I led the procession up the steep path to the village.

When we finally panted our way to the top of the path, we found several people who had obviously been watching our trek up the hill. They were sitting on a bench in the shade of the single tree which was growing in front of the cluster of houses. 'Where d'you reckon the supermarket is then?' asked Nick. It did not look too promising

Looking down from the village, at Thalassi *anchored in Blacksmith's Bay.*

for much in the way of shopping. The houses were little more than shacks, and none of them looked like a shop.

Nods and smiles were exchanged with the row of watchers. Between the three of us, we discussed whether we should attack the next section of path, which vanished up the mountain. It looked even steeper than the one we had just struggled up. Nick, never one for unnecessary exercise, was for once eager to try, in case we might be able to find a cigarette shop. Chris and I were less enthusiastic. We were still debating what to do when a young man stood up, walked over and introduced himself. To our ears, his name was totally unpronounceable, and it sounded different each time we got him to repeat it. The closest we could get was 'Himself', so Himself he became for the duration of our visit.

By dint of some fractured Spanish, a lot of sign language and a few drawings in the dust, we understood that Himself was offering to take us to the valley where the villagers grew their food.

He led us along a narrow rocky track over the escarpment to the east. We crested a ridge, and suddenly the valley was there in front of us; a splash of brilliant green among the dusty, barren red hills that made up most of the island. As we walked down the side of the valley, Himself showed us a large stone cistern, brimming full of water. This, he explained, was where they got their drinking water, and then, as if to prove how good the water was, he peeled off his shirt and jumped in. He beckoned us to join him, and I must admit it looked tempting, but we wondered how the village elders might feel if they found three very sweaty yachties frolicking in their drinking water. We declined as graciously as we could.

We were very curious, however, about the source of the water. It was obvious from the parched countryside that it rarely if ever rained, and yet in this little valley, they had water apparently to spare.

Once we could get Himself out of the water tank, he gave us the answer, or at least a part of it. He took us past the rocky outcrop against which the big stone tank nestled, and showed us the beginning, or I suppose more technically the end, of a long, intricate series of stone aqueducts.

We could see the network of supporting stone walls zigzagging its way up the mountain, at least a couple of miles from the valley. Offshoots went down into the valley itself, while one branch ensured that the cistern remained full. There was not a lot of water coming down the stone channel, but there was at least a steady trickle. The clouds which were gathered round the tops of the mountains suggested that there would always be water up there, even if it never rained down where we were.

We wanted to know who had undertaken this immense engineering project. Clearly it would have been beyond the scope of the few villagers who lived there. We asked Himself who had built the aqueducts. His reply was puzzling, and a little disturbing. Nobody had built them, he said, and he was adamant on this point. Nobody had built them, they had always been there. It was an enigma for somebody with a better grasp of the Portuguese language to solve.

He showed us an ancient grindstone, where the villagers crushed sugar cane. The cane juice was used to brew the local hooch. When he asked us if we would like something to drink, I feared that he was about to produce some of the home brew. The boys said yes, they

(Opposite) Nick walking along one of the mystery aquaducts on Brava. Our guide, 'Himself', insisted that nobody had built them, they had always been there.

were thirsty, and I had visions of them becoming blind or going mad through drinking the local grog.

I was much relieved when our man nipped up the nearest palm tree and cut a young coconut for each of us. Once he was safely back on terra firma, Himself cut the top off each nut, and we gratefully drank the surprisingly cool milk. It was sweet and refreshing and, more to the point, would not make the boys go blind!

The expedition was deemed complete, and Himself led us back down through the village. He vanished momentarily inside a house, to reappear clutching three eggs. He gave one to each of us. We asked if they were cooked, but he said they were not, they had just been laid. Each of us solemnly carrying an egg, we walked back down to the beach.

We took our guide out to the boat, together with two of his young friends. How could we repay them? All we could think of was a can of Coke each, and a packet of biscuits. Then Chris had a bright idea, and produced a couple of old T-shirts. It was little enough to repay their generosity when they had so little, and we appeared to have so much.

As the sun began to set, we could see a group of people gathering beneath the tree. Motoring out of the bay, I blew the horn in salute to our audience.

We made sail as darkness fell with tropical rapidity. As we looked back towards the bay, there was not a single glimmer of light to be seen. There was not even a moon to silhouette the island, and the perpetual dusty haze hid the stars. It was as black as the inside of a cow. Only the radar told us that the island, and no doubt the people of Blacksmith's Bay, were still there. As each of us took a piece of the three-egg omelette that Lana had made, we drank a toast to them.

Aboard the *Beagle*, things were continuing to look up. They too had a fair wind and warmer weather. Darwin began to take more of an interest in his studies as his sea legs developed. He made a bag to tow behind the ship, in order to collect plankton. When he examined his catch under the microscope, he saw a bewildering array of tiny plants and animals of every conceivable shape and form. In his journal he expressed 'an unhappy wonder at so much beauty for, it seems, so little purpose'.

Like us, Darwin read a lot on passage. I am afraid that at sea our reading is mainly limited to 'airport' novels. Most of the time we find it difficult to concentrate on anything more erudite when sailing. We did have our moments though. There was a full set of Encyclopaedia Britannica on board, and that was used almost every day to settle an argument, or to start another. Chris was especially good at checking facts and figures, and it got to the point when one could hardly make any statement at all without every nuance being verified by Chris.

Darwin spent a lot of time reading a recently published tome on geology. Much of what it said went against the current religious dogma relating to the age of the earth. The author of the book was convinced that the world was much older than the Bible would allow.

As they approached the islands, the visibility was about as bad as we were experiencing. However, they were without any of the modern electronics that made navigation so easy for us. Fitzroy had only his sextant and a compass to work with, so their exact position was often a little uncertain.

The persistent haze made star sights impossible and sun sights difficult. To take a sextant sight of the sun, or indeed any heavenly body, as the stars and planets are quaintly called, one has to be able to see the horizon. One trick when taking sights in reduced visibility is to get low down, as close to the water as possible. This has the effect of bringing one's horizon closer, hopefully within the limits of the visibility. Captain Fitzroy took sights whenever he was able, and breathed a small sigh of relief when the first land eventually appeared through the haze.

Darwin noticed the same red dust landing on the decks as we had, but instead of cursing it for making more clean-up work, he carefully swept up samples and examined them under his microscope.

We had assumed that it was dust blowing out from the Sahara Desert. After all, the easterly trade winds were always blowing over the desert and out to sea, and deserts must be dusty old places.

We were almost correct, but not quite. Darwin described the dust as being composed of 'Infusoria, with siliceous shields'. Our dictionary says that 'Infusoria' are 'a group of protozoans frequently developed in infusions of decaying matter and stagnant water'. So what we had dismissed as dust was actually lots of little one-celled animals which had come from stagnant water. Stagnant water in the desert?

By the time he had sifted through his various samples of dust, Darwin had identified sixty-seven types of protozoa, including flagellates, amoebas and ciliates. We had guessed that the wind had carried them over the 300 miles from the mainland, so it was not too surprising that he found that all but two were fresh rather than seawater species.

The big surprise came later, when he got back to England and identified some that he was having trouble with. He found that two species were not to be found in Africa at all. They were unique to South America. Had some of the red dust which landed on the *Beagle*, and even now was being crunched underfoot on *Thalassi's* deck, originated in South America? If so, the trade winds had carried the little animals almost three-quarters of the way round the world before dropping them on us.

In 1832, the Cape Verde Islands were a Portuguese colony, inhabited by a few hardy settlers from West Africa and from Portugal itself. In the 1970s, when colonialism was becoming a dirty word, the islands achieved a quasi-independence. When Portuguese Guinea broke away from Portugal to become Guinea Bissau, the islands were lumped in with them, to be ruled by the same political party.

That state of affairs did not last long. By the time we arrived, they had been a completely independent country for five years, largely supported, it seems, by the many Cape Verdians who have emigrated to the north-eastern USA.

Beagle sailed into the port of Praia, on the island of Santiago, which is now the country's capital. The total population of the Cape Verde Islands is about 350,000, and almost half of that number live on the island of Santiago. Praia, which Darwin describes as a small village, now has in excess of 60,000 inhabitants.

He describes Puerto Praia as having a desolate aspect, saying that volcanic activity and the searing sun had rendered much of the soil unfit for cultivation. However, he was still interested to get ashore, to start his field work, and put his new-found geological knowledge to the test. After so long at sea, it was exciting to be walking through a strange land, and to stroll through his first grove of coconut trees was an added thrill.

He remarked that compared with the English countryside, the landscape looked sterile. Indeed, there was almost nothing green to be seen growing on the lava plains, yet there were goats and a few cattle that seemed able to survive. When he asked some of the settlers about this, he was told that, on average, it rained there but once or twice a year. But when it does rain, the vegetation springs up quickly, much of it literally growing up overnight. It soon dies down again in the hot sun, but it forms a natural hay for the animals to eat, and survive on until the next time it rains.

Darwin was able to make a couple of expeditions with Rowlett, the purser, and Byrne, the assistant surgeon, who both shared his interest in exploration. One day they rode over to Ribera Grande, a village to the east. There they found the remains of a large stone fort, and a big cathedral. They had been built when the adjacent bay was the main anchorage for the ships visiting the island. Now, for some reason, the bay had become silted and too shallow for ships to enter. The town had been more or less abandoned, and everybody moved lock stock and barrel to Praia, where the anchorage was still deep.

Another day they crossed the central plain to a little village called St Domingo. On the plain itself, Darwin was intrigued by the stunted acacia trees growing there. Every one was leaning to the south-west, sculpted by the incessant wind. The village, they found, was in a small valley, which was fed by a little stream. The whole valley was a veritable oasis. Fruits, vegetables and plants of all descriptions were growing in profusion there, in stark contrast to the rest of the island.

There was so much for him to see, and he wanted to see it all. Everything was very different from what he was used to in England, and every new sight stimulated new thoughts.

While at Praia, he did a little marine biology, scouring the rock pools at low tide. He found some sea slugs and watched octopuses change colour as he teased them, but it was geology that really drew his attention.

He decided to try and draw a map of the geological structure of the whole island. One day, while working on his map, he took a rest at the foot of a low lava cliff. He was marvelling at the sun, the bright coral reef and the tropical plants, when he had a sudden vision of where his life's work might lead. He began by thinking that instead of just recording everything for the Admiralty, perhaps he should try and write a book comparing the geological aspects of the various lands he was about to visit. Then it occurred to him that he should include his other studies. He was already finding that his books on tropical flora and fauna were woefully inadequate. Maybe he could add to and improve on them. So really it was here, sitting on the water's edge in the Cape Verdes, that the seeds were sown for *The Origin of Species*, which was to make him famous.

Chapter 5

St Peter and St Paul Rocks

*B*eagle left the Cape Verdes, and set off across the Atlantic towards the north-east corner of Brazil. Their course took them close to the St Peter and St Paul Rocks, so naturally Darwin was anxious to stop and visit them.

The rocks – they can hardly be called islands – are just over 50 miles north of the Equator and 540 miles off the coast of Brazil, to whom they nominally belong. They stick up only about 50ft above the sea, and there is deep water close up to them. It was not going to be an easy landfall for Captain Fitzroy to make.

Almost as soon as they left the Cape Verdes, Darwin became seasick once again. A couple of days out, they met a north-bound packet-ship called the *Lyra*. Captain Fitzroy ordered the *Beagle* hove to so that he could stop and talk to the other captain. The *Lyra* stopped and *Beagle's* gig was launched to take Captain Fitzroy over for a visit.

The *Lyra* was bound for England, and offered to take mail for them. Despite feeling wretched with seasickness, Darwin wrote a hasty letter to his father. He was surprisingly enthusiastic, and said that he was 'Unreservedly glad that he had not missed the opportunity of the century'. He intimated, even at this early stage, that he might be able to do some original work in some branch of natural history.

Underway once more, Darwin began to settle into the shipboard routine, and despite the lethargy caused by the seasickness, he kept busy sorting his collections and writing his notes. He began to enjoy the imposed regularity of the ship's routine, and he got on well with the officers. They nicknamed him the Flycatcher, and despite the fact that he was younger than all of them, just twenty three-years old, they often referred to him as the Dear Old Philosopher.

As they neared the rocks, Captain Fitzroy grew more and more nervous. He took sights of the stars at dawn and dusk, and at least three sights of the sun by day. His star sights at dawn on their eighth day out, put him a scant 15 miles off the rocks. They sailed cautiously onwards, and as soon as the sun rose, the mast-head lookout spotted the rocks to the south, gleaming white in the early light.

Landfall at St Peter and St Paul Rocks. Our electronic navigation aids made our landfall easy. Captain Fitzroy must have been very nervous of approaching these tiny rocks, in the middle of the ocean, with only his celestial navigation to guide him.

They hove to near to the rocks, and put a boat over the side. It is far too deep to anchor, even very close to the rocks, so the ship stood off, and one of the whale-boats took Darwin and a few of the officers ashore. They landed in the little bay between the two islands, which is rather hopefully marked on the Admiralty chart as an anchorage.

Darwin scrambled ashore and set to work. Part of his interest in the rocks was their actual structure. With his new-found geological knowledge, he discovered that they were composed of two types of rock, chert and feldspar. He realised that this was unusual, since all the other offshore, remote islands in the world, with the exception of the Seychelles in the Indian Ocean, are composed of either coral or volcanic matter. With his chipping hammer he knocked off a few pieces of rock to add to his collection.

He was also fascinated by the white coating that covered much of the rock. He found that it was very hard – hard enough in fact to scratch glass. The coating was about ⅒in thick, and consisted of many thin layers. He decided that it was probably formed by the action of rain and salt spray on the accumulated bird droppings. What intrigued him was the similarity of this coating to the mother of pearl

which lines living shells. It was almost as if the rock itself was alive and secreting the covering.

Darwin found that there are only two types of bird living on the rocks. The bigger is the booby, a type of gannet. Much smaller is the little noddy tern. Both birds are very prolific. The booby does not bother to build a nest, it just lays its eggs on the bare rock. The little terns, however, build quite intricate nests. They use the only materials available to them – seaweed and their own droppings.

In his journal, Darwin enumerates the spiders and other insects that he found there, including a woodlouse that lives beneath the guano. When we landed there, however, we were not about to pick through the bird droppings to see whether the lice were still there.

The only other fauna are the many bright red crabs and flora is non existent. Other than seaweed in the tidal zone, there are no living plants on the rocks, not even a lichen.

While Darwin was ashore, listing the species for scientific posterity, many of the crew were off in the boats also looking for fauna, but of the edible variety. All around the rocks they found the fishing to be good, although they sometimes had difficulty landing hooked fish before they were stolen by sharks. Nevertheless, enough was caught for all the crew to enjoy a meal of fresh fish. This made a welcome change from the normal diet of salted and dried food. The leftovers were hung in the rigging, to be dried for later use.

Late in the afternoon Darwin was summoned from his labours. Captain Fitzroy was anxious to get clear of the rocks before the dark. The boats were hoisted on board, sails loosened and a course set for the Equator, which they crossed early the next morning.

There is a strong tradition amongst most seafarers that people crossing the Equator for the first time (called pollywogs) are initiated by King Neptune (a seasoned sailor in disguise). After a suitable ceremony, usually involving some kind of penance, they are promoted to the rank of shellback. Surprisingly, Darwin makes no mention in his journal of being initiated, and in his account Captain Fiztroy rather disdainfully dismisses the ceremony as 'one to divert the childish minds of the men'. But *Thalassi*'s crew was not going to get off as lightly as Darwin – they were going to suffer thoroughly at the hands of the childishly-minded skipper.

(Opposite) The birds nesting on the rocks have little in the way of raw materials to construct their nests – just a few bits of seaweed and their own droppings.

Our course from the Cape Verdes towards Brazil was nearer
south than west. I do not think any of us had realised quite
how far east the continent of South America lies. Indeed, it
was only when Chris dug out the atlas that we could see that almost
the whole of South America is further east than most of the east coast
of North America. Since we were aiming for the easternmost bulge of
the continent, we had very little westing to make.

It felt a little odd to be crossing the Atlantic by sailing south, but at
least this course gave us fairly comfortable sailing on a broad reach
across the trade winds, rather than a roly-poly downwind run. The
Cape Verdes were quickly left far astern.

Unfortunately we soon ran out of the trade winds, into the area of
fluky winds known as the doldrums. We had plenty of fuel, however,
and the engine kept us right on schedule, averaging about 170 miles
a day.

The fishing was good – we caught two large dorado and a wahoo.
Lana cooked them all, and after the fourth consecutive meal of fish,
the crew unanimously agreed to stop fishing.

Each of us found different ways to help pass the time. Lana did
some sketching. Jeff got his sextant out and took at least three sights
a day for practice. Chris worked hard on his suntan and hair bleach-
ing, while Nick grew grumpier by the day now that his cigarettes
were but a distant memory.

Our landfall on St Peter and St Paul Rocks were easy enough – in
fact it was a little anti-climactic. Jeff's sights and the satellite navigator both told us that we were getting close, and they appeared as two
little green blips on the radar when they were still over 30 miles away
– no anxiously peering lookout at the mast-head for us.

If finding them was almost too easy, getting ashore certainly was
not. Although the wind had been light for several days, there was
quite a big swell running. The rocks were not big enough to give us
much shelter, and *Thalassi* was rolling heavily.

Thalassi has two boats on deck: 16ft hard-bottomed inflatable with
a 40-horsepower outboard, and a smaller, but almost as heavy, fibreglass pulling boat. We tried to put the inflatable over. In calm water
it is easy enough, lifting it over the rail with the mizzen staysail
halyard on a hydraulic winch. But with *Thalassi* rolling it was a different matter. As soon as we lifted the dinghy clear of its chocks, despite
everybody hanging on to it, it started crashing from side to side.
Somebody was going to get hurt.

Hastily we dropped it back onto the deck and lashed it down again.
What to do next? The pulling boat was almost as heavy, and it would
probably not be much easier to handle. Should we abandon the

project, and sail on for Brazil?

Jeff was all for pressing on. Nick was by now desperate for cigarettes and was eager to get to the mainland. Lana did not want the skipper to leave the boat in mid-Atlantic. Only Chris shared my enthusiasm to try and land on the rocks.

We decided to swim in. Jeff was well able to handle *Thalassi*. He would take her in near to the rocks, drop us off for the swim in, then stand by at a safe distance. When he saw us getting ready to come back, he would bring *Thalassi* back in close, to save us having to swim too far. Lana thought we were mad, and retreated to the galley.

Chris and I both put on diving fins to help with the swim, and as Jeff brought *Thalassi* to a stop, about 75yd from the rocks, we jumped off the stern. Despite being so close to the rocks, the depth sounder said the water was over 500ft deep. It was a dark inky blue. Although neither of us would admit it to the other, I think we were both a bit worried about swimming in such deep water. It is entirely irrational, since once one is out of one's depth, it is academic whether it is by 1ft or several hundred. Despite knowing this, and trying hard to rationalise it, I swam as fast as I could to get to the rocks, and Chris was going even faster than me.

About halfway there, a large and excessively curious booby tried to land on Chris's head. The bird had probably never seen a human head swimming off its rock before, and had decided to investigate. Between giggles I told Chris that I thought it was attracted to the lemon juice he was still using to bleach his hair 'beach-bum blond'.

At first Chris was amused, but after the second or third aborted landing, he began to get annoyed. Finally I think the big bird frightened him, because his stroke rate almost doubled, and he beat me to the rock with some 20yd to spare.

Having reached the nearest rock – we were not sure whether it was St Peter or St Paul – we found that landing was not going to be easy. Although we were on the lee side, the swell was breaking on the rocks, and the water was rising and dropping 4 or 5ft every few seconds, with each wave. After a quick discussion we decided the thing to do was to take our fins off, so that once we did gain terra firma, we could scramble up the rocks unimpeded. We threw the fins ashore, above the wave line. Now we were committed to landing, if only to recover the fins.

Chris went first, and timed it to perfection. He grabbed hold of a rock as a wave lifted him high, and as the water fell away, scrambled nimbly ashore. I did not manage it quite so gracefully. As I crawled up the rocks I made a Darwinian observation. He had noted that the pearly white concretion on the rocks was hard enough to scratch glass. I discovered that it was also well able to cut knees. As a corollary to this observation, I later found that these cuts took over two months to heal. Whatever the white stuff is, not only is it hard, but it is also powerful.

Notwithstanding the slight loss of blood, I followed Chris up to the summit of the rock. The birds were going crazy. There were hundreds, maybe thousands, of them swooping low over us, all wanting to take a look at these strange creatures that had emerged from the sea.

We found the bird-dropping nests, but did not dig into them to see if the woodlice were still living there. There were also crabs by the million. Everywhere we looked there were these bright red creatures scuttling to and fro across the rocks. Indeed, close to the water's edge, it was hard to walk without treading on them, there were so many.

From our perch on the top of the northernmost rock, we could look down into the so-called anchorage. It was a veritable cauldron from the swell that day. We realised that even if we had been able to launch the inflatable, we would have been hard pressed to get ashore without swimming the last bit. It must have been exceptionally calm for Darwin's visit if they were able to step dry-shod from the whaleboat.

Looking across at the other rock, we could see the tangled, rusted remains of what looked like a light tower. In bad weather, waves must have washed right over the rocks, taking everything, including the bird-dropping nests and most of the light tower with them. The birds, with an infinite supply of building materials, had rebuilt their nests, but it did not look as if anybody had been near the tower for several years.

Feeling well satisfied that we had accomplished our mission, we waved at the distant Jeff to bring *Thalassi* closer and made our way down the rocks ready for the swim back to the boat.

It was only once we were back on board, and reread Darwin's account, in which he mentioned the numerous sharks, that we thought that perhaps we had been a little rash, especially as both my knees were leaving a steady stream of blood behind us on the swim back to the boat.

I was determined that our crew of pollywogs would be properly initiated at the Equator, and I spent most of my night watch making up a King Neptune costume, which actually turned out rather more like Father Time.

Having broken the watch schedule while we messed about at St Peter and St Paul Rocks, I decided to move the Equator 93 miles south, so that we could cross it at 'happy hour', just before supper,

The Author ashore on St Paul Rock. The birds were very interested in us – they don't get many visitors.

rather than at 5.30 a.m.

Nick was on watch for the geographical crossing just before dawn. He took a series of photographs of the satellite navigator counting the latitude down to zero, and finally clicking over to south. Although he still had no cigarettes, he was a little more cheerful to be back in 'his' hemisphere.

For the ceremonial crossing later that day, I had to be a little circumspect, since I was the only shellback and so was outnumbered four to one.

Once King Neptune appeared, clad in his Father Time disguise, the first thing he did was to co-opt a queen. Since Lana was the only candidate, and following the maxim of never upsetting the cook, she got the mildest of initiations. She was made to promise not to cook any more of the King's fishy subjects, and 'tattooed' with 'save the fish'

49

slogans in marker pen. After taking the solemn oath, she became a shellback, and Neptune's Queen. That evened the numbers a little.

We decided to set about Jeff first. King Neptune accused him of being a perpetually oily engineer who left cigarette ash everywhere. Both accusations were patently false, as Jeff was always clean and tidy in his work, but mere facts were not going to stop the King. After being made to promise to do better, he was anointed with an evil mixture of olive oil and cigarette ash. A good squirt of aerosol shaving soap completed the job; Jeff was now a shellback and could help us with the boys, who were both looking a little apprehensive by this time.

Nick was next. I had been trying to persuade him to let Lana cut his long and straggly hair before our landfall in Brazil. I wanted to arrive with a smart-looking crew, not a bunch of hippies. He had steadfastly refused, so King Neptune took matters, and a large pair of scissors, into his own hands. Nick got the shortest haircut he had ever had. By the time the Queen had tidied up the King's enthusiastic work, he no longer looked like a hippy, more like a bottle brush.

That left Chris as the last pollywog. He was actually shaking, perhaps more in anticipation than fear. The King told him that putting lemon juice on his hair was not a very macho, salty thing to do, and if he was to be shellback, then he must use the King's mixture. For a moment or two Chris looked relieved that he was not to get the same haircut as Nick, but when he saw that the mixture which the King was holding had burned through the bottom of the plastic cup containing it, fear returned. The mixture contained quick-setting epoxy, which the King used to make two large spikes out of Chris's hair.

Poor Chris took it in good part, even when the epoxy started burning his scalp. He had to virtually shave the crown of his head, almost like a monk's tonsure, to get rid of the epoxy. His suffering was compounded over the next few days when his newly acquired bald spot became badly sunburned, but at least he, like all the rest of the crew, was now officially a shellback.

Chapter 6

Fernando de Noronha and Natal

O ur first destination in Brazil was to be Natal, where we were to meet the Boss and friends. From the telex we learned that he was bringing two Spanish film-makers with him, and we would back-track a little to take them to the island of Fernando de Noronha, to make a documentary film.

B *eagle* did not have any owners to collect, so from St Peter and St Paul Rocks, they sailed straight for Fernando de Noronha. Although they were not faced with deadlines as rigid as ours, Fitzroy was still concerned about being behind schedule, so once again they lingered for only one short day. The moment the anchor was down, Darwin went ashore. He was determined to make the most of the short visit.

The most prominent feature of the island is the gigantic spike of rock which overlooks the north-western corner of the island. It rises straight up for some 1000ft, and actually overhangs its base on one side. It was this rock that drew Darwin's attention first. He put on his geologist's hat, so to speak, and attacked the rock with his chipping hammer. He found that the pinnacle was composed of a rock called phonolite, which is volcanic in origin.

Once he had finished his studies of the rock, there was time for only a short walk in the woods. At least he got a taste of the tropical rain forest which lay in store for him on the mainland.

All too soon it was time for him to return on board. He was not too disappointed to leave after such a short visit, because he was becoming more and more excited about what lay ahead.

The curious spire of rock, overlooking the anchorage at Fernando do Noronha.
Darwin, of course, went over to chip a piece off it, to analyse what it was made of.

Our course to Natal took us close by Fernando, but as time was pressing, and we were due to come back with the Boss, we did not stop, but sailed onwards towards Natal.

We made our landfall off Cabo São Roque, the north-eastern tip of Brazil. Natal lies about 50 miles south of the cape, a couple of miles up the Potengi River. Looking at the chart, we could see that shallow water extends out to sea for several miles, with a distant bar across the entrance to the river. Although the channel into the river is clearly shown on the chart, and there appeared to be plenty of water for us to get over the bar, I was still a bit nervous. The south-east trade winds were blowing hard onshore, and the shallow water was likely to be breaking. I knew we would have to get it right first time; it would be difficult or impossible to turn the boat round if we missed the channel or ran aground.

Through the night we had slowed the boat down, so I could time our arrival on the bar just before high tide. This would give us a few extra feet of water, and if we could carry the very last of the flood tide into the river, the seas on the bar would be calmest – or rather least rough.

As we closed the shore we raised the centreboard. With the board up *Thalassi* draws almost 9ft of water, which can cause problems enough, but with it down, she needs all of 16ft. The board was almost up when we heard a loud 'clunk', and the boat lurched. I almost had cardiac arrest. Just for an instant, I thought we had run aground, but the depth sounder showed 30ft. We could not be aground.

'Did we hit a log or something?' asked Jeff.

Nick ran to the stern and looked back. 'Nothing came out this end,' he reported.

'What the hell was it then?' I wondered.

Jeff and I had the same thought at the same time. It must be the centreboard hoist. 'We need somebody to go and take a look,' I suggested hopefully. Without any discussion, all eyes turned on Nick, who was the youngest and was usually 'volunteered' for any nasty jobs.

He hardly grumbled at all as we strapped him into a facemask and tied a rope around his waist. He hesitated for a moment on the boarding ladder, when Chris started making unhelpful comments about shark bait, but he was far enough down for a gentle shove from Jeff to ensure that he did not change his mind.

He had not been in the water more than thirty seconds before he confirmed our worst fears. 'The bloody board's all the way down.' Some part of the mechanism joining the hydraulic ram to the board had broken. The ram was all the way up and the board was all the way down.

There was not much we could do rolling about in the open sea, so while Chris and Jeff retrieved Nick, I recalculated the depth of water over the bar. It looked as though there would be just about enough for us to get over with the board down. Even if we touched, the board would probably swing back safely as long as we were going forwards. The only danger would be if the board hit the seabed as a wave dropped us straight down, or if we were swept sideways by the current onto a shoal. Then the board would certainly be damaged, and perhaps the hull as well.

We crept in over the bar in our deep-draught mode. At times there were just inches to spare, but we did not touch at all. Finally we were able to anchor in the middle of the river, off the little yacht club, just as the ebb tide started. I calculated that there would be just enough water for us at low tide.

We were still getting organised for a celebratory end-of-passage drink when a very agitated Harbour-master appeared in his launch. He took great exception to our being anchored in the middle of the channel, which, he explained, is used by big commercial ships. He wanted us to move closer to the yacht club, and refused to believe that we drew some 5m of water. At low tide, we would be close enough to touching bottom where we were, never mind moving in any nearer to the shore. I had hoped to postpone raising the board until the next day, but it was obviously not going to be. We would have to do it now, or risk the wrath of the harbour authorities.

The river was a muddy chocolate brown, not the best water for diving in, but there was no other way. The board weighed almost 2 tons, so we would have to find some way to secure a rope under its tip and winch it up with the hydraulic sheet winches.

A year or two previously, in a very similar-looking river in Panama, I had seen numerous big crocodiles (I suppose technically they were caymans, but they all look the same to me, or at least their big teeth do). I was very nervous about diving in what was obviously going to be near zero visibility. It is all too easy to imagine big jaws full of crocodile teeth appearing out of the muddy water to remove a leg or an arm in a single munch. I decided that a quick expedition ashore to the yacht club would be prudent, to ask them about crocodiles in the river.

The woman in the club office was young, attractive and spoke good English. Our three bachelor crew members immediately, and to a man, fell in lust with her. There were no crocodiles in the river, she assured us. Then, as we turned to leave, she added that there were hardly any piranha either.

We had all read accounts of how schools of these voracious fish are supposed to be able to strip a cow to its bare bones in a matter of moments, and we had no wish to test the veracity of these tales, in the flesh, as it were. There was a discussion about who was to go in the water. Chris had never scuba dived, so he was off the hook. 'I've done a bit,' conceded Jeff, 'but I never did get certified.' If I had known Jeff better than, I would have realised that for him to admit to having done a bit meant he was a very accomplished diver – as he turned out to be. Lana, who is a qualified dive-master, sloped off to the galley, muttering, 'If you want feeding tonight, you can count me out.' Nick, who had already regaled us all with tales of diving in Australia, could not come up with an excuse. So it came down to him and me to brave the piranhas, and attach the rope to the board.

It was not easy. The ebb current was by now quite strong. The visibility was close to zero, and in my imagination, swarms of hungry piranhas circled us, licking their fishy little lips. It took us about an hour to position, move and refasten ropes, but finally the board was near enough up, held in place by a rope passing under the hull from side to side. We weighed anchor and moved *Thalassi* out of the channel into her designated anchorage off the yacht club. The postponed arrival celebrations could begin.

The next job was to prove even more time-consuming. We had to clear Customs and Immigration, or as they came to be known on *Thalassi*, 'Costumes and Intimidation'. It was to take three days to get all the paperwork in order. On the way across the Atlantic, I had managed to speak on the radio to several hams in Brazil. Having made contact with one, I was introduced to several more, and finally spoke to one in Natal. He was a German called Peter, who had lived there for several years. He met us at the yacht club, and explained how to change money on the black market at almost double the official rate, and how, and in what order, to deal with officialdom. He gave us a street map with all the various offices marked.

The first part of the procedure was a visit to the hospital for clearance by the Ministry of Health. Lana came with me. We took a taxi, and despite having the map with all the streets named, we got hopelessly lost. The taxi driver had very thick glasses, and it transpired that even with them on, he was still so short-sighted that he could not see the map – and perhaps not very much of the other traffic either. As soon as we realised that, we paid him off and searched for another taxi.

The second driver had better eyesight, at least sufficient to read the map, but we did not fare much better. He stopped twice to ask the way, and eventually, more by a process of elimination than anything else, we found the hospital. We arrived at 5.25 p.m., to be told that they closed at 5.30 and we should come back the next day! At least we now had a fix on where the hospital lay.

On our return the following morning, they said a doctor had to go down to the boat to check for rats and breeding mosquitoes. We piled into a hospital jeep and drove down to the yacht club for the inspection. It turned out to be a very cursory one, and once it was finished the doctor announced that we all had to get yellow fever injections. To do this, we had to go back up to the hospital! There was no charge for the shots, but they did economise by using the same needle on all five of us. It pays to know your shipmates well!

Fortunately that was the only time we had to deal with the Ministry of Health. Now all that was left was to have papers stamped by the Port Captain, the Federal Police and the Customs. The papers had to be obtained and stamped in a specific order, and naturally the offices were far apart and kept different hours. Peter warned us that this procedure was going to have to be repeated at every port we visited. Without exception, the officials were friendly and helpful, but it was annoying to say the least.

What was even more confusing than dealing with officialdom was the currency. Just a few months before our arrival, as part of the grand economic plan for Brazil, the government had knocked three zeros off the value of the notes. Some new notes had been printed, but many of the old ones were still in circulation. Lana almost came to blows with one taxi driver when she insisted on trying to pay him one thousandth of what he wanted, as that was what was showing on the meter. We would go shopping with a fistful of notes with a lot of zeros and feel quite well off. When we came to work out the actual value in 'real' money, however, it was worth almost nothing.

Between tracking down the officials and placating taxi drivers, we did get to see quite a bit of the town. Natal is a very old place, founded by the Portuguese in 1597. Indeed, many of the ramshackle buildings looked as though they dated back almost that far. It is the main port and capital of the northern state of Rio Grande.

Much to everyone's relief, Nick found a tobacconist, renewed his habit and quickly became his old cheerful self again. Lana located the market, and arrived back laden with fresh fruit and vegetables. Meanwhile Jeff had tracked down a good hardware shop and got most of the various bits and pieces he needed for the engine room. The stern gland, which stops water coming into the boat along the propeller shaft, was leaking, and Jeff was doing his best to stop it. While all this was going on, Chris had almost taken up residence in the yacht club, where he was trying to learn Portuguese (he said), from the lovely secretary.

Natal is a busy fishing port, and every morning and evening we could watch the fleet sailing in and out. Almost all the boats were engineless, and relied completely on sail power. There were two distinct types. One was like a raft, with almost no freeboard, while the other was larger, and more like a conventional boat. Although the two designs were so different, they shared the same rig. Without exception the boats had a curious mast, with the top third bent back through about 45 degrees. This does make for a very efficiently shaped sail, and perhaps it had evolved over the years because of the prevailing onshore winds. Every trip out across the bar would entail a heavy beat to windward, and the more efficiently this could be done, the quicker and easier it would be for the crew to reach their fishing grounds.

Nick and Chris befriended a young Brazilian man who worked as a translator for one of the oil companies. With his help Jeff managed to find somebody who would deliver diesel oil to the dock, and got permission for us to go alongside to receive it.

All too soon, it seemed, the Boss and his two friends arrived. His friends were brothers, but very different from each other. One was small, serious and eternally pessimistic, while the other was tall, always joking and a born optimist. Their names were, respectively, Paco and Pedro, but before the first day was over, they became known as Paco and Wacko.

On our way back out to the offshore islands, we were surprised to see the little boats from Natal 30 miles or more from shore. They were well out of sight of land, bobbing along, apparently quite happily, in the big swell and brisk trade wind – rather them than me.

Our first stop was to be a little atoll called Atol das Rocas, about 150 miles from the mainland. The Boss wanted to stand a watch during the night, and insisted that Paco and Wacko do likewise. It was a mistake to leave them unsupervised. When I came up on deck at the end of the Boss's watch, he proudly announced that he had been able to steer a lot closer to the wind than the compass course I had given him. Meanwhile one of the trio had been fiddling with the satellite navigator, and had got it so confused that it had stopped working.

So there we were, barrelling along through a dark night, sailing towards an unlit coral reef, and we did not have a clue where we were. Being virtually awash, the reef would not even show up on the radar. The only prudent thing to do was to heave to while we tried to get the satellite navigator running again, or took dawn star sights if we could not make it work by then.

The film crew started to complain that we were wasting time – they wanted a full day on the atoll for filming. The Boss did not seem to be able to grasp that I did not know where we were, nor what course to steer for our destination, and retired to his cabin in a bit of a huff.

Despite the navigational problems, we found our way to Atol das Rocas by mid morning. Paco and Wacko had been seasick since leaving Natal, and they were dismayed to find that the little atoll gave almost no lee. We were rolling at anchor worse than we had been while sailing. They were more than anxious to get ashore. Nick and Chris wanted to help them and were also eager to see what lay ashore. I stayed on board, ostensibly to help Jeff with a few engine-room problems, while Lana was to cope with the domestic chores. In fact the three of us were just glad to have a break from the film team.

The shore party set off in the inflatable dinghy, with film equipment, dive gear and a lot of optimism. Nick returned about half an hour later with a deflated dinghy and an account of how everybody and everything was dumped in the surf. They had underestimated the size of the waves, gone straight into the beach, and been tipped over by the first wave. The dinghy had been punctured by the sharp coral.

We had another smaller inflatable dinghy stowed in the lazarette, so we hoisted the big one on deck for repairs and sent Nick back ashore in the little one.

When the film crew returned, they were still damp and a little chastened. It had been too rough to dive, and apart from an overwhelming number of birds, there had been little of interest to film ashore. Almost as a final insult, between the five of them they managed to puncture the second inflatable on *Thalassi's* exhaust pipe while unloading the film gear. It joined the big one on deck to be repaired. It was not an auspicious start to the film expedition.

On the overnight sail to Fernando de Noronha, I decided that we would keep a better eye on the Boss and his friends. This time I would do the watch with Paco and Wacko, while Jeff could keep a surreptitious eye on the Boss. Everybody was forbidden to touch the satellite navigator.

During the watch, I quizzed the brothers about their proposed film. Paco explained that the island of Fernando was little visited, and in his words 'pristine'. Living among the coral along its shores, he told me, is a particular worm, which is unique to this island. Their intention was to do a background of this 'pristine' island, then study and film the worm. The fact that they had only five days to do it, and that they were not quite sure what the worm looked like, did not seem to bother them at all.

We spotted Fernando's rock pinnacle soon after dawn, and by lunch time we were anchored in its shadow, in Bahia Antonio towards the northern end of the island. The trade winds were blowing hard, and there was some swell working its way into the anchorage. Through the binoculars, we could see a good-sized surf breaking on the beach.

Paco was visibly disappointed to find eleven other yachts anchored in the bay, which he had expected to find deserted – and 'pristine'.

On their first foray ashore, with the Boss in command of the repaired dinghy, they again misjudged the size of the waves, and were dumped in the surf one more. When they finally got ashore to find a rather scruffy little town, Paco reached hitherto unplumbed depths of gloom. 'This is like a little New York,' he said – surely the biggest exaggeration of the voyage so far. Wacko took his unexpected swim in good part, and officially named the landing area 'Killer Beach'.

Despite the problems of negotiating Killer Beach, we enjoyed our visits ashore. We found the island interesting, and learned a little of its colourful history. It was given to its Portuguese discoverer, after whom it is named, in 1504. History does not relate what Fernando did with his island, but it was soon seen to be of strategic importance. As a result it was attacked several times by various nations in the seventeenth and eighteenth centuries. It remained under Portuguese control until as recently as 1942, when it became a territory of Brazil.

Shortly after Darwin's visit, it became a penal colony – Portugal's equivalent of Devil's Island. During this period much of the forest that Darwin walked through was cut down. Some was used for fuel, but much was destroyed to stop the prisoners building boats in which they could escape to the mainland.

In the late 1950s and early 1960s, the Americans built a tracking station on the island to monitor the early space shots from Cape Canaveral. The buildings of the defunct tracking station have now become a very low-key hotel. From a peak of several thousand in its heyday, the island's population is down to a little over 900, and is steadily declining. There is little work to be had, and like so many other island communities, the young are leaving for the bright lights of the mainland.

The Boss and his men went to do some research for their film, and quickly met another setback. The only dive operation on the island was fully booked for the next two weeks by, insult of insults, another film crew. They would not be able to dive with our men at all, and if they knew anything about Paco's coral worm, they were not saying.

Wacko, the cameraman of the duo, seemed content to move the operation ashore and film birds instead of worms. The three of them piled into a rented jeep, and with the Boss in command, vanished off to the other end of the island in a cloud of dust.

Guns guarding the main anchorage at Fernando. We found British Admiralty arrows still visible on the guns. How did British guns end up here?

Their departure gave the rest of us a little time to explore the town. We found a very large abandoned church, and then a big stone fort overlooking our anchorage. In the fort we found some rusty old cannon, which still bore the imprint of the British Admiralty. It would be interesting to track down where they came from: the island has never been British, so the cannon must have been captured elsewhere, in some battle, and brought there. Alas, there was no time on that visit to find out more – maybe one day we can go back, when everybody is not in such a hurry.

The Boss told us that he wanted his men to film us sailing *Thalassi* into a small bay which they had found further down the coast. The three of them would be on the cliff top, Wacko filming, while the Boss controlled the operation by radio. We dutifully hoisted anchor and sails, and found the bay we were supposed to sail into. Perhaps it looked bigger from the top of the high cliffs, but from where we were, it hardly looked big enough for *Thalassi* to turn around in.

The Boss was very emphatic with his instructions over the radio. We were to sail into the bay, and we were not to begin to turn until he gave us the appropriate order. As we got into the bay, Jeff must have seen that I was getting a bit nervous. 'Should I fire up the main engine, just in case?' He asked. I nodded.

We got closer and closer to the rocks. The Boss's voice on the radio kept saying, 'Don't turn yet. Don't turn yet.'

Jeff commented, 'If we don't turn soon they'll be able to film the sucker running up the rocks.' Finally I put the engine into astern to

Looking across the anchorage and 'Killer Beach' at Fernando.

slow us down. We crept closer and closer to the shore. Seemingly inches from the rocks, the Boss was finally satisfied. 'Turn now,' came the order.

'About bloody time,' responded Nick as he got ready to release the jib sheet for tacking. There really was not room to turn, so with the engine hard astern we backed out, with sails still set and drawing.

Chris gave a chuckle, and said 'That'll look like they've got the film running backwards.

Back in the anchorage off Killer Beach, we were able to talk to the crews of a few of the other yachts there. They all told us that we had to visit Dolphin Bay, at the south end of the island. For some reason a large group of dolphin have chosen to live in this bay, and provided one does not wear scuba tanks, they are happy for people to swim with them. But everybody warned us that the dolphin are frightened of divers with tanks.

The film crew wanted to continue their work ashore the next day, so after depositing them again at Killer Beach, Lana and I took the dinghy down the coast to Dolphin Bay. As we got close, dolphins came to inspect us, jumping in the bow-wave of the dinghy. The motor did not frighten them at all – the faster we went, the more they seemed to enjoy it.

We anchored the dinghy at the head of the bay, put on masks and fins, and jumped in the water. Immediately we were surrounded by fifty or more dolphins. They appeared to be as intrigued by us as we were by them. What surprised us most was the noise. We could clearly hear the squeaks and grunts as the dolphins talked to each other and examined us with their sonar.

As we swam along, they swam with us. If we dived, they dived. We saw several mother and child pairs, and as they swam close to us we could see the child occasionally reaching out to touch its mother, as if for reassurance. Sometimes if the baby lagged behind a little so that the mother could no longer see it, she would reach out a fin to feel if it was still there. We felt a bit like animals in a zoo, as parents showed their children these funny creatures that had dropped into their world from above. They did not want us to get near enough to touch them, but they would frequently swim up close in front of us and gaze into our masks. It was a strange feeling to make such intimate eye contact with a wild animal.

When we were physically and emotionally exhausted, we climbed back into the dinghy and headed back to *Thalassi*. Jeff, Nick and Chris were eager to have a visit, and came back as excited by the experience as we had been.

Over dinner that night, the five of us were going on so much about the dolphins that the Boss became a bit irritated that we had done it first. He intimated that it had always been their plan to film the dolphins, and that they would do so the next day.

We weighed anchor right after breakfast, and sailed to the south end of the island. The Boss was taking Paco and Wacko in the dinghy so that they could film us along the way. The dolphins came out to play in *Thalassi*'s bow wave and escorted us the last little bit into their bay.

We anchored in the middle of the bay, and the trio started to get their gear together. When the Boss told Nick to get three sets of scuba gear ready, I repeated the warnings we had heard about the dolphins being frightened of tanks. The Boss dismissed it as irrelevant, and said, 'We need to be wearing tanks if we are to make a professional film.'

We could only do as we were told, and helped them load all their gear into the dinghy. But all five of us stayed on board *Thalassi*. We watched them anchor the dinghy near where we had anchored it the previous afternoon. The Boss put his tank on and was the first to jump into the water. I doubt whether he had drawn a single breath from his tank before the dolphins came together in a tight group and, leaping from wave to wave, left the bay *en masse* and headed straight out to sea.

The Boss and his men were oblivious to what had happened, and spent half an hour searching in vain for the dolphins. They eventually came back to the boat and tried to blame us for coming to the wrong spot, arriving too late, or maybe even exaggerating the whole thing.

We spent the rest of the day there, waiting, but in vain. No more dolphins appeared. Two boats from the hotel came past, also searching for the dolphins to show to their guests, but they too were destined to be disappointed.

After retreating to Killer Beach for the night, we tried again the next morning. This time we managed to persuade them at least to have one dive first without tanks. They finally agreed and off they went, with the camera but without tanks. Once more the expedition degenerated into a farce. Wacko was first in this time, and since he was without a tank, he was immediately surrounded by dolphins. True to form he became overly excited and yelled at the Boss to pass him the camera quickly. In the rush and excitement, he dropped the camera, and it soon sank from sight into 50ft of water. It was a chastened trio that returned on board; that was their only underwater camera.

Out came the scuba gear once more. They were determined to

look for the camera, and to hell with the dolphins. It was a fairly small area to search, and there was a good chance of finding it. Nick and I agreed to dive with them, to help them look, while Chris followed us in the dinghy. We made up several floats on long ropes that we could anchor, in order to mark out the area and search it methodically.

But there appears to be something in the Spanish nature that precludes doing anything in a methodical way. No sooner had we reached the seabed, than the three of them swam off hither and yonder, leaving Nick and me with an armful of floats, gazing at each other. Of course we found no camera.

We finally retreated to *Thalassi* for lunch. The Boss decided that the camera was a lost cause, but Nick was keen to have another go. During siesta time, he, Jeff and I donned scuba gear, and once more Chris manned the dinghy. We established a base line with the floats, and began a systematic search pattern with the three of us in line abreast, just in sight of each other. On the second pass, Nick spotted the camera, and we were back on board before siesta was over.

Of course with all the scuba activity the dolphins were far away, and since we had to leave the next day for our men to catch their flight out from Recife on the mainland, that was the end of the filming exploits.

Just like Darwin, we did not feel we had done justice to the island, but also like him, we were excited about the prospect of seeing more of the mainland of Brazil.

Chapter 7

Recife and Salvador

On their way south from Fernando de Noronha, *Beagle* bypassed Recife, or Pernambuco as it was called then, and went straight to Salvador. They did, however, stop there on their way back to England, towards the end of their voyage. However, to avoid confusion I intend to describe their ports of call geographically, rather than strictly chronologically.

When the *Beagle* reached Recife, Fitzroy decided to anchor outside the reef which shelters the town. It was his intention to stop for only six days, to check and rate the chronometers. He soon realised, however, that even for a short stay, it was going to be too uncomfortable. The ship was rolling heavily in the swell. They hoisted the anchor once again, and sailed in through the gap in the reef to anchor off the town.

Darwin was not impressed with the town, to put it mildly. In his journal, he says: 'It is in all parts disgusting, the streets are narrow, ill paved and filthy.' If that were not enough, he goes on to say, 'the people are sullen and unfriendly'. Even remembering that this was towards the end of the voyage, when he was becoming very anxious to be home, it was not exactly a glowing report.

Darwin was particularly upset about the slavery which was still very common in Brazil at this time. A woman in Rio had shown him the thumbscrews that she used to keep her maid up to the mark. He had seen children horsewhipped and adults too cowed by their 'masters' to ward off blows. Now, here in Recife, he heard the screams of people being tortured. This was to be his last port in Brazil, and he wrote, 'I am happy to leave the country, and hope never to return while slavery survives.'

About fifty years after Darwin left, Recife had another distinguished nautical visitor – Joshua Slocum. This was a few years before he made the single-handed circumnavigation for which he is remembered. At this time, in 1888, he was Captain of the trading ship *Aquidneck*. He had the misfortune to lose the ship on the reefs off the city, but he, his wife and children survived.

Transport in those days was not as easy as it is now. The only way he could get himself and his family back north was to build a boat and sail them home. He designed and built the junk-rigged *Liberdade* on the beach right there in Recife. To fasten the wooden planks, he cast his own nails from melted coins. After his wife, Hettie, had made them a suit of sails, he traded her sewing machine for an anchor, about the only thing he felt unable to make. They sailed north and, a couple of months later, safely reached home.

In contrast, once we reached Recife, the Boss and his friends were able to take a taxi to the airport and fly back to Spain the same day.

The first part of our passage down to Recife from Fernando was not very comfortable. When we left the shelter of the island, the trades were blowing hard, and a big swell was running. The boat was crashing and jumping about. Just as Lana was getting ready to serve up dinner, an extra big lurch almost dumped the whole lot on the deck.

Through the night even Nick complained that he could not sleep, and it takes a lot to keep him awake. When it is rough, it is very hard to sleep. Despite having a canvas lee-cloth to stop you falling out, you are rolled from side to side in your bunk, and then every few minutes the boat falls off a wave with a bang loud enough to waken the dead. Fortunately the wind eased around dawn and became, if anything, a bit too light for optimum speed. However, at least with the lighter wind the sea went down, and the motion was more pleasant, even if progress was not as fast.

As the wind dropped, the heavy mainsail began to slat and bang about. As usual we had a preventer rigged to stop the boom from crashing around, but as we went to lower the mainsail, off the entrance to Recife, we discovered that its slatting had cracked the aluminium boom. That was going to have to be mended before we went much further. For once the telex machine was a blessing – I was able to send a telex off to the spar-makers in Holland before we even got ashore.

As we entered the harbour we found that a naval exercise was just about to begin, and ten or twelve big warships were getting ready to leave the harbour. As we passed each, Jeff dipped the British Ensign in salute, as is the proper custom. The first two were slow to respond, but then somebody must have got on the radio to warn the other ships that some foreign yacht was going to salute the fleet, because all the rest saluted us smartly as we passed.

We spotted an empty wharf and tied up alongside. We had not been there five minutes before somebody came to tell us that we could not stay there, as a ship was expected soon. The only obvious alternative was to go and anchor in an open area at the south end of the harbour. Unfortunately the bottom was thin silt, and the anchor just could not get a grip. After four attempts we gave up, and almost in desperation tied up alongside a very rusty derelict ship that did not look as if it would ever sail again.

We were no sooner settled there when somebody else came round and said we should not stay there. Fortunately this man spoke English. He was not an official, just a concerned yachtsman. He told us that this side of town was dangerous, and if we stayed there we would certainly be robbed.

By now my opinion of Recife was if anything lower than Darwin's, but our new-found friend, Hermano, told us that all was not lost. He suggested that we tie up in the middle of town, alongside the wall of a small ornamental park. There we would be much less likely to be attacked. He jumped back into his car, and drove round to catch our lines. We were finally secured, at the seventh attempt.

Hermano not only found us the best spot to tie up, but he also introduced us to the Brazilian phenomenon of the *churascaria*. After we had waved goodbye to the Boss and the would-be film-makers, I suggested to Lana that we eat ashore that evening to give her a break. I did not want to leave the boat unattended, so we would have to go in shifts. Lana asked Hermano to recommend a restaurant, and he suggested that if we collected his wife he would take us to a *churascaria*.

We drove across the city to his house. After he had gone through the third traffic light on red, and virtually stopped at the only green one we saw, I felt compelled to say something. He told us that traffic lights were a favourite place for muggers to lie in wait, and warned us that if we rented a car in any Brazilian city, we should never stop at a red light. The reason for stopping at the green one was because he knew people would be coming through the other way against the red light. This was not a place I would like to live!

We safely crossed the city to his house, met his wife and a very large pet toucan that ate whole bananas, skin and all. Once the toucan had finished its supper, we set off for the *churascaria*

A *churascaria* is a sort of barbecue restaurant. One gets the basic salads, vegetables and bread, usually from a buffet, then waiters bring round great slabs of meat, each of which is impaled on a sword. They rest the tip of the sword on one's plate, and cut off slices of meat. The meat is cooked over an open flame, so just the outside is cooked.

As they slice bits off and it starts to get a bit rare, they throw it back on the fire and grab another swordful.

The serving method is very clever. They start serving the cheapest items like chicken livers and sausages first, hoping the customers will fill up quickly, before they serve the more expensive cuts of meat. Those in the know refuse the first six or eight offerings to save room for the better stuff. There was beef, pork and chicken, and the waiters kept coming with more and more until we begged for mercy.

Once Chris and Nick discovered the *churascarias*, there was never a problem in getting them to eat ashore while we were in Brazil. For one fixed, and remarkably low price, they could eat until they could hardly move.

Once the Boss and his team had gone, there was no reason to linger in Recife, so we set off the next day towards the *Beagle's* next anchorage, Salvador, some 400 miles to the south. This was *Beagle's* first stop on the mainland.

After an easy passage down the coast, with mostly light winds, we found that it was much easier to find a spot to anchor at Salvador than it had been in Recife. There was plenty of room off the town, in the lee of the big breakwater.

Salvador is at the mouth of a very large, island-studded bay, which rather reminded us of the Chesapeake Bay in the USA. The bay is rather unimaginatively called Bahia, which in Portuguese means simply 'bay'.

Salvador is a very old city, indeed one of Brazil's oldest. It was founded in 1549, and was the capital when Brazil was a Portuguese colony. The Dutch held it for a brief period in 1624, but otherwise it remained Portuguese until the Brazilian war of independence in 1823.

The city is unusual, if not unique, in that it is built on two levels. The lower part is virtually at sea level, while the higher one is on a rocky bluff over 200ft above it. There are a few roads connecting the two, but the principal mode of transport between them is several gigantic lifts that climb up and down the cliff face.

As usual, Lana made a beeline for the market, which was conveniently situated right at the water's edge. It was kept well stocked by a non-stop procession of local boats, which kept arriving all day long, laden with fruit and vegetables of all descriptions. Chris took the dinghy right to the edge of the market to collect Lana's purchases. It was as well that he could get the dinghy so close, because she had bought far more than the two of them could possibly have carried. If only provisioning was always that easy.

Chris was less enarmoured of the city than we were. He wanted to change some money, and when he was offered about 50 per cent

Local dugout canoes in Salvador, used for fishing and bringing produce to the waterfront market. Although the harbour has been improved since Beagle*'s visit, the local boats are still the same.*

more than the usual black market rate, he thought it was too good to be true. It was. He handed over his $50 to one of a pair of men who had offered the deal. One took the money, ostensibly to change it, leaving the second as a kind of hostage. Of course he never came back, and after about fifteen minutes Chris and Nick began to smell a rat. Suddenly the second man took off down the side streets, and without pausing to think of the consequences, the boys set off in pursuit.

Fortunately they could not catch him, and only lost the $50. Had they had a confrontation up some little back alley, it is possible they could have lost a lot more. They did not even have the satisfaction of reporting the incident to the police, because what they were doing, changing money on the black market, is in fact illegal.

The town was very noisy. Preparations were in full swing for carnival season. Usually the boys were all for the bright lights and action, but after the money-changing episode they lost interest in the town. They were happy enough when I suggested that we look for a more secluded anchorage on the other side of the bay where we could hopefully find a bit of peace and quiet for a day off.

Thalassi *anchored off the island of Itaparica in Bahia, for our well earned day off.*

We found a wonderful anchorage, which we had to ourselves, behind the island of Itaparica. There was a beautiful little palm-fringed beach, with, as we discovered, an icy cold waterfall tumbling down the rocks behind it. Had *Beagle* been anchored here, it would have been easy for them to top up their tanks with the cool clear water. There was deep water almost right up to the beach, so they could have got the ship in very close.

We had heard from some cruising boats that there was another spring a bit further up the bay, which produced unlimited supplies of fizzy water. It was claimed to be every bit as good as Perrier. Apparently it was a popular spot for the cruising boats to visit, armed with every empty bottle they could scrounge. We did not get a chance to look for it, however, as our time was limited by the Boss's schedule for us to reach Rio, still another 700 miles to the south. One realises what a big country Brazil is, when one sails along its coast!

Meanwhile, there was a day off to enjoy. We were happy enough with our own little waterfall, even if it was not fizzy. We explored the beach soon after we arrived, and Chris, in a fit of machismo, shinned up one of the overhanging coconut trees. Even though it was leaning over, which made it easier than most to climb, it was a tall one and he did well to reach the top.

He was going to throw down some coconuts to us, and had the first one in his hand, when a machete-wielding man emerged from the jungle and started yelling at him. We were all a bit surprised, as we had thought we had the place to ourselves. We could not understand a word the man was saying, but got the message loud and clear – he did not want Chris to remove any of what were presumably his coconuts.

Chris was perhaps the most surprised of all of us, and promptly slid down the length of the tree. He came down a little faster than was wise, and since he was only wearing a thin pair of shorts, he skinned his chest and his knees, and a good part of everything inbetween.

For the official day off, it was decreed that no boat work would be done – a rare occurrence. We had a leisurely breakfast in the cockpit, watching one of the local sailing boats, heaped high with fruit, trying to work its way through the lee of the island. She was obviously headed for the market, but with the foul tide and light breeze, it was slow going.

As we watched, they made a few yards, then as the current became stronger than the wind, one of the crew heaved a kedge anchor over the bows so that they would not lose their hard-earned distance. The second crew stoked up the little open fire burning near the stern, and on went the kettle for a cup of tea.

Once the tea was finished, the anchor came up with the next puff of wind, and a few more yards were gained. As the breeze died again, so the process was repeated. Anchor, kettle and a leisurely cup of tea. It must have taken them seven or eight cups to clear the island, but they did not seem to be perturbed.

I guess it was watching their peaceful progress that inspired Jeff. He suggested that we launch the pulling boat and, using oars and sails only, see how far we could get up the river that we could see at the head of our anchorage. That did not offer enough action for the boys. They thought they would rather water ski the day away. Lana wanted to catch up on her letter writing, and then do some gentle windsurfing.

That was fine. Everybody could do their own thing on their day off. Jeff and I packed a picnic and some suntan cream, and feeling a bit like Darwin himself, set off for the river.

We hoisted sail and made quite good progress – for almost 100yd. Then we ran aground on the unseen bar that blocked the entrance to the river. We were still in sight of *Thalassi*, and our pride could not allow the major expedition to end there. Lowering a tentative leg over the side into the warm, chocolate-brown water, we found that the mud, although it was very soft, was only 3 or 4in deep. We would wade and skid the dinghy over the bar, and hope that the river itself would be deep enough for it to float in.

We had covered 10 or 15ft, when Jeff let out a shriek, and jumped almost clear of the water. He had trodden on something that had wriggled under his bare toes. I was still calling him a wimp, teasing him that it was probably a little piranha, when I trod on one. It was a horrible feeling – some unknown creature wriggling about under-foot, with what we called the primeval ooze squeezing up between our toes. If we had had any sense, we would have gone back to the boat for shoes.

Squealing like a pair of schoolgirls, we covered the next 50yd in as many seconds. Then the water became a little deeper and we both leaped back into the boat, almost capsizing it in the process.

I feel certain that Darwin would have captured whatever it was that we were treading on, and identified it as to genus and species, but we were just happy enough to be back in the boat, and hoisted sail once more to continue our voyage of exploration.

We had no idea where we were going. The chart showed the entrance to the river, but only as a dotted line, which suggested that

(Opposite) Chris up the coconut tree at Itaparica. He came down much quicker then he got up, when the owner of the tree arrived.

it was unsurveyed. Even the dotted line went for only half a mile or so before becoming a blank space on the chart.

The river became narrower, and because of the high mangrove trees, the wind was becoming more fitful. What little there was, was basically blowing down the river, against us. Undaunted, we furled the sails, and shipped the oars. We had two pairs of oars, and with both of us rowing, we made good progress.

We had covered perhaps 4 or 5 miles when we came to a clearing on the river-bank, and there was a group of Indians busy washing clothes. We paused in our rowing long enough to wave to them. They seemed a bit perplexed to see two white people rowing up their river in the middle of nowhere, and nobody waved back. Their heads just swivelled in unison as they watched the apparition pass them.

We carried on for another couple of miles, but the river showed no sign of ending, so we pulled the boat up on a handy sand-bank, and ate what bits of the picnic we had not already devoured on our way up the river. If we were to be back at *Thalassi* before dark – and neither of us fancied wading back across the bar in the dark – then it was time to start back down the river.

The current was with us now, so spells of rowing were interspersed with periods of drifting and listening to the birds that remained largely hidden in the mangroves. We reached the river entrance just as dusk was falling, to be met by Chris and Nick in the big dinghy. They had been sent to look for us by Lana, who was anxious not to lose both skipper and engineer at the same time. The tide had come in enough for us to sail across the bar dry-shod. We refused Nick and Chris's offer of a tow and sailed back down the bay on the last of the evening breeze. It had been a fine day.

One could spend weeks exploring the bay, but for us it was not to be. It was time to head for Rio.

Darwin actually enjoyed the trip south from Fernando to Salvador. They had light winds for the whole passage, and he was getting his sea legs at long last. He did suffer a bit from the heat, and often took to pacing the decks in the cool of the night. He was fascinated by the new and strange constellations of stars that appeared each night as they headed south.

He marvelled at the fact that just six months before he had not even thought of the possibility of making such a voyage. Now he had seen

the sun pass north of him at noon, and was about to set foot in the 'New World'. He was contented enough, but still a little astonished to find himself there.

I can understand his feelings. When things are going well for us, I sometimes find it hard to believe that we are being paid for doing what we do. Then we get a spell doing a refit, a long passage in bad weather or a charter with difficult guests and we know that we are not paid nearly enough. It is an emotional roller coaster.

Despite his euphoria, Darwin was feeling a little homesick. Although he was still looking forward to the rest of the voyage, he was already looking forward to it being over, and anticipating his return to England.

Eight days after leaving Fernando, the *Beagle* anchored off Salvador. Darwin wasted no time in getting ashore to start his studies. He collected botanical and entomological specimens and then, strange for a naturalist, had a day on a shooting expedition with some of the officers. Still eager to expand his newest interest of geology, he spent some time examining one of the big granite outcroppings, many of which are found up and down the Brazilian coast. He could not understand how they had been formed.

He also took his first walk in the jungle. Loud insect noises could easily be heard from on board the ship when it was anchored in the bay, yet once he got deep into the jungle, he found what he called a 'universal silence'; it was so quiet it was eerie. He was fascinated by the many parasitic plants, such as orchids, and the general profusion of vegetation. It was all beyond his previous experiences.

Most of his time was spent in the jungle, and he largely ignored the shore and its plants and animals. He devoted just one afternoon to exploring the beach. He spotted a puffer fish swimming close enough to be caught, and spent the next hour or two tormenting the poor thing, making it puff up like a spikey football, both in the water and out. He was curious to discover how it managed to inflate itself.

Fitzroy wrote his first homeward reports, and praised Darwin as 'a very sensible, hard-working man, and a pleasant messmate'. Darwin also had a high opinion of his Captain, both personally as a man, and for the care and sympathy he had shown him when he was seasick. He admired him too for his seemingly limitless mental and physical energy.

Yet it was here in Salvador that they had a violent argument, which almost caused Darwin to leave the ship. Even though Darwin had yet to experience it at first hand, he was most strongly opposed to slavery. By contrast, Fitzroy, with his Tory upbringing, would defend slavery to anyone, in the name of property rights.

One evening, they entertained a Captain Pagett from another naval ship in the anchorage. He brought up the subject, and Fitzroy became irritated at having to defend his position on board his own ship. After their visitor had left, Fitzroy continued the conversation, and told Darwin of comments he had heard from slaves he had met. Darwin queried the validity of such statements if the slaves had made them in front of their master, of whom they were probably frightened. At this Fitzroy exploded, saying that if Mr Darwin doubted his word, then he would never sleep under the same deck as him again.

Darwin was actually beginning to pack, ready to leave the ship for good, when the officers of the gunroom asked him to move in with them. Fitzroy exhausted his anger upon the luckless Lieutenant Wickham, who just happened to walk in at the wrong time. Once he had finished with him, Fitzroy went to Darwin and apologised completely and sincerely.

Although such outbursts were not common, it was not an isolated incident. As much as anything else, it was probably an indication of the pressures of living so close together. We had discovered for ourselves how difficult it can be when it is impossible to get more than a boat length away from people, sometimes for weeks at a time. Nick's grouchiness and withdrawal symptoms probably would not have appeared nearly so bad on our crossing if we, or he, had been able to go off for a long walk, or maybe to spend an evening at the pub.

Although Fitzroy usually seemed calm and in control, he was actually under a lot of pressure. It is worth remembering, that at this stage in the voyage he was still only twenty-seven years old. Sometimes the tremendous responsibility weighed him down, and he felt he was not achieving the ideals that he set for himself. For a while he was very close to a nervous breakdown, and several years after the voyage he ended his days tragically, cutting his throat in a fit of depression.

Beagle did not linger in Salvador – they too were in a hurry to get to Rio. The whole crew was eager to see the city, whose reputation for partying, even then, had reached England.

Chapter 8

Towards Rio

Our disappointment at leaving Bahia largely unexplored was somewhat tempered by the prospect of sailing to Rio de Janeiro. Who would not be excited by the thought of sailing to Rio? The boys were also hoping to find *the* girl from Ipanema. Moreover, Christmas was fast approaching, and our Christmas mail was supposed to be waiting for us in Rio. It can be a bit frustrating getting mail only every six or eight weeks, but we were doing a lot better than the *Beagle*. They often went as long as a year without mail, or indeed any news from home. On *Thalassi*, as on *Beagle*, the arrival of mail is very important and long anticipated.

About halfway between Salvador and Rio, there is a small group of reef-strewn islands called Dos Abrolhos. The Boss, who was not with us for the passage (he was still back home in Spain), had asked us to stop there and take some photographs. We thought it a little peculiar, but much later we found that he liked to be able to say of some remote spot, 'My boat has been there', the inference being that he had been there too. I did not mind. By sheer coincidence the *Beagle* had stopped there on her way south, so it was another anchorage we could share with her.

We were told that Dos Abrolhos colloquially translates as 'two wide open eyes'. Despite making our landfall soon after dawn, there were ten very wide open eyes on *Thalassi* as we gingerly felt our way in through the reef. The chart was vague as to the location of the reefs, and even had a warning printed on it that they might be in positions other than those indicated. As we closed the western of the two main islands, Lana spotted the wreck of a good-sized yacht on the beach – a salutary warning to go carefully.

We passed south around the island, and anchored to the east of it, in the lee of the larger one. The only sign of humanity was the light-house on the latter. We were not sure whether it was manned or not, but decided not to go over, in case there were officials there who said we should not be there. We contented ourselves with exploring the smaller, uninhabited island.

There were hundreds and hundreds of birds, which were totally

Once through the reef, we found a good anchorage at Dos Abrolhos. Beagle, without an engine, could not get into this anchorage. They hove-to offshore, while Darwin and some of the crew went ashore.

unafraid of us – probably because very few people visit the islands, and they have yet to learn to be afraid.

We walked over to the north side of the island, to take a look at the wreck. She was a ketch of about 45ft, and the waves had thrown her well above the high-water mark. What a desolate spot to get ship-wrecked. I wondered whether they had hit the island in the dark? Perhaps the lighthouse was not working. And did the crew survive?

Back in the anchorage we all went snorkelling. The coral was a bit disappointing, but we did see a lot of fish, including several very large blue and yellow angel fish. Chris had been trying to persuade me to let him try diving with the scuba gear. He had watched the film crew with a mixture of envy and scorn, and was very keen to try it. I am a firm believer that potential divers should be taught by professionals but, for the sake of a happy ship, I finally gave in and said I would take him on one dive, on the firm understanding that this was a one-off, and if he wanted to go again, he would have to find somebody to teach him properly. I made it very plain that he and Nick were not to go off diving together on the strength of this one experience. The last thing we needed was a corpse or two on our hands.

We spent half an hour or so on deck, going through the basics, then I made him take off and replace his face mask under water. Finally we strapped on tanks and went down the anchor chain to the seabed. We stayed down about half an hour, exploring the area around the boat. He did very well, and was quite relaxed in the water. He thoroughly enjoyed the experience, and said he would make sure he became certified.

I broke my own resolution a bit later. I let Chris dive again in Rio, when we had to scrub the weed off *Thalassi*'s bottom. I did not see why he should get out of helping, just because of my stubbornness.

The day slipped by all too quickly. I wanted to be well clear of the reef before dusk, so we weighed anchor soon after 3 p.m., while the sun was still high enough for us to see the coral heads. The southern passage out was a little easier than the way in from the north had been. Soon we were in deep water, and could set sail again.

The second part of the passage was not as comfortable as the first. The breeze had picked up, and we were rolling a bit in the beam seas. In these stronger winds, the watch routine was altered to include a regular inspection of the cracks in the boom. Jeff had drilled holes at the ends of the cracks to try to stop them getting longer. They did not seem to be getting worse, but to be on the safe side, we kept the mainsail well reefed down to reduce the strain. Despite not being able to use full sail, we were making good progress, averaging around 200 miles a day.

Lana's equatorial promises to King Neptune were forgotten. We caught two fish. One was a good-sized tuna, but it escaped just as we were pulling it over the guard rail. The second was not so lucky. It was a 16lb male dorado, a brilliant blue and gold. He was in the oven within ten minutes of hitting the deck.

One reason why we had resumed fishing again was the lack of meat to buy in the shops. Although there was no shortage in the restaurants, as our visits to the *churascarias* showed, it was near enough impossible to buy meat at the retail level. We eventually discovered that there was a farmer's strike. The Government, in an attempt to control the country's galloping inflation, had fixed the retail price of meat, eggs, dairy products and, for some reason, beer. The producers said they would not sell at these prices, so refused to supply. There was a black market trade of course, but for outsiders that was harder to penetrate than the currency one. Supplies continued to be hard to find in Brazil, so a supper of fresh dorado was very welcome.

Our dawn landfall off Rio was spectacular. Rio is one of the few harbours we have visited that actually look as good in reality as in the tourist brochures. From the harbour you do not see the dirt, poverty or crime of the *barrios*, just the city nestling at the foot of high, tree-covered mountains. It is guarded on one side by the Sugarloaf Mountain, and on the other by the even higher Corcovado, topped by a gigantic statue of Christ.

It was easy enough to find space to anchor among the many yachts in the southern part of the harbour, but what turned out to be much more difficult was to find a place to get ashore. We went into the yacht club and got a very frosty reception. Later we discovered that the crews on one of the round-the-world yacht races had celebrated too hard there one year. Things had got out of hand and the party had finished with the riot police being called. Their solution was to teargas everybody, members and rowdy visitors alike. The yacht club in Rio has wonderful facilities, and the members pay dearly for privilege of using them. To see the place being abused by a bunch of drunken foreigners did not go down well, so the members voted to exclude all visitors, unless they had a personal introduction from a member. As so often happens, the few had spoiled it for the many. We were not allowed even to land there with the dinghy, and they could not offer any other suggestions.

We returned to the boat and the telex machine. With the Boss's help we managed to find a member of the club who had been at the races in Spain. With his help and introduction, we eventually got permission to use the club's dinghy dock, and to pass through their gates. We were not to use their bar, restaurant or swimming pool, and for some reason Lana and I were to use the main gate, but Jeff and the boys had to use the tradesman's entrance. Nick was incensed by this, taking it as a slight against Australia.

The most important job was to get the boom mended. The spar makers had sent us drawings showing how to repair it, and told us to get it welded locally. Through an unlikely string of contacts arranged by the spar-maker, we were introduced to Fernando Duarte and his son Paulo, who were the local fixers of things nautical in Rio.

Rounding 'The Sugarloaf' at dawn, to enter the harbour of Rio de Janeiro. From the seaward side, it does not have it's characteristic shape, nor did it seem very big. The landfall was not as spectacular as we had imagined.

Paulo arranged for a welder, and offered to translate our needs to him. All we had to do was get the boom ashore.

Thalassi's boom is over 30ft long, and weighs about 300lb, so it is not feasible just to pop it into the dinghy and run it ashore. Paulo got permission for us to take *Thalassi* alongside the fuel dock at the yacht club, and for a truck to take the boom to the welders. It was easy to lift it off the boat with two halyards, straight onto the truck. Everything went remarkably smoothly, and with the promise that it would be returned in three days, the boom vanished into the city.

I did not want to leave the boat unattended, so we staggered our time off. Nick and Chris were sent off for their day first. I think they spent most of their time on the beach at Copacabana, watching the girls with their backless bikinis. They did manage to tear themselves away long enough to take a trip up the Sugarloaf, and returned well contented with their day.

Jeff spent most of the day with Paulo, in the never-ending quest for bits and pieces for the engine room. I tried to find out what had happened to our expected consignment of parts from Britain, including the replacement part for the centreboard, which was still being held in the 'up' position with a piece of rope. Even with Paulo's help, it took four days to trace it, and then a couple of bribes to get it through Customs.

Despite all these problems, Lana and I managed to take our day off to play at tourists. We left Nick and Chris to varnish the toe-rail round the edge of the deck, and Jeff came with us to go up the Sugarloaf. We walked to the base of the mountain, glad of the chance to stretch our legs, then took the cable car which goes to the top in two stages. And what a spectacular view we had from the top. We could look down onto *Thalassi*, which appeared to be lying almost directly beneath us, 1300ft below. Through one of the coin-in-the-slot tourist telescopes, I could see the boys stretched out on deck, sunbathing, all thoughts of sanding and varnishing apparently forgotten.

Whenever any of us go ashore, we carry a portable VHF radio, and the ship's radio in the cockpit is left tuned to a relatively quiet, little-used frequency. Thus, when we are ready to be collected, we can call up whoever is on board. Feeling just a little evil, I turned on the portable radio. 'This is your conscience speaking. Don't you think you'd better get on with the sanding?' We could see them jump up and look around in surprise. Nick went back to the cockpit and asked us on the radio where we were – he was a little bit put out when I said we were keeping an eye on them from the top of the Sugarloaf.

We recuperated from our trip up the Sugarloaf by having lunch on the beach at a *churascaria*. We had intended to walk up the Corcovado in the afternoon, but as we could hardly move after our big lunch, we went by taxi. It is probably as well that we did, as the mountain is 2300ft high, and the walk would probably have been too much for our legs which, because of all the time spent at sea, had not had much use recently.

Looking down on 'The Sugarloaf' and Rio's harbour, from the Corcovado.

The statue on the top of the mountain is enormous, almost 100ft tall, and the views from the Corcovado are even better than those from the Sugarloaf. To the north we could see the bay and the city, while to the south we looked down on the beaches of Ipanema and Copacabana. On the far side of the bay was the little blue speck which was *Thalassi*. It is hard to describe such views without digging out all the old clichés.

The days were slipping by. We got the boom back and repainted then refitted it. We got our spare parts on board, and Lana provisioned as best she could with the continuing strike. The Boss had agreed that we could stay there for Christmas Day, but then we were to go to the Falklands as quickly as we could. He was to join us again there, and our hearts sank a little when he told us that Paco and Wacko would be coming again, to make another film.

Christmas Eve dawned, and brought two events of momentous

importance. We finally received our long-awaited mail, and I found that the mast was cracked.

I always go aloft and check the rig before an offshore passage, and since we were about to venture into the Southern Ocean, I was giving *Thalassi*'s rig an especially good look. I had started at the top of the mainmast and was making my way down, inspecting every fitting on the way. When I came to the top spreaders, which hold the cap shrouds away from the mast, I noticed a crack in the paint where the spreader fittings join the mast. I scraped away the paint and then the filler, and found that the weld itself was cracked.

I called down for Jeff to come up and take a look. Nick fetched the second bosun's chair, and pulled Jeff up on another halyard to join me. Together we scraped the paint and filler off all the joints, on both sets of spreaders. Of the eight welds, six were cracked.

That was a setback, to put it mildly. I was certainly not going to venture into the Roaring Forties with cracks in the mast. A quick telex to Holland found the mast-maker about to close for the Christmas holiday. He wanted photographs of the cracks before he would comment, so Jeff was back up the mast with a camera, then over the road to a one-hour processing place in the nearby shopping centre. We sent the photographs by courier so the mast-maker would have them when he reopened immediately after Christmas. While Jeff was doing this, I was on the telex trying to track down the Boss to break the news.

Everything in and around Rio shuts for the week between Christmas and the New Year, so nothing was going to happen until January. Paulo told us about a big shipyard at Angra dos Reis, further south, which had one of the few cranes tall enough to lift out *Thalassi*'s mast. A quick phone call revealed that they were already closed for the holidays.

After a rash of transatlantic telexes, it was decided that we would go down to the shipyard to see if they could do the job when they reopened. If that was possible, then the mast-maker would send out one of their engineers. He would bring the correct welding rod, and would help us unstep and restep the mast as well as supervise the repair.

Suddenly we were no longer in rush. What a change – we could enjoy Christmas and, much to the boys' delight, New Year's Eve in Rio. They had heard about the New Year's Eve fireworks and beach parties, and had already been asking if we could delay our departure. Now their wish had come true. The boys produced a Christmas tree from somewhere, Jeff rigged up some lights and Lana made lots of decorations. The boat took on a festive air.

Christmas morning dawned overcast and rainy. Although the wet season was officially over, we were getting more than our fair share of rain. Fortunately it cleared up soon enough to let the Christians among us go to church while the heathens slept in. Then Lana cooked a proper Christmas dinner, with turkey, stuffing, bread sauce and roast potatoes, followed by the obligatory Christmas pudding. Nobody could do much after that, except digest it. After a suitable pause, we opened presents and felt a bit homesick. It was a nice Christmas.

For the next few days, we did a few maintenance jobs on the boat, but it was all pretty low-key. Nick and Chris went off for a few days with Paulo to help him sail a friend's boat down to Angra dos Reis with his family. It was good for them, and for us, to have a break for a while. However well everybody gets on, there are inevitable irritations from living together in close quarters, and a spell away from each other does wonders. Darwin was very lucky to be able to spend several long periods ashore, including one in Rio. We were envious of the time he was able to devote to exploring on land; just to be able to spend *some* time off the boat would have been nice.

Although we had been happy to see the boys go for a few days, we were pleased to see them back in time for New Year's Eve. We were starting to feel rather like a family, and indeed the boys often jokingly called us Mum and Dad when they thought we were fussing over them unnecessarily.

The boys had been trying to talk me into taking *Thalassi* round to the beach off Copacabana for the fireworks. I did not fancy being out there in the dark, with speedboats racing about with drunken drivers and fireworks shooting off around us. We had enough boat problems already, without risking any other damage. They were a bit put out, but Lana and I offered to do the anchor watch, and I told them they could leave the little dinghy at the yacht club, and get themselves back any time they wanted. That mollified them a little.

Jeff must have had enough of parties, because he surprisingly decided to stay on board with us. We did our celebrating at 9 p.m., which was midnight GMT. We listened to the BBC World Service, and heard the chimes of Big Ben. As far as we were concerned, the New Year had begun, and we could have an early night.

At midnight local time we were woken up. All around us boats were hooting and we could hear the crash of fireworks from the beach. It was impossible to sleep – at least we thought so, but Jeff seemed to be managing.

We got up again to see if we could watch any of the fireworks, but the hills to the south of the Sugarloaf hid most of them from us. We were heading back to bed, when Lana spotted a lot of lights down on the Botofogo beach, off on our starboard side.

Through the binoculars we could see a group of people launching model sailing boats into the harbour. Each boat had candles in it. Some of the bigger ones had a dozen or more flickering away. The gentle breeze wafted them out into the bay, like an armada of tiny fireships.

Hand in hand we stood on deck, watching them sail off into the distance, on their infinite voyage. One by one the candles began to burn out, as if they were memories of the old year fading. Finally the bay was dark again. We kissed each other Happy Brazilian New Year, and retreated to a still warm bunk. It was a much more peaceful way to welcome the New Year than with noisy fireworks and rowdy parties.

On New Year's Day, Lana and I left the boys sleeping and went off on a last little expedition. We wanted to see the Botanical Gardens that Darwin had visited. Unfortunately, when we reached the gates, we found that the gardens were closed for the day. Not wanting to go back to the boat, we went for a long walk on the interconnecting beaches of Copacabana and Ipanema. Along the beach, there were people sleeping off the excesses of the night before, amid signs of the mayhem that we had missed. We enjoyed the walk, munching first on ice cream and then on corn on the cob sold at little stands along the beach.

On Copacabana beach we saw a group of people looking at something in the surf which was breaking on the beach. As we walked by we saw it was a dead man, wearing nothing but a plastic bag over his head. Was it suicide, murder or the result of a drunken prank? We would never know, but feeling like doting parents, we were glad the boys had arrived home intact the previous night. Rio can be a tough place.

We finally got the word that we were to head to the shipyard at Angra, who would do the repairs. We motored for eleven hours down the coast, on a hot and windless day, to the Verholme shipyard, which is about 5 miles from the town of Angra. Despite the presence of the enormous shipyard, the biggest, they claim, in the southern hemisphere, the area was one of the prettiest we had ever seen. There were many small bays off the main one, separated and surrounded by high, green, wooded hills, with only the occasional house peeking out.

The shipyard itself is at the head of one bay. The whole complex covers several square miles and employs over 2000 people. Indeed, we were to discover that it is like a small city itself, with its own housing, shopping and recreation centres for the employees. As well as the company store, there is a company school, company bank and company church, all within the compound.

On the ways there was an enormous bulk carrier that they were building, which was nearing completion. Close by were three gigantic drilling platforms which were being repaired. Yet right in front of the yard was a pristine white beach, and the water where we were anchored was crystal clear. In stark contrast to the harbour in Rio, there was absolutely no sign of pollution at all. We swam from the boat every day – what a nice change.

Before we could start work, there were the obligatory visits to Costumes and Intimidation. Once that was out of the way, we could begin to get ready to take the mast out. This is not a quick or easy job on an eighty-three footer, with a 100ft mast. The first job is to take off all the sails. The lightest weighs almost 200lb, so it was lucky that we did not have to shift them far. We folded them as best we could, and stacked them on deck. Then comes the task of unpinning and slackening all the rigging, which is perhaps the most time-consuming part of the job.

The most complicated part, however, turned out to be getting the Dutch engineer, Jan, from the airport in Rio, almost 100 miles away, down to the boat. Nobody hired cars locally. After exploring many possibilities, the plan we came up with was to get a bus to Rio, then take a taxi from the city to the airport, where we could meet Jan. There we would be able to hire a car to drive back to the boat, and hopefully at the end of the project Jan could return the car and himself to the airport. I co-opted Jeff for moral support, and off we set. It all went surprisingly smoothly, although four hours on the local bus was a bit gruelling. We were back on the boat with Jan by about 1 a.m.

Early next morning we set the jet-lagged Jan to work, and by lunch time the mast was out of the boat and safely on the ground. The actual welding went a lot more slowly. They could only weld an inch or two at a time; then Jan insisted that they stop to let it all cool down, so as to avoid distorting and possibly bending the mast. Even the cooling down was slow, because the air temperature was close to 100 degrees. We built a little tent over the welding area to give some shade, but it was still hot. Any metal tool left in the sun for more than a minute or two became too hot to pick up. Flip-flop sandals had to be left face down, otherwise they were too hot to put back on.

We all swam a lot, but even that did not cool us down very much. The sea water off the shallow beach where we were anchored was as hot as a warm bath – well over 90 degrees.

Lana and I did get one chance to cool off. The Boss had told us to hire a surveyor to keep an eye on the repairs, which was how we came to meet Arthur. He was the resident surveyor from the American Bureau of Shipping, who was watching the bulk carrier being built. One day he invited Lana and me to visit his country home, with our swimming things. He had a surprise in store: his favourite swimming hole in the river, under what felt like the world's coldest waterfall. We were all goosebumps and chattering teeth in an instant, but it felt wonderful to be cold.

Arthur helped in another, more serious, way by introducing Lana to the intricacies of the provisioning black market. He managed to track down long-life milk, and to the boys' delight and relief, beer. Lana had not been able to buy either of these on her own. Then he produced some beef and some chicken. The only thing that was proving really difficult was butter. He solved that by going back to the shipyard and telling them they had better keep the surveyor happy if they wanted to launch their ship on schedule! Soon afterwards, somebody came down the dock with a 5lb block of butter, compliments of the company store. We were reprovisioned!

As a final favour, Arthur took the whole crew to see over the new ship. We all donned hard hats and followed him through the bowels of the ship. It was enormous. Jeff envied the air-conditioned control centre for the engine room, but the boys were glad not to have to scrub a deck that big.

By the end of the week, the welding was complete and we managed to step the mast before the yard shut for the weekend. Jan left us to set up the rig and bend on all the sails again. He was anxious to get back to Holland.

For trials and tuning, we sailed up and down the big bay a couple of times, and then across to Isla Grande at the mouth of the bay. Arthur had suggested a nice anchorage there, and I thought a last day of 'R and R' before the long sail south would do us all good.

The island is beautiful. It is about 10 miles long, hilly, wooded and not too developed. There is one small hotel, a few houses and, at the southern end of the island, a prison. Arthur warned us that prisoners escaped on a fairly regular basis, and usually hitch a lift ashore on a passing yacht. He said that if an escapee came to the boat, we should take him over to the mainland and drop him off; then we would have no problems! But we stayed away from the prison, and the prisoners stayed away from us. Lana and I walked over to the beach on the windward side to swim and snorkel. Jeff vanished into the hills for the day, and the boys looked in vain for waves big enough to surf. We all enjoyed our last days in warm waters. It was going to be a long

time before we were in weather this warm again.

Soon after leaving Bahia, *Beagle* sailed through a red tide – great areas of the sea stained a brownish red colour. As might be expected, Darwin took samples and found the colour was caused by plankton. There were literally millions of microscopic cylindrical animals. He did not know where they had come from, nor why they should have reproduced in such vast numbers, and he was not alone. Even now, I do not think that anybody has come up with a satisfactory explanation of what makes the plankton that cause the red tides suddenly multiply and bloom. What is well known is the damage they can cause. A red tide can kill other sea life or render them poisonous to humans.

For most of the passage down to Rio the weather was fair, and Darwin found the easy sailing quite pleasant. For once he was not seasick, and he began to hope that perhaps it was a thing of the past. He settled into, and began to enjoy, the shipboard routine. Breakfast was served at eight, and when that was over he would usually work on his specimens. It took many hours to identify them all and record their details. The chart table in the poop cabin would often be covered by his bits and pieces, and he would fight for space with the fortunately good-natured Lieutenants Stokes and King, the navigating officers of the forenoon watch.

The midday meal was much more formal than breakfast. It was called dinner, and was in fact the main meal of the day. The officers were served at 1 p.m., and Darwin usually ate with Fitzroy in his cabin. In the afternoons, Darwin either worked with his collection again or retired to his hammock to catch up with his reading. What they called tea was the last meal of the day. It was served at 5 p.m., so that all could be cleared away before dark. When we are at sea, we also try to eat our last meal of the day before dark. It is easier and more pleasant when we can see what we are eating. Unless the weather is bad, we like to eat in the cockpit rather than below, where the heat and cooking smells can sometimes stifle even the strongest appetite.

On *Thalassi*, there is virtually unlimited electric lighting. The generators run so much for the water maker and freezers that there is a surplus of electricity for lighting. The *Beagle,* of course, had no electricity. The officers had a lantern in their accommodation, but for the crew before the mast, the stub of a candle was as much as they could hope for. As the voyage progressed and fuel supplies dwindled, even the officers would be discouraged from burning a lantern unnecessarily.

If he could get a lantern, then Darwin would sometimes work again or read in the evening. More often, however, he would just pace the deck, sometimes chatting with the officers of the watch. He seemed to get on well with all of them.

During the passage, they sighted a waterspout, caught a shark, and one morning Lieutenant Sullivan hailed Darwin. 'Come quickly. There's a grampus bear swimming off the port side.' Darwin abandoned his specimens, and rushed up on deck, to find the whole crew laughing at him. It was 1 April, and the Flycatcher had been caught.

Although he agreed to stop at Dos Abrolhos, Fitzroy quite rightly decided not to take the ship in through the reef. If we had not had a big, reliable engine, I would certainly not have taken *Thalassi* in there either. It is not an anchorage to try to sail into, or indeed out of.

They hove to off the islands and launched one of the whale-boats to take Darwin ashore. His time was limited, because Fitzroy wanted to be clear of the land before dark – there was no lighthouse there at that time. Darwin dashed about collecting samples of every plant he could find ashore; once again there was no mention of his looking at the coral or the sea life. Almost the only time he ever seems to have studied sea life was when they were at sea and he had no terrestrial life to observe.

They reached Rio a couple of days later, and anchored off Botafogo, which he describes as a pretty little fishing village. He would not recognise the place now; his pretty little village has become a series of high-rise apartments and shopping centres.

Waiting for them in Rio was their first mail from Britain, and probably only a long-distance sailor can fully understand how important that was for them. Darwin felt a little homesick, reading the letters from his family. The feeling was not to last long, because ashore he met an Englishman who was about to ride out to an estate he owned. It was about 100 miles to the north, near Cabo Frio, and he invited Darwin along for the ride. Of course Darwin did not need asking twice, and he set off with the Englishman and his five companions. It took them five days to reach the estate, and they passed through a wide variety of landscapes along the way. Close to Rio much of the land was cultivated, but as they moved out into the country, this soon gave way to thick forest, interspersed with swampy areas surrounding a series of lakes.

Most nights they found an inn to stay at, but Darwin described

them as basic, invariably dirty, and with owners who were not very friendly. They often had to go out and kill, then cook, their own supper. Riding for ten hours a day was hard on both riders and horses, but the horses suffered the most. At night, they were often bitten by vampire bats. Apart from the blood loss, the bites had a tendency to chafe and fester for days afterwards. Darwin, of course, had to catch one of the vampire bats to study it and add it to his collection.

On the third day, they reached a plantation belonging to a relative of one of the group. Darwin found the estate to be somewhat of a paradox. The furnishings in the main house were very ornate – gilded chairs and sofas – yet the rooms containing them had rough whitewashed walls, and no glass in the windows.

The main crop of the plantation was coffee, but a secondary cash crop was manioc, or cassava as it is also known. Cassava is a curious plant: its root is poisonous until cooked. The fresh juice is said to be strong enough to kill a cow. It makes one wonder how people discovered that it was safe to eat when cooked, if they had already discovered that it was poisonous when raw. All parts of the plant are used. The leaves and stalks are fed to the horses, and the roots are ground to a pulp, dried and baked to make farinha. We first came across farinha in the West Indies, where it is still commonly eaten, usually with stews or other juicy meals. The usual way to eat it is to pull a piece off the pile and roll it into a ball – it has the consistency of uncooked bread dough – then dip the ball in the stew and eat it with the fingers.

The plantation kept a few cattle for milk as well as for meat. They also grew beans and rice for food. In the surrounding forests, there was an abundance of deer and game birds for the taking, so nobody on the plantation went hungry. In fact, Darwin suffered from over-consumption. They sat down to a prodigious meal that evening and he thought it would be impolite not to try everything that was offered. He was just about at bursting point, and was congratulating himself on having managed to taste a bit of each dish, when the servants brought in a roast suckling pig, and a gigantic stuffed turkey!

Although he was most strongly opposed to slavery, he did grudgingly concede that the slaves on this plantation were not badly off. They only worked five days a week for the plantation, and the other two for themselves. He did not see any of the physical abuse that he knew was common. But the slaves were not free to leave, nor were they paid.

The party headed north the next day, towards the Englishman's plantation. When Darwin asked him how big the estate was, the

owner replied, 'I know it's about 2½ miles long, but I don't recall the breadth!'

The roads, such as they were, were very overgrown in places. Often somebody had to walk ahead of the horses, using a machete to cut a path through the vines and creepers that were blocking their way. Progress was slow, and Darwin had plenty of time to gather more bugs and plants for his collection as they travelled.

After a few days on the estate, they headed back to Rio. *Beagle* had gone back to Bahia Salvador to survey the bay, so Darwin moved into a rented house in Botafogo. I cannot help but feel that he would have found more of interest on the survey expedition around Salvador, but he seems to have been happy enough to be ashore. Perhaps it also did him good to escape the confines of shipboard living for a while.

During his stay ashore, he concentrated mainly on insect collecting. His usual programme was to spend one day collecting and the next studying and cataloguing. Between his collecting and his studying, he did manage to leave some time for his social pleasures too. He was invited to most of the naval events, and attended the Admiral's inspection of HMS *Warspite*, which was the social event of the month.

Darwin's house faced the Sugarloaf across the bay, and from his back garden he could see the Corcovado. He spent many hours watching the clouds form just below the peak of the Corcovado, which they did almost every afternoon. He did not get to the top of either peak. Of course at that time there was no cable car up the Sugarloaf, nor had the road been built up the Corcovado, so it would have been a fairly serious expedition to get up them.

His favourite time of the day was the evening. He enjoyed sitting out in the garden with a drink, and liked to watch the sun go down and the night come racing across from the east. In the tropics, nightfall is the signal for the tree frogs and cicadas to start up with their noisy chorus. The noise they make between them is surprisingly loud. The curious chirp that the tree frogs make is, for me, very evocative of tropical evenings spent in a quiet anchorage.

It goes without saying that even in these moments of relaxation, Darwin still had to satisfy his curiosity and track down and capture one of each of the noise makers. I am not sure whether he was surprised when he caught his first tree frog, but the first time I saw one, I was amazed that such a little creature could make such a big noise. They are tiny – only an inch or so long – and almost completely transparent. On the end of each toe they have a disproportionately large sucker, and can defy gravity by walking up vertical surfaces, even those as smooth as glass.

The other creatures that caught his attention, and suffered the inevitable consequences, were fireflies. He was fascinated by their bright flashes as they darted around his garden every evening. Under closer scrutiny he found that the flash comes from two bands around the body of the insect. Then he discovered that if he decapitated an insect, the bands stayed lit, often for as long as twenty-four hours. From this he deduced that the glow itself was involuntary, and the insect controlled the flashes by switching the glow off. (A sailor might say that the fireflies do not in fact flash, but rather occult.)

Darwin enjoyed his visit to the Botanical Gardens which we had tried in vain to see on New Year's Day. He was amused to see what he termed 'useful' trees growing there. It was the first time that he had seen cinnamon, camphor, clove and other aromatic trees growing. Then he found mango and breadfruit trees, important for their fruit, as well as timber trees such as mahogany and teak.

He spent some time studying spiders, comparing the ways in which they caught and devoured their prey. He also enjoyed watching the tiny humming-birds darting from flower to flower. There was much to occupy his mind, his days were full, and the time passed quickly. One morning, he awoke to see the *Beagle* anchored out in the bay once more. It was time to move back on board. It was time to head south again.

Chapter 9

South to the Falklands

*B*eagle sailed south for the River Plate, which was to be its base for the next stage of the surveys. On the second day out they sailed through a gigantic school of dolphins, which obviously excited Darwin. He was fascinated by some that came to play in the bow-wave of the ship, but mainly he was overwhelmed by the sheer numbers in the school, which took several hours to pass.

We often see dolphins when we are sailing, but usually only in small groups. Only once, about twenty years ago in the Pacific, did I ever see a school approaching the size that Darwin describes. I wonder if such big schools still exist, or whether we have killed so many of them that only the small schools survive?

Fitzroy decided to base their operations at Maldonado, in the wide estuary of the River Plate. It is on the Uruguay side, close to the entrance. As they sailed into the estuary, Darwin was intrigued to see how the muddy fresh water from the river seemed reluctant to mix with the clear blue sea water. Their wake left a swirling band of blue across the surface of the brown water, which was only a few inches deep, floating on top of the denser sea water.

Although they were based at Maldonado, they did sail up to Montevideo at one stage. Darwin, however, dismissed it as a dull and dirty town. Another day they sailed across to the Argentinian side, to visit Buenos Aires. Political tensions were running fairly high at the time, and when Fitzroy failed to heed a warning shot, they were fired upon by an Argentinian warship. Fitzroy retreated in an almost blind fury. His anger, for once, was shared by Darwin. Fitzroy sent a message to the Argentinians. 'If I had known I was entering an uncivilised port, I would have had my broadside ready for answering.' Of course *Beagle's* few guns would have been no match against those of a full-blown warship.

They sailed to Montevideo, and there Captain Fitzroy asked the Captain of a British frigate to go over and demand an apology, or sink the offending vessel. Perhaps fortunately for all concerned, cooler heads prevailed and the incident was eventually forgotten.

Darwin was very busy writing letters home, and getting the first of

his collection ready for shipping to Professor Henslow back in Cambridge. A fast packet-ship was getting ready to sail to England, and it would carry mail back for them.

Darwin had already collected several hundred samples, and there would have been even more if it had not been for the time he had spent on his meticulous notes. He had written some 600 pages in his journal by this stage, and that was increased to over 2000 by the end of the voyage.

His journal and geological notes were in fact to prove more valuable, in many cases, than the samples themselves. It turned out that he was a better note-taker than dissector, which is not surprising considering his lack of training. Some of his biological samples were so mutilated, and his drawings so poor, as to be almost valueless, but his descriptions were generally full and accurate.

In a covering note to Professor Henslow, Darwin apologised for the fact that the collection was not larger, but he protested that he had not been idle. I do not think anybody could argue with that. He said, 'Anybody who complains that my geological samples are small, should try carrying rocks for a mile or two under the tropical sun.'

From the River Plate, *Beagle* made a foray south for a month or two, to start the survey work. The weather was rough, and Darwin was very unhappy to find that once more he was desperately seasick. He spent much of his time at sea in his hammock, but whenever they stopped he was usually first ashore, reaping his usual harvest.

At Punta Alta, some 400 miles south-west of Maldonado, he found an enormous number of fossils embedded in an outcropping of soft rock. The fossils were from all kinds of beasts. One was of the skull of a creature that looked like a rhinoceros, but the real puzzler was what he was sure was a horse's tooth. It was generally acknowledged that horses were a modern introduction to the continent of South America, yet here was proof that they, or a very close relative, had existed there for thousands of years. What, he was often to ponder, had caused their extinction?

To help the survey work along, Captain Fitzroy hired two local schooners. He put two of his officers aboard each, and retreated north once more to Maldonado, leaving them to their work. Darwin complained from time to time that the *Beagle*, seemed to spend more time in port refitting than she did at sea. I know the feeling well! It seems to me that boats require at least two hours of work for every hour spent sailing.

Darwin had a bad case of depression while they were there. He began to wonder whether he could in fact endure the coming months and years. When he was ashore, and the ship confined in port, he was longing to be at sea, moving on to the next adventure. Yet once the ship was sailing, and seasickness reared its ugly head yet again, he wished fervently to be ashore. It is easy to criticise him, but we should remember that he was still only in his early twenties. It was hard for Lana or me to imagine 'our own' Nick or Chris taking responsibility for such an undertaking, or having the skill and patience to collect and describe all the specimens that he did.

While the ship was in port or surveying, Darwin did manage to make several long trips inland. We often envied the fact that he had the time for these expeditions. He rode and lived with the gauchos, the cowboys of the plains, for several weeks at a time. They carried no food on their travels, but ate whatever they could catch – armadillo, ostrich and puma. The puma, Darwin said, compares favourably with veal. Imagine the furore now, if one of the popular television naturalists sat down to a plate of puma and chips!

When the gauchos were out on the plains herding cattle, he found that they lived on a diet of beef, and nothing else. When the time came to eat, they would kill a cow and eat it. Darwin noted that 'like any other purely carnivorous animal, they were able to go for long periods between eating, without apparent discomfort'. Three days between meals was common. Compared to our crew, that was truly amazing – it was hard for them to go three hours without eating! Maybe Lana should have fed them more meat!

While he was with the gauchos, they had several of what he called 'skirmishes' with the Indians, all of whom were generally hostile, apart from a 'tame' colony near Punta Gorda.

When he could not find gauchos to ride with, the ever restless Darwin organised his own expeditions. For one such trip he hired two men and a team of twelve horses. This cost him the princely sum of $2 a day, which in those days amounted to about 8 shillings (40p). On meeting his guides he was a bit perturbed by the assortment of pistols and sabres they were carrying. They positively bristled with weapons, and he felt they were overdoing it a bit for what he saw as a little ride into the country. He changed his mind, however, when, just as they were about to leave, reports came in about a traveller found on the Montevideo road with his throat cut.

They spent their first night at a small country house, about 30 miles from Maldonado. After supper, while planning their next day's route on the map, Darwin's little pocket compass caused great astonishment. The locals were amazed that this gringo-stranger knew in which direction the next settlement lay without having been there before. His reputation as something of a sorcerer preceded him, and from then on, everywhere they went, he had to produce and demonstrate his compass. At one settlement, he was summoned to the bedside of a very sick woman, to 'show her the compass', in the hope that it might cure her.

Just as the compass was a source of wonder for the locals, Darwin was equally amazed by what he perceived as the ignorance, not of the peasants but of wealthy owners of huge estates, with many thousands of cattle. They treated him as the fount of all knowledge, and he was stunned by some of the questions they asked: 'Is it the sun or the earth that moves?', 'Where is Spain?', 'Is it hotter or colder in the north?' He was quite put out when he discovered that most people thought that North America, England and London were different names for the same place. One such owner, better informed than most, knew that North America and London were countries close beside each other, and he was equally certain that England was a town in London. And that was just over 150 years ago, only four or five generations.

While staying at one of these ranches, Darwin went out before breakfast to the water pump beside the house. He filled a bucket with water and washed his face. This caused great consternation, and he was closely questioned about the curious practice. Somebody said that they had heard Muslims did such a thing, but none of them had witnessed it before!

He spent one night at a particularly large and wealthy estate belonging to gentleman who was actually called Don Juan. It covered many square miles and he owned thousands of cattle, which were tended by several dozen gauchos. He was obviously a wealthy man by any standards, yet his house had a packed earth floor, a few rough chairs and tables for furniture, and no glass in the windows. Darwin was appalled at the evening meal, which consisted of two gigantic platters heaped high with beef. One pile was roast, and the other boiled, so their guest could have a choice! There were a few bits of pumpkin added more or less as an afterthought, but no other vegetables or bread. Everybody drank from the communal water jug in the middle of the table. For a young man with his strict upper-middle-class upbringing, it must have seemed truly barbaric.

On his rides with the gauchos, he became fascinated by their skill with *bolas*. The *bolas* are made with two, or sometimes three, balls joined together with a leather thong, and are used to catch animals. The method is to hold onto one ball, and whirl the whole thing around your head to get it spinning. Once up to speed, it is thrown into the fleeing animals' legs. Because of the spinning motion, the balls and thongs became entangled in the legs and with each other, effectively tying up the animal by remote control. The gauchos use

balls of different sizes and of different materials, depending on the animal they are chasing. Stones are often used to make heavy balls for bigger animals, and wood for the lighter ones.

The gauchos showed amazing dexterity at throwing the *bolas*, and naturally Darwin had to try to learn. He found it was easy to use them while standing still, but it was a different matter altogether when galloping fast over rough ground. On one of his attempts on horseback, he caused great amusement. He was galloping along, and got the balls swinging successfully around his head. Just at the crucial moment, as he was about to let go, one of the balls touched a bush they were passing, which upset the rhythm. The ball ricocheted off the bush and into the horse's legs. The entanglement was swift and comprehensive. Horse and rider were instantly stretched out on the ground. The gauchos almost died laughing. They said they had seen many animals successfully caught by *bolas*, but they had never seen anybody capture themselves so effectively. Luckily no more than his pride was hurt. He might easily have broken his neck, and then who knows when we would have been introduced to evolution.

When he got back to Maldonado, political tensions had eased a little, so he was able to take a short trip to Buenos Aires. He does not offer much description of it, save to call it a big city of 60,000 people. What would he make of it now, with a population well over 3 million? A big change in a comparatively short time. Will it be fifty times bigger again in another 150 years? I am glad I will not be around to find out!

Finally, and to Darwin's barely concealed relief, Fitzroy announced that they were ready to head south again. On 6 December they left the River Plate for the last time, or as Darwin eloquently put it, they 'were never again to enter its muddy stream'.

He was anxious to press on south, as he now saw Cape Horn as the 'gateway to further adventures'.

We left Isla Grande on 17 January. For the first couple of days the sailing was pleasant – a beam reach, with the wind staying around 15–20 knots. Because by now my faith in the rig was close to zero, and because the mast was still liable to bend alarmingly despite our best efforts at retuning the rigging, we kept a permanent reef in the mainsail. Even so we were ticking off around 200 miles a day: an average speed better than 8 knots. The sun was shining, and all was well with the world.

I had hoped to be able to stop in Punta del Este, in Uruguay. This is where the round-the-world races now usually stop, since making themselves unwelcome in Rio. It is the port for Maldonado, and is fairly close to Montevideo. It would have been interesting to sail up the River Plate and take a look at Darwin's 'muddy stream". Unfortunately, time was passing by all too quickly. We were already past the middle of the southern summer, and if we were to have time to explore Patagonia, we had to press on. For once we were as eager as the Boss to hurry. He was still planning to meet us in the Falklands, ostensibly with his film crew, so we steered a direct course for Port Stanley.

The good conditions could not last. We knew we were heading into one of the stormiest areas in the world, but that did not stop us enjoying the fair breeze while we could.

We had our first taste of what lay in store when we were passing the entrance to the River Plate. The pilot book warns of the strong squalls that can come down the river valley from the high plains. I thought that by staying about 250 miles off the coast we would avoid them. I was wrong! The squall came out of nowhere, at about tea time. There were no dark clouds, no warning; the wind just increased from about 15 to 50 knots in a matter of milliseconds. Fortunately we had the precautionary reef in the mainsail, but even so we had far too much sail set.

It was Nick's watch, but I was in the cockpit with him. We ran off before the wind. Lana came to take over the steering while Nick and I went forward to get the mainsail reefed some more. Jeff heard the commotion and got on deck in record time. Without waiting to be told, he rolled up most of the jib, then came forward to help us. Nick and I struggled to pull the mainsail down. The wind from astern was pressing it against the rigging, making it very hard to drag the sail down. The wind was really howling, but it had increased so suddenly that there had not been time for the waves to build up. The tops were blowing off the waves in a continuous sheet of spray, which made it hard to see where we were going.

The main came down slowly. Although Nick and Jeff were only inches away, I had to yell at them to be heard. 'Don't stop at the second reef. Let's keep going for the third one.' I did not dare look up the mast to see how much it was bending. As Nick and I dragged the sail down, Jeff was winching in the reefing pendant at the leech of the sail as fast as he could. The boom was flailing about as the sail flogged, when suddenly there was a bang and the after end of the boom hit the deck with an almighty crash.

The hydraulic vang had burst. This type of vang not only holds the boom down against the force of the sail, but also supports it when the sail is being lowered. Now it had collapsed and there was nothing to hold the boom up until we got the reef pendant tight. It was just good fortune that nobody was beneath the boom when it crashed down. We already knew how heavy it was, having had to lift it off for the welding in Brazil. Had it landed on somebody's head, it could well have killed them.

Jeff kept winching in the reef pendant, and slowly the boom returned to its horizontal position. As luck would have it, by the time we had tied in the reef points along the foot of the sail, the squall had passed, and the wind was back down to a pleasant 20 knots. Those three reefs stayed firmly tied in, however, until we were well south of the River Plate. We were not going to be caught by any repeat squall.

Once we had passed the River Plate, the night watches became distinctly nippy, and we dug out various woollies that had lain dormant in the bottoms of lockers for many a month. The water temperature had fallen by about 25 degrees Fahrenheit since leaving Brazil, showing that we had reached the cold Falklands current, which flows up from the Antarctic, around Cape Horn. Not only was it making things colder for us, but it was running against us at almost 2 knots, which meant we had to sail an extra 50 miles a day.

Nick and Chris became excited as we crossed the fortieth parallel. We were now in what the old sailors called the Roaring Forties, named after the number of gales encountered in those latitudes. We were lucky, however, for us they were the Whispering Forties. The wind stayed mostly light, and to keep to our schedule we motorsailed in the calm patches. Although the wind never blew really hard, we had a couple of very uncomfortable days when it went well south of west, and we were beating into the wind and weather. Every time *Thalassi* came off the top of a big wave, she slammed; it felt as if she was being dropped from a great height onto solid concrete. Under these conditions it was difficult to eat, harder still for Lana to prepare the food, and almost impossible to sleep. Not much fun.

Just past the halfway mark we had another good day's sailing – a beam reach with 25 knots of wind, and not too much sea. Despite keeping an extra reef in the mainsail, we did over 9 knots all day long. Everybody started to be a bit more optimistic about our arrival date in the Falklands, hoping that these conditions might hold for the

---

(Opposite) Our downwind rig. A following breeze was all too rare, it was usually on the nose. A headwind was bad enough for us, but would have been almost impossible for the Beagle.

last 900 miles.

It was wishful thinking. That night the wind went back round to the south again, right on the nose. I did not want to sail *Thalassi* too hard, not only for the comfort of the crew but also to try and keep the rig intact. We reefed the sails right down, and used the engine as well. The motion was awful. The best speed we could make was about 5 knots. Any more and she would start slamming so hard into the confused sea that Chris was convinced that the motion was going to shake the fillings out of his teeth. With the Falklands current also slowing us down, we made only about 40 miles in the next twenty-four hours. If the wind stayed like this, it was going to take us weeks to reach the Falklands. Jeff was becoming concerned about the amount of fuel we had used. We did not have enough to motor all the way to the Falklands, so we had to hope for a change in the weather.

Fortunately the wind co-operated and went back into the west, and life on board once more assumed a degree of normality. Everybody caught up on their sleep and began to take a bit more interest in the surroundings.

We saw a large sea-lion, which was investigating a big patch of seaweed. It gave us a whiskery grin as we passed. Our first albatross had visited us a day or two before, and now there was scarcely a moment when there were not at least one or two circling the boat. Darwin made no mention of the albatross visiting them while *Beagle* was at sea; he only described the nesting and feeding habits of the birds ashore. Perhaps because the Forties were roaring for the *Beagle* and Darwin was confined to his hammock, he missed seeing them circle the ship. We made the very Darwinian observation that almost without exception they circled us in a clockwise direction. Was this to do the Coriolis effect, which determines the direction in which bathwater goes down the plughole in each hemisphere? Unfortunately albatross are not found in the northern hemisphere, otherwise we might have been able to confirm that they circled in an anticlockwise direction there.

When the first albatross came to visit us, we were a little disappointed. It did not look as big as we had expected, just like a big seagull. Because they are so well proportioned, and there is nothing to scale them against, they really do not look very big when they are flying. Only when one comes face to face with one ashore, does one realise just how enormous they are. The biggest species have a span of up to 11ft.

Some types of albatross will spend five years or even more at sea without ever touching land, so we should not have been surprised to see them 600 miles from shore. It was fascinating to watch them glide, apparently effortlessly, often for minutes at a time.

An albatross will swoop down into the trough between two waves, often actually touching the breaking crest of the wave with one exploratory wingtip. The air being pushed along by the wave gives them enough momentum to enable them to bank sharply round up the face of the wave, and then soar up high enough to complete at least one complete clockwise circuit of the boat, all without a single flap of their long slender wings. They appeared to be able to repeat the process, without effort, *ad infinitum*. When it was rough, we kept waiting to see one dumped by a breaker. They flew so close to the waves that it seemed to be only a matter of time before a breaking wave would catch one, but it never happened. The rougher it became, the easier it was for them to soar.

The only time we ever saw an albatross struggling was in flat calm weather. It is very difficult for them to take off from smooth water, as their long wings hit the water. They run along the surface with their big feet, trying to get up enough speed for take-off, but if there is no wind to help them, they more often than not, flop back into the water, exhausted, after 100yd or so. By contrast, when it is windy and there is a good sea running, they can take off with scarcely a flap. They sit, bobbing about in the water, then by timing the spread of their wings to the arrival of the crest of a wave, they take off. By swooping down into the trough to gain momentum, they can start their endless soaring without a single flap.

For the same reason, an albatross will not willingly land on flat ground. With its long wings and short undercarriage, it may not be able to take off again. They will always nest at the top of a cliff, so that by stepping off the edge, they are airborne with no effort. It is almost as if it is 'nonU' in the albatross world to flap one's wings.

If we had not expected to see the albatross so far from land, what came as an even bigger surprise was a group of penguins swimming along when we were still some 500 miles from the Falklands, the nearest land. At first we thought they were seals when Lana spotted them in the distance. Having nothing better to do, we hardened up and sailed over for a closer look. There were half a dozen small penguins bobbing along, heading north, even further away from land. Were they lost? Were they migrating? Were they going back whence they came? Even allowing for the favourable current they would have had from the Falklands, it seemed a very long way for a penguin to paddle with its short, fat legs.

Every day now, we were seeing more and more birds, including tiny storm petrels, which looked too frail to be out there among the waves. The old sailors called them Mother Carey's chickens and it is easy to see why: they appear to run about among the waves rather than fly. They look just like inquisitive chickens poking around in a farmyard. Why these little birds are not drowned by each passing wave is one of nature's secrets.

Being able to watch the wildlife made the daylight watches pass a little quicker, but it was a little spooky at night, as the eternally circling albatross kept flying through the glow cast by the navigation lights.

We had 350 miles to go, and a bit of a race was developing. On the maps we were receiving from the weather fax, we could see a very deep low approaching Cape Horn. Would we reach the Falklands before it did? Neither Nick or Chris had experienced a bad storm at sea, and nothing that Jeff, Lana nor I could say would convince them that the experience was to be avoided at almost any cost. They were excited at the prospect of the impending gale; we were scared.

I came on deck just before dawn. Jeff and Chris had the watch, and we were roaring along at over 10 knots. It was comfortable enough, and at this rate we would easily beat the gale to the Falklands. As the sky started to lighten, we could see the high cirrus clouds or mare's tails, a sure sign of an approaching front. I went forward to take a look up the mast. It was bending too much. I waved for Jeff to come and help me pull down another reef. At first he tried to talk me out of reefing. 'Don't be a wimp,' he said. 'She's going fine. Let's get in before this gale.'

I did not say anything. I just pointed up the mast. He leaned over, sighted up it and without saying another word started uncoiling the reef pendant. It was frustrating not being able to sail the boat properly, just because the mast could not take it, but to lose the mast at this stage would be disastrous.

With the third reef down, we were doing 8 knots, perhaps still fast enough to beat the storm. The conditions stayed pretty much the same all that night, although the wind may have picked up a little more. We were making excellent progress, and it began to look as if we would win the race.

Then at dawn, quite unexpectedly, the wind dropped, leaving us slatting around in a confused sea. We did not waste time trying to sail; on went the engine. Was this the calm before the storm? Did we have enough fuel to motor the last 180 miles? Maybe, but it would be close.

We motored all day, at what Jeff judged to be our most economical speed. He was monitoring our fuel consumption very closely, using a dipstick to measure what fuel was left, since the gauges were already reading virtually empty. The wind stayed light, and we motored all night.

We sighted land at dawn, and as we motored down the east coast into the lee of the land I breathed a huge sigh of relief. As soon as we were in the calmer water, we hoisted the main anchor up out of the forepeak and shackled it onto the chain – before leaving Isla Grande, we had cleared everything we could off the deck in anticipation of the Roaring Forties. As we reached Port Stanley, we rounded up into the wind to drop the sails, and with almost literally the last bucketful of fuel we motored through the narrow entrance into the harbour.

Over the radio, the Harbour-Master directed us to tie up at a very ramshackle-looking jetty, more or less in the middle of town. It would be convenient enough, but the way the barometer was heading, I

The anchorage off Port Stanley, in the Falklands. We were happy enough to get in before this gale struck, even though it was too rough to get ashore.

thought there was a good chance of us pulling the whole thing out by the roots as soon as the wind got up. When I expressed my concern, he told us that we could anchor in the harbour if we preferred. The only proviso was that we would have to go and fetch the man from Costumes and Intimidation, and bring him out to the boat to clear us in. No problem.

The anchor and the big dinghy hit the water at about the same time. Nick and Chris zoomed to the shore, while Jeff paid out the chain. We were in about 20ft of water. Thinking about the forecast, and since there was plenty of room, I had Jeff let out some 200ft of chain. The harbour is long and narrow, and its only design fault is that it runs east–west. Every Cape Horn gale blows from the west, and where we were anchored there would be a fetch of at least a mile. If only the bay had formed running north–south, it would have been perfect. Even as it was, it looked a lot better than being out at sea with a big gale on its way.

The boys were soon back, bringing a very helpful and friendly gentleman who was to do all the official business. We settled him down in the saloon, with all his papers and a drink, but he seemed to be in a hurry, and suddenly announced that he had done enough for now; we could finish the rest ashore later. As we came back on deck I realised why he was in such a rush. He had sensed that the gale was all but upon us, and he wanted to get ashore before he was stranded on board, perhaps for the night. The boys drove him back in, and by the time they got back, the wind had arrived and was already blowing over 50 knots. It was howling.

We brought a second anchor up on deck, shackled it onto its rode, then made several abortive attempts to drop it up to windward using the dinghy. I did not want to motor *Thalassi* forward to drop it, for fear of letting the boat fall back onto the main anchor chain with a jerk, which might make the anchor drag, or even snap the chain. We struggled ineffectually for about half an hour. The second anchor weighed 140lb and the dinghy was bouncing around – somebody was going to get hurt.

I called a halt. The best we could do was to drop the second anchor under the bows of the boat and then carefully let out another 100ft of chain on the main anchor. That meant 300ft of chain in 20ft of water. If we dragged or the chain snapped, then at least the second anchor was ready, even if it could not share the strain yet.

We retired below to a well-earned lunch that Lana had prepared. Even the boys agreed that we had been lucky to get in when we did. They conceded that they would rather be here in Port Stanley than still out at sea. If we had been at sea, we would have been hove to by now. Progress against this wind would have been impossible, particularly with our suspect rig. We would have been losing ground to the east, and then be faced with a long beat back after the gale had passed. It felt good to be well anchored in a secure harbour. The wind was gusting well over 60 knots now, almost up to Force 12 on the Beaufort scale. We had been lucky. Welcome to the Falklands!

Government House at Port Stanley. A timely surrender by the Governor saved it from getting flattened by the Argentinian invaders.

Chapter 10

The Falkland Islands: In and Around Port Stanley

The *Beagle* made several trips to the Falklands during her stay in the south. She zigzagged through Patagonia, and to and from the Falklands. She retreated there more than once for a bit of wound licking and repair after the boisterous conditions off Cape Horn. Once again, rather than follow their adventures in a chronological order, I will do it geographically, relating their adventures to our progress along their route.

Captain Fitzroy was becoming almost as frustrated as Darwin about the lack of progress. The survey work was going much more slowly than he had hoped and expected. They were still using the two chartered schooners, and now he bought a third, slightly larger one out of his own pocket. He was hoping to be reimbursed by the Admiralty, but for the time being he was happy enough to pay for her himself so that the survey could be speeded up. Remembering the ship that had accompanied *Beagle* on her first voyage, he renamed her the *Adventure*, and sent her off to look for the other two schooners, which were still surveying the east coast of the mainland.

On her first visit, *Beagle* spent five weeks anchored off East Falkland. Darwin describes this as a dismal time. It was March, pretty much at the end of the southern summer. If he had been there a month or two sooner, perhaps his eye would not have been so jaundiced. He describes the land as 'having a wretched and desolate aspect, being barren and treeless, with only a few miserable inhabitants'. After his book was published, Darwin received a letter from Captain Sullivan, who had been one of the lieutenants who had stayed on in the Falklands to complete the survey after *Beagle* had left. Sullivan told Darwin that he had painted a falsely bleak picture of the climate and the islands, a fact which Darwin acknowledged in later editions of his book.

The general mood on board the *Beagle* was not improved when the Captain's Clerk, Hellyer, was drowned while on a shooting expedition. The funeral further depressed the ship's crew.

Darwin made a foray ashore with one of the shooting parties, but he found that his blood lust had left him. Geology was now more interesting to him than killing birds or animals for sport. In the last batch of mail they had received before leaving Montevideo, he had received another geology book, which had just been published in Britain. He read it from cover to cover on the sail south. The book expressed the very latest thinking in geology. Indeed the whole consignment of mail was very up to date – it had reached them in what Darwin felt was the remarkably quick time of five months.

He was treating geology as a mental exercise as much as anything else. He enjoyed taxing his brain trying to answer the various puzzles that he discovered during his geological forays.

Darwin took a six-day ride across East Falkland, escorted by two gauchos and six horses. Without the geology to hold his interest, he said, the ride would have been boring. For most of the time they were riding over undulating moorland, covered with light brown, withered grass interspersed with a few small shrubs. The soil was mostly a springy peat, except for the rocky hills they crossed in the middle of the island. These were barren, rocky, and difficult for the horses to cross.

In the valleys between the hills, they saw some geese and a few snipe, but not many other birds. Once they crossed the hills to the southern plains, they spotted several herds of wild cattle. According to the gauchos, these had once been more numerous, but were now declining – hardly surprisingly, because that day the gauchos killed a cow for a single meal for the three of them.

They found a small herd of cattle, and one of the gauchos separated the chosen cow from the herd. Using his *bolas* and a lasso, he managed to bring it down, and then with some difficulty killed it with a knife. They cut out the meat that they needed and carried it to the place where they had decided to camp for the night.

Darwin was fascinated by the way the gauchos were able to make a fire, even though it had been raining for most of the day. They scrabbled around beneath small bushes and tufts of grass to find two or three small, fairly dry twigs. They rubbed these into fine fibres, then surrounded them with other twigs, rather like a bird's nest. Then they produced a small piece of rag from a saddlebag, and sparked it with a tinder box. The rag with the glowing spark was laid over the centre of the nest, and the whole thing held up into the wind. It soon began to smoke, then quite suddenly burst into flames. They put it back on the ground, and built a fire round it.

There are virtually no trees on the Falklands, but the gauchos showed Darwin how well beef bones burned as fuel. Older bones burn better, but even fresh bones, with the meat picked off, will burn well enough. They also pointed out one particular shrub which will burn reasonably well even while it is still green.

To cook the slab of beef, they did not bother to skin it. They laid it out skin side down, and roasted it on the embers of the fire. It was moulded into the shape of a saucer to contain all the gravy. The gauchos called it *carne con cuero* – meat with skin. Darwin thought it was about the best beef he had ever eaten, saying it was 'a delicacy fit to serve to a London Alderman'. He did not seem to have any pangs of conscience about killing such a big animal for a single meal for the three of them.

It was mainly the cows that were killed, presumably because they were an easier prey. As a result there were disproportionately more bulls than cows, often roaming in small groups of three or four. The conditions on East Falkland obviously suited them, because they were much larger than any cattle Darwin had seen before. The gauchos were wary of the bulls, saying they could be very fierce. They warned Darwin that a bull would sometimes charge a rider and horse, often with fatal results.

On their long ride, they met a big bull while they were trying to cross a small stream. The bull stood its ground, even when the gauchos tried to chase it away. For its pains, the gauchos decided to emasculate it, supposedly to take the fire out of it and prevent it from making trouble in the future. One suspects, however, that it was more a matter of Latin macho pride, to prove that they were braver and stronger than the bull. The gauchos ran the bull down and caught it with their *bolas* and lassos. After a bit of a struggle, they were able to tie it up sufficiently for them to do the dirty deed. Once again, Darwin did not seem to be concerned about these antics, or if he was he kept his feelings entirely to himself.

They came across a herd of wild horses near the southern end of the island. These had been brought there by the French in 1764 and, according to the gauchos, had proliferated. They had no natural enemies, yet after a while their numbers stabilised, and then began to decline. Now only a few remained. Why this had happened was a mystery. Had some sickness decimated the herds? Had they eaten all the good grazing?

There was another paradox concerning the horses for Darwin to ponder upon. The cattle had grown to be larger than usual yet the horses, under the same conditions, were becoming smaller and smaller with each generation. Now, they were almost like Shetland ponies. Why?

There were a lot of rabbits, which had also been introduced and had prospered. For some reason the gauchos did not bother to eat them; it seems they preferred to kill the cattle for food.

The animals the gauchos liked to kill for sport were foxes. They were the only native quadrupeds, and by the time of Darwin's visit, the gauchos had all but wiped them out. They killed them by holding out a piece of meat for them in one hand, while holding a knife at the ready in the other. Darwin noted in his journal that the activities of the gauchos was likely to reduce the fox to the level of the dodo, but he did not seem to be too worried. What was one species more or less?

Another aspect of the fox did concern Darwin, however, and he had a long and passionate discussion with Fitzroy about it. The fox on the islands was similar in many ways to the Patagonian fox of the mainland, yet different enough to be distinct. Darwin was convinced that they were different species. Fitzroy was equally certain that they were the same species, but had changed through successive generations because of the modifying influences of climate, food and habitat in the two different places. In other words, Fitzroy felt they had evolved, but Darwin dismissed the theory. The way had been shown to him, but he had ignored it.

For much of his ride Darwin was to concentrate on geology. In fact he noted in his journal that there was little to say about the zoology of the islands, a comment I find hard to understand in view of our own experiences there; but more of that shortly.

He mentions seeing hawks, carrion vultures and owls, but few other land birds. He does say the waterfowl were numerous, and spent considerable time watching a cormorant playing with a fish it had caught. Eight times it let the hapless fish go, and eight times it caught it again. He likened it to the way a cat might play with a mouse before killing it. He had seen an otter do the same thing with a fish, but otherwise such actions are rare enough in nature. Most hunters kill their prey quickly; few will torment and play with them.

He describes the upland goose, which is commonly found in pairs or small flocks. It is a big bird, which does not migrate. It nests on the outer islands, presumably to escape the attentions of the foxes, and is a vegetarian, eating mainly grass. They are hunted even now, not for the pot – they do not taste very good – but because of the amount of grass they eat. Most of the farmers today rear sheep. The grazing is poor enough, and it is said that a full-grown goose will eat as much grass as a sheep.

There is a smaller goose called the rock goose, which lives exclusively on the beach areas. Then there is the bird which amused us on many occasions, the steamer duck. It gets it name from its peculiar

method of locomotion. It cannot fly, and rushes across the water in a cloud of spray like a desperate little paddle steamer in a hurry. Its wings and legs move at a furious rate, much like a farmyard duck's when it is being chased across a pond by an excited dog. It seemed to Darwin – and to us – that it uses its wings alternately, like somebody swimming crawl, rather than together, as other birds do when flying, or even swimming. No doubt someone has by now discovered whether this is true, perhaps with slow motion photography. However they do it, they always seem to be in a hurry, and they are fun to watch as they bustle about in their own furious way. They cannot dive very deep, so feed exclusively on the shellfish that live among the kelp which is found in the tidal zones.

Magellanic penguins at Cow Bay. Where Darwin reported seeing the odd one or two penguins, we found them in their thousands. Have they increased, or did he just not visit the areas where they live?

The only other bird that Darwin describes, is a solitary Jackass penguin or Magellanic penguin. It gets its nickname from the fact that its call sounds for all the world like a donkey that is being tormented. I find hard to understand that Darwin did not see, or if he did see, did not record, more penguins. Apart from the Jackass, we saw Gentoos, Rockhoppers, Macaroni and King penguins – not just a few but, with the exception of the kings, many thousands of each. I doubt whether they can have proliferated so much in the last 150 years. Perhaps he was just very unfortunate in the choice of areas where he went ashore. Maybe he got so involved in his geology that he largely ignored the shoreline, but the huge flocks of penguins we saw would have been impossible to ignore.

Surprisingly, the other bird that he appears to have missed was the albatross. We saw great colonies of these birds nesting on the cliff tops, so unafraid of us that we could walk among them.

What caught his attention geologically, and what I think are possibly unique to these islands, are what he called the 'streams of stones'. From a distance they do indeed look like mountain streams, tumbling down the sides of the valleys. When one gets close to them though, one finds that they are made of jagged, angular rocks that are too sharp ever to have been rolled and polished by flowing water. The individual rocks are quite big: the smallest are usually at least 1ft across, and many of them are as much as 10ft or more. They are not thrown up in heaps, but spread out in level streams – there really is no other word to describe how they look. The streams vary in width from a few feet to perhaps as much as a mile across. Darwin talks about crossing one such stream, jumping from rock to rock for at least half a mile. Some of the rocks were so big that when it started to rain, he had no difficulty finding a rock big enough to shelter under.

The crevices between the rocks are not filled with sand, which suggested to Darwin that the streams had been formed after the land had emerged from the sea. And although the rocks themselves obviously had not been part of a river-bed as such, at several of the streams Darwin could hear water running far beneath them. How deep down the water lay he could not tell, as he lacked the time and equipment to move the rocks. He was also frustrated at not being able to ascertain how deep the rocks themselves went. He had to content himself with measuring the angle of the slopes down which the streams appeared to flow.

Because of the size of the rocks, this was difficult enough to do. It was obvious that few of the streams were steep enough for the rocks slide down; most slopes appeared to be about 10 degrees, and some were almost horizontal. He followed one stream up a valley, to the

crest of a hill, where he found rocks, some as big as houses, seemingly poised to begin their journey down the valley.

What had caused the streams? What had propelled the rocks down the shallow inclines? He was to ponder this long and often. Perhaps his most plausible theory was that they were streams of lava which had solidified before being broken to fragments by some cataclysmic upheaval. Has anybody come up with a better theory?

Had he not been so interested in these streams, had the weather been a little kinder and had Captain Fitzroy put him ashore in an area with more wildlife, perhaps the Falklands would have interested him at least as much as the Galapagos were to do. We certainly found them and their wildlife more interesting. We shared Captain Sullivan's opinion: Darwin failed to do the Falklands justice.

Although we were happy enough to be safe in the harbour, it was a little frustrating to be anchored off Stanley but not able to get ashore. It had become far too rough to risk venturing out in the dinghy. We had to content ourselves with minutely studying the town through the binoculars. The wind howled all that afternoon and most of the night.

By the time we woke up the next morning, however, it had finally abated and the sun was shining. The world looked like a different place. After a quick breakfast we all piled into the dinghy and headed ashore. Lana made a beeline for the Post Office to look for our mail, while I went to visit the Harbour-Master.

He was every bit as friendly and helpful as the man who had come out to the boat, and gave me a lot of useful local information. He told me that the population of Stanley was about 1500, with about the same number living on outlying farms, or 'in the camp' as he put it. Additionally, there were still some 3000 British troops stationed there, mostly living in a new base built at the recently completed airport, near the centre of the island.

The most important thing he wanted to give me, however, was a minefield map. Although the war with Argentina was already a fading memory, the legacy of that war will be with the islands for ever. All of the land has been graded to three levels with regard to the risk of mines. The first grade is deemed to be safe. This land has been minutely searched, and there are no mines or other unexploded ordnance. Such areas are close to Stanley and the other settlements, as well as areas where there was no fighting, such as some of the off-shore islands. The middle grade covers most of the island. These areas are thought to be safe, but no guarantees are given. They have not been closely swept, and people go there at their own risk.

The third grade, shaded in red on the map, covers known mine-fields that have not been, and probably never will be, cleared. Some of these areas are around Stanley, others along potential landing sites where the Argentinians thought attacking troops might land in any attempt to retake the islands. In many cases the Argentinians had made no effort to record the positions or even the numbers of the mines, and the modern plastic one are difficult to sweep for without setting them off. These minefields will be there for many years to come.

Known minefields are well marked, both on the map we were given, and around the perimeter. Some of the minefields will never be cleared, because of the difficulty of finding the plastic mines.

Formalities completed, I met up with a rather downcast Lana. There was no mail at the Post Office yet. We walked down the road to the Company Store, where she was a bit happier at what she found. This is the general store run by the Falkland Island Company, and it is about the only shop in town.

We learned that much of the land, and almost all of the commerce, in the Falklands is controlled by the Falkland Island Company. The main business for the islanders is ranching sheep, some on land owned by the company, some on private property. The company, however, seemed to have a monopoly on collecting the wool from the farms and shipping it to Britain to be sold. Its ship makes a regular run between Port Stanley and the outlying farms. In the shearing season the ship collects the wool, and the rest of the year it delivers supplies to the farms. These goods are usually ordered by radio from the Company Store, with payment offset against wool collected and sold. We were to find that many of the people living on the outer islands visited Stanley only once or twice a year. The rest of the time all their shopping, and most of their socialising was done by radio.

Every farm has a radio, and it is very important to the way the community survives. Not only is most business done this way, but it is also the medium for gossip. There are twice-daily sessions reserved just for idle chatter. Other periods are for school work. Many of the children are educated at home, using the radio to talk to the teacher, and for class discussions. The doctor also has a period reserved for him. Each remote farm has a standard medical box, with all the medications numbered. In non-serious cases, or if the weather prevents him from flying in for a house call, the doctor discusses the symptoms with the patient, and then prescribes by numbers – perhaps 'three Number 18 every six hours.' It must be difficult sometimes, discussing personal illnesses with the doctor, knowing that half the population of the islands is probably also listening. An ongoing illness could probably be a fair substitute for the TV soap operas that have yet to arrive here.

In the Company Store, Lana found all sorts of canned and packaged goods from Britain – Branston Pickle, digestive biscuits and Marmite, things we had not seen for months. There was a small amount of frozen food, but no fresh vegetables or meat. We discovered that everybody grows their own vegetables, but fruit is virtually unknown because it is too windy for the trees to survive. The only meat the islanders ever eat is lamb or, more accurately as we were to discover, mutton. The locals jokingly refer to mutton as 365, because they eat it every day.

While we were at the store, Jeff had found out which jetty we could come alongside to get fuel. We did not have enough money to fill up, as we were waiting for a transfer of funds from the Boss. We had enough to get 150 gallons, but Jeff was worried that if we used the generator much more, there would not be enough fuel to get the boat to the dock, our fuel was so low, so he had arranged for us to go to the fuel dock right after lunch. Nick and Chris had toured the town and discovered the southernmost fish and chip shop in the world.

As we went back down to the dock where we had left the dinghy, we saw that the company supply ship had come in and tied up across the end of the dock. She was a happy-looking little green ship called *Monsunen*. Perhaps she was a little past her prime, but she looked capable enough and well cared for. The skipper saw us looking at her, guessed we were from *Thalassi* and invited us aboard. George was obviously proud of his little ship. He gave us a guided tour and a lot of useful local knowledge. There can be few people who know these islands and the anchorages as well as George does.

He offered to allow *Thalassi* to lie alongside *Monsunen* for a few days, until his next trip. That would be much safer for us than against one of the other rickety docks, and a lot more convenient than having to go to and fro in the dinghy all the time.

There are half a dozen docks sticking out into the harbour from in front of the town. Some are more substantial than others, with the company dock, where *Monsunen* lay, being the biggest. George explained that the docks have all been built by sinking old ships, filling them with rocks, and boarding over the top with planks.

There are numerous hulks of old sailing ships scattered around the harbour, one or two looking almost intact and still partially rigged. Others have been built up with wooden structures to make small warehouses. Then there are all the ships that were sunk to become jetties. When I asked about the wrecks, I was told an interesting tale. In the days of sail, ships would often struggle through appalling conditions, trying to round nearby Cape Horn against the prevailing westerlies. All too often they would suffer damage and run back to what the skipper might perceive to be the safety of Port Stanley.

Unfortunately for the ship owners, the local Lloyd's adjuster was also the only shipwright. If a damaged ship which came in for repairs had the misfortune to be insured, this gentleman (using the term loosely), would metaphorically put on his Lloyd's hat, inspect the damage, and insist on a quote for repairs. He would then put on his shipwright's hat and proceed to give an absolutely outrageous quote for repairs. Back once more in his Lloyd's persona, he would assess the value of the ship, find that the quote for repairs exceeded the insured value and promptly condemn the ship. There was nothing

One of the many wrecks in Port Stanley. This one is at the eastern end of the harbour. Disabled ships seeking shelter were often condemned by the Lloyds Surveyor, and they provided a ready source of timber in a place where virtually no trees can grow.

the captain or owners could do. The hapless ship would become a storage hulk or a jetty, or even be broken up for the timber, which was always in short supply in the treeless islands.

One ship to suffer such a fate was an American clipper by the name of *Snowsquall.* She had become part of the jetty next to the main company dock. She and four or five other ships had been tied side by side and sunk to form the foundation. Now a group of people from Maine were working on her, trying to cut off and salvage about 35ft of her bows that stuck out from the side of the jetty. They claimed that she was the only surviving American clipper ship, although to say that she had 'survived' is perhaps stretching the point.

The cold water that had preserved her timber so well, made it difficult for the divers who were trying to saw through her salt-hardened timbers. We watched their progress daily, and shared their excitement when the bow section finally broke free. It was lifted on to a specially made cradle on board a big container ship, which was eventually going to carry it back to a museum in Maine.

Our first evening ashore was to be a cook's night off. We reconnoitred the one and only hotel, the Upland Goose, which George had recommended. Much to our surprise, they said they were fully booked for the next several nights. So instead we ended up at Emma's Guest House, which happened to be where the *Snowsquall* people were staying. We had a good meal, and enjoyed chatting with the divers.

The waterfront of Port Stanley is dotted with jetties leading out to grounded hulks of old sailing ships, which are used as ready-made warehouses.

We thought we had completed a full and interesting day, but it was not to be. The boys wanted to stop for a drink at a bar called the Globe. Lana and I were feeling like tired little sailors, but finally agreed that we would stop for just one drink before heading back. The boys could drink the night away if they wanted, but we were ready for sleep. The pub was rather noisy, very smoky and quite busy. The clientele looked like about an equal mix of islanders and soldiers – who was whom was immediately apparent by the haircuts!

We were about to leave when we saw a young soldier come in and start to assemble his bagpipes, so we decided we would stay a few minutes more. He played one short skirl, then started to pack the pipes away. Lana went over to ask him why he was not playing more, and he explained that the barman had told him he could not play in there. He went on to tell her that there was a folk club meeting in the Town Hall that night, and he was going to be playing there.

Lana was keen to go and investigate – by now she was getting her second wind. Off we set, back down the road to the Town Hall, thinking that the piper was right behind us. When we got there, we found the show had already started. Two soldiers were singing with a local girl, accompanying themselves on guitars, and they were good. The piper was supposed to perform for the second half, but did not show up, so members of the audience filled in instead. Midnight was approaching, and we had just about given up on the piper when he and his friend stumbled in. They were both so drunk that they could hardly stand. A minor problem like that was not going to stop him from playing, however, and play he did. He was amazing. His equally inebriated friend accompanied him on the accordion. We later learned that the piper had won the Scottish National Championship two years running. It was an excellent end to a busy day.

The next few days were almost as busy. We had had word that the Boss was coming in a week's time. After he had learned the price of the air tickets, he had abandoned the film crew, and was coming on his own, which would make the provisioning and catering a little easier. There was plenty of cleaning and polishing to do before his arrival, but we were determined to do a little exploring as well.

Jeff and I were keen to go up into the hills overlooking Stanley, where the fiercest battles of the war had been fought. I do not want to dwell too much on the war, but it did obviously have a great impact on the islands, and has changed, perhaps for ever, the way they are perceived by the rest of the world. After a longstanding dispute over sovereignty, the Argentinians invaded the Falklands on 2 April 1982. The British sent an almost unprecented task force of 100 ships 8000 miles to fight them, and the combined cost of the war was 1000 lives.

Argentina surrendered the islands once more on 14 June.

During the war, while we were living and working in the Virgin Islands, we had listened regularly to the BBC World Service, following the progress of the fighting. Now it was a very moving experience to walk over the sites of the battles, and visit the places that, for a short time at least, had become household names.

The Argentinians had built a defensive horseshoe around Stanley and the harbour, fortifying all the high ground, from Wireless Ridge across Mount Longdon, Tumbledown Mountain and Sapper Hill. Jeff, Nick and I set out to walk this ridge line. The first mile or two was easy enough, along the road to the western end of the harbour. We had our first glimpse of the war when we found the ruins of the Moody Brook Barracks, which had been levelled in a mortar attack during the first assault.

From the barracks we headed north for Wireless Ridge. As soon as we left the road, we realised that the going was not going to be easy. The land is mostly peat bog covered in a wiry, coarse grass. For the most part we were able to keep our feet dry, but every now and then, usually with a loud curse, one of us would break through a particularly boggy bit and squelch into knee-deep muddy water. It was hard going. The struggle we were having brought home to us just how fit the marines had been who force marched some 26 miles across the island in the dark, carrying full kit. The fact that they were able to surprise the Argentinians by arriving behind them suggests that the Argentinians too had thought the feat would be impossible.

Huffing and puffing, we scrambled up onto the ridge. On the pretext of admiring the view of the harbour below us, I suggested a pause, and sat down on the driest spot I could find. All around us were craters in the peat from mortars and shells that must have literally rained down on the defending Argentinians.

Jeff, lighting a cigarette, joined me. Nick, ever the restless one, was roaming about along the ridge. He called us over to see what he had found. We ambled over, to see him poking at something sticking out of the side of the crater. He was scraping the mud away from a brown cylindrical object, about 18in long. Nick reckoned it was a fire extinguisher, and was all for digging it out and taking it back as a souvenir. Jeff pointed out that fire extinguishers do not have fins on the end, and started to back away in a tactical retreat. It could have been an unexploded shell of some sort. We were in one of the areas thought to be safe, but not closely swept, so it was entirely possible. We gathered a few stones and a couple of sticks to mark the spot, and decided that we would report it when we got back down to Stanley. Let the experts decide what to do with it.

We struck off westwards along the ridge, towards Mount Longdon, trying to be careful about where we trod. We had been grumbling about stepping into mud holes on the way up, but it would be a lot worse to tread on a mine! As we struggled up the flank of Mount Longdon, there were ever-increasing signs of the battle. Dozens of slit trenches had been cut into the hill, and even though the battle had been fought several years before, there were many things inside left by the surrendering troops. We found mess kits, bits and pieces of clothing and boots galore. Inside one, wedged in a niche in the rocks, Nick found a comic book in Spanish. Many of the Argentinian troops had been teenage conscripts. We could just visualise a cold, wet, homesick, young kid, huddled in the trench, probably scared out of his mind, seeking solace from his magazine. The war suddenly took on a personal touch. Real people had fought and died here.

The slopes of Mount Longdon were closely covered with trenches, many of them still connected by wires from field telephones. All around them were craters, big and small, where falling shells had exploded. It must have been truly awful to have been there, for soldiers on both sides.

On the top of Mount Longdon, 600ft above the harbour, was a small memorial and some wilted flowers. Fairly recently, somebody had taken the trouble to climb all the way up there to leave flowers. Sad. We ate lunch, and nobody talked much.

We scrambled back down to the road, skirted a well-marked minefield, and began the hardest climb of the day, up the rugged side of Mount Tumbledown. It is aptly named – the top is little more than a heap of gigantic boulders. It is steep enough to make the climb hard work. We reminded ourselves that we were doing it on a summer's day; the troops attacking the mountain had done it on a winter's night, carrying weapons and fighting kit, with people trying their hardest to shoot them. After a struggle we reached the top, and found another memorial and a magnificent view down the harbour and across the town.

On the mountain were the remains of quite intricate bunkers, built in among the rocks. Some were connected by passages, some were out on their own. Again there was still a surprising amount of abandoned personal gear in the bunkers. Real people had been hiding here as well.

After catching our breath, and waiting for my pulse to go below 200, we made our way down the eastern flank, towards Sapper Hill. This was the last high ground before Stanley, although it was much lower than the other hills. Much of that was still fenced off with minefield markers, so we skirted the edge and dropped down into Stanley.

A bunker on the top of Tumbledown Mountain, that has now become a memorial. Looking down the length of Port Stanley harbour.

The next morning Jeff and I went to report the 'fire extinguisher' that we had found on Wireless Ridge. We met Captain King, who was in charge of the bomb-disposal crew. He asked us to describe the thing and as soon as we mentioned two yellow stripes, he said they would have to go and attend to it. Yellow stripes, he explained, are the international symbol for high explosive. As the Boss's arrival was increasingly imminent, I explained that we did not have time to walk all the way back up there. He laughed and told us that he was not going to walk either; we would all drive.

The Captain said we could take the rest of the crew, so Jeff ran back for the others and we all piled into a very curious vehicle. It looked like a small tank towing a trailer, but in fact it was all one vehicle, articulated in the middle. The part that looked like a trailer had tracks like the front section, and both sets of tracks were driven. Lana and I got the last two seats in front with the bomb crew while Jeff and the boys were put in the back where, the soldiers warned them, the ride was much rougher. We trundled off down the road.

At the foot of the ridge, the driver just turned off the road and headed straight up the hill. Boggy peat or jagged rocks all seemed the same to this vehicle. We went straight up the side of the hill that we had stumbled up with so much effort the day before, and found the 'fire extinguisher' without too much effort. The boys emerged from the back of the vehicle looking a little pale. It was rough enough for us in the front, but apparently in the back they had been well shaken about.

One quick look by the bomb crew confirmed that it was an unexploded Argentinian mortar shell. Captain King tied a long piece of wire round the tail and, from what he deemed to be a safe distance, pulled it out of the mud. It did not go bang, so with what was perhaps

Captain King examines the unexploded mortar shell we found. He decided it was too rusty to take back to their depot, so blew it up on site.

a touch of bravado, he picked it up. It was pretty rusty, so he said it was not safe to defuse and take back to Stanley, which was fine by me; I would not have wanted to ride back down that bumpy mountain inside a tin box with a live bomb!

He decided to blow it up right there on the ridge. He put it into one of the deeper craters to minimise the chance of shrapnel flying about. Next he stuck a piece of plastic explosive and a detonator on the side. We needed no encouragement to stand back. It went off with a surprisingly loud bang, and the crater where it had been sitting was now about 4ft across. We tried to imagine what it must have been like to be hiding in a trench with these things raining down all night long. Awful.

Back on the boat, the preparations continued. *Monsunen* left to do her rounds, so we had to move out to anchor. Her place on the dock was taken by one of the British Antarctic Survey ships, the *John Biscoe*. Somehow we managed to get ourselves invited on board for a cocktail party, and her Captain, Chris, offered to let *Thalassi* lie alongside as she had done with *Monsunen*. He also told us some fascinating tales about his many trips into the Antarctic, supplying the various bases.

Monday was a festive day. It was Nick's birthday, and Lana found our mail at the Post Office. Our excitement at getting the mail was somewhat overshadowed when we opened our bank statement. We had not been paid for the last three months. That would give us a good opening conversation with the Boss when he arrived.

We celebrated Nick's birthday with lunch at the southernmost fish and chip shop in the world. It was fortuitous that we did, because Lana found out that the owner of the shop also imported fruit and vegetables, and he was expecting his monthly shipment that very night. She went back at 4 p.m. to find she was at the back of a long queue. By the time she had worked her way up to the front, there was not much left, but she did get some apples, a few grapefruit and a big bag of onions.

The butcher came to *Thalassi* to deliver Lana's order. Ostensibly we got lamb chops, legs of lamb and several pounds of lamb mince, as per Lana's request. It was only after the butcher had been paid, and we were chatting over a drink in the cockpit, that he explained the economics of sheep farming. In the Falklands sheep are reared primarily for their wool. They will produce good wool for four or perhaps five years, after which the quality falls off, so the animals are killed. That is when the butcher gets his hands on them. Young lambs are not killed for meat, because they are too valuable for their five years' worth of wool. So we had just filled the freezer with what turned out to be very tough five-year-old sheep. When Lana roasted the first of the legs, it looked and smelled delicious, but it blunted the sharpest knife and defied the strongest teeth. The expression 'tough as an old boot', could be rewritten as 'tough as an old sheep'. It was like rubber. The only way we could eat any of it was minced up as lamb burgers.

The second BAS ship came in. She was newer and bigger than the *Biscoe*, and was painted the same striking red colour. Her name was the *Bransfield*, and it did not take us long to be invited on board for a tour. She had much more modern equipment than the *Biscoe*, and I was especially fascinated by a TV display which gave a real-time picture from a satellite above. They used it mainly for spotting big icebergs, but it was equally valuable for looking at what sort of weather was coming. The cloud lines of approaching fronts were clearly visible. I wanted one!

During the tour, we met a young doctor, Tony. He had just been picked up by the ship after spending a winter with fifteen others at Halley Base, deep in the Antarctic. Apart from looking after the health of everybody on the base, he had been doing various experiments. Now he had several months to wait until his samples reached Britain before he could complete his projects. He asked if we needed any more crew. The timing was fortuitous. Chris was waiting to hear about a date to go back to a job in the 'real world', so we were casting around for another crew member to replace him. Since the insurance company insisted on five crew, I thought it better to have one extra for a few weeks than to end up one short in Patagonia. We told him to come over to *Thalassi* for a talk.

I let him talk to Nick and Jeff first. They could explain to him about the martinet skipper, the cantankerous cook and the wayward owner, and then if he was still interested, he could talk to Lana and me. We took an instant liking to him. He was extremely intelligent, quick on the uptake, and had a good sense of humour. Jeff liked him and Nick seemed ambivalent. Chris was a bit put out that we would even consider replacing him with somebody who had never sailed before. I said that I felt he could learn the sailing, but what he already had was the ability to rub along with other people in a confined space. If he could live underground in the big plywood tube which was Halley Base with fifteen other people for a year, then he would probably manage to fit in with us.

It was agreed, and we signed him on. He would join us just in time for the Boss's arrival.

Chapter 11

In and Around the Falkland Islands

The day of the Boss's arrival dawned. We all made an early start to finish off the last bits of cleaning and polishing. Just before breakfast, we received a message that he had missed one of his flight connections, and the next plane was not due for another four days. Suddenly the pressure was off. The boat was near enough ready, so we could take a few days to play with a clear conscience. We could do a bit of serious exploring. Jeff decided to celebrate by going back to sleep. It was agreed among the rest of us that we would have a lazy day in Stanley, then make a short expedition to one or two of the nearby islands for a couple of days.

A couple of hours later I received another interesting piece of news on the radio. While we are travelling, I try and make daily contact on the ham radio with a couple of friends. One lives in Michigan, near Lana's family, and the other is in Ireland. We had a house in Baltimore, in west Cork, where we spent some time when we were not sailing, and our friend Neilie lives a few miles away in Skibbereen. I am still not sure quite how he managed it, but Neilie had unearthed an old newspaper cutting about Conor O'Brien, and the building of a boat in Baltimore for the Falkland Island Company in 1926. Neilie asked us to enquire about the boat, called the *Ilen*, and see if we could find out what had happened to her.

After the radio contact, I went back up into the cockpit and scouted around the harbour with the binoculars. I had noticed an old green ketch anchored behind us, only because she was the same colour as the *Monsunen*. Sure enough, as she swung on her anchor, I saw the name *Ilen* on her stern. Lana and I went ashore to ask in the company office if we could go on board. No problem, they said, so off we went. That she was still in commission after more than fifty years in these stormy waters is surely a tribute to her builders. Her engine has been replaced, but otherwise she is as built.

Conor O'Brien had stopped in the Falklands in the course of a circumnavigation. People from the company had admired his boat, the *Saoirse*, and tried to buy it. He refused to sell, and instead offered to build a new boat and deliver it the 8000 miles from Baltimore. The

The Ilen, *built in Baltimore in West Cork, where at the time we had our home. She was sailed out from Baltimore by Conor O'Brien in 1926, and is still in regular use.*

result was the 56ft ketch *Ilen*.

She had no sails bent on when we saw her, but they do still regularly use her under power for short-haul deliveries, mainly running supplies out to the fishing boats anchored in the bay outside Stanley. In the wheelhouse, the builder's brass plaque naming Baltimore made us feel intensely homesick.

Tony moved on board *Thalassi*, and was happy enough to find that he would have a few days to get to know his way around the boat before the Boss arrived. It was all new to him, but it was uncanny how quickly he was able to learn things. Nothing ever had to be explained twice.

The anchorage recommended in the Admiralty Pilot Book, in the centre of St Peter and St Paul's Rocks. Darwin landed at this spot from Beagle's *whaleboat, so it must have been calmer for him than it was for us. The only way we could get ashore was to swim.*

Swimming with the dolphin at Fernando. Darwin never mentions swimming, let alone diving. What would he have made of swimming underwater with the dolphin? We loved it.

Waiting for a breeze. Local boat becalmed in the lee of Itaparica, on her way to the market in Salvador.

Above: Any time the penguins got fed up with us following them, they would head into the sea, with a look as if to say 'Are you going to follow us now?'

Right: The skipper out on the end of the pole, checking for chafe; a common enemy that we shared with the Beagle.

It was only when we got close to the albatross that we realised how big they are. They were totally unafraid of us, and it was the size of their beaks that made us keep a respectful distance.

The fluffy albatross chicks sat on their pedestal-like nests waiting to be fed. Their feathers are not yet developed enough for them to fly. Neither they nor their parents minded us getting close to them.

Once they had enough of us photographing them, the King penguins walked down into the breakers and swam out to sea, confident that we would not follow them into the icy water.

Going ashore at Keppel Island. Many of these farms are so remote that the inhabitants only get to visit Stanley but once or twice a year. They rely on George and the Monsunen *for all their supplies.*

Thalassi *sailing past the Romanche glacier in the Beagle Channel – the blue of the ice almost matching the colour of her hull. This was the first big glacier we saw, and it was probably on the beach opposite the glacier, that Darwin and crew nearly perished when an icefall sent a wave across the channel which almost washed their boats away.*

Off the Garibaldi glacier, where we spent a worrysome night in the worst anchorage we found in Patagonia.

Thalassi *moored in 300 feet of water in front of Glacier Asia. We did not need to anchor – the ice held her snugly.*

Estero Peel, near Glacier Asia.

Thalassi *anchored off the beach at Puyuguapi, waiting for Jose to join us.*

Our first little expedition, and Tony's first sail, was up the coast a few miles to Cow Bay. We anchored in the bay and dinghied over to the beach. It was a bit of a scramble up the low cliffs to get to the grassy meadowland that overlooked the bay. We could hear the Magellanic penguins well before we got to the top. They sounded uncannily like a herd of donkeys. After hearing all this noise, we were surprised when we saw how small they were, only about 18in tall. Instead of the solitary bird that Darwin described, we found a colony of hundreds, maybe even thousands. There were a few sheep grazing unconcernedly in among the penguins. They were very shy of us, and ran off if we walked anywhere near them, but the little penguins were much braver. They would stand their ground as we walked up to them.

Magellanic penguins at Cow Bay. They were quite unafraid of us, unless we got too close, when they would dive into the nearest burrow, often to the digust of the occupant.

Magellanics are unusual in the world of penguins in that they live in burrows, just like rabbits. In fact the only other birds that I can think of which live in burrows are puffins, but there may be others.

Although the Magellanics are remarkably brave little birds, there are limits to how near they would let us come. If we got too close, then they would panic, and bolt into their burrows. Sometimes, in its haste, one would dive down what was obviously the wrong burrow. A cacophony of donkey noises would then accompany it as it came flying out backwards. It would usually give us a reproachful look before dashing off to try its luck down the next burrow.

Some of the penguins liked to stay and watch us from the safety of their burrow entrances, seemingly as interested in us as we were in them. They did not seem to be able to look straight ahead, but swivelled their heads from side to side as they studied us, first with one eye, then the other. If we stood over their burrow, their heads would turn round through 180 degrees to look at us. When they stood watching us like that, it looked as if they had their heads on back to front. Kodak shares must have gone up at least ten points in the hour or two we spent there.

From Cow Bay, we walked a couple of miles along the shore to Victory Beach, a wonderful white beach, that really *was* pristine. It stretched unbroken for at least half a mile across a shallow bay. We climbed down to it, and spotted half a dozen King penguins among many hundreds more Magellanics. They are the biggest, and least common, of the five types of penguins found in the Falklands. They are at least 3ft tall, and strut about imperiously among their lesser subjects. They are better groomed than the Magellanics, some of which have a tendency to look a bit scruffy. The Kings dress in smooth grey-blue coats, very white shirts and smart yellow cravats.

The Magellanics, when they are dashing about on the land, often use their wings like front legs; nothing so ungainly for the kings. When they had finally had enough of the paparazzi and their clicking cameras, they walked slowly and majestically down the beach into the surf. With a last royal look at us over their shoulders, they took off through the waves, as if daring us to follow.

Our second expedition was to Kidney Island, a very small island a few miles from Stanley. Kidney is interesting for two reasons. Probably because it is so small, it has never had sheep grazed on it, and so it still has the original vegetation of tussock grass. The locals had also told us that there was a colony of fur seals living there.

We found a nice anchorage to the south of the island, and took the dinghy in to the stony beach. Across the front of the beach there was a broad band of kelp, thick and rubbery seaweed which seemed designed to tangle propellers on outboard motors. I stopped the engine just before it ground to a halt, and Nick and Chris paddled the last few yards to the beach. There were two large male fur seals, together with three smaller females, at one end of the beach. The males were growling, roaring and puffing up their necks as we approached, so we diplomatically chose the other end of the beach to make our landing.

Tony, our new resident expert, told us about the differences between seals and sea-lions. He explained that the first things to look at are their ears. Most seals do not have external ears, and all these so-called earless seals swim by using their back flippers for propulsion and their front ones for steering. The back flippers have become well adapted for this, almost fusing together to form a single tail. Whilst this tail is very good in the water, it is not much use on land. When these seals come ashore, they have to more or less flop along in a rather ungainly manner.

A baby fur seal on the north side of Kidney Island. We didn't want to get too close, in case Mum or Dad were watching. A big fur seal is an intimidating proposition.

131

The seals with external ears, which include the fur seals, and sea-lions, move in a different way. They swim by using mainly their forward fins for propulsion, and the back ones for steering. On shore, they are able to swivel the rear flippers forward, to make them effectively four-legged. As a result, Tony warned us, they can move very quickly on land, and as they have big, ugly teeth, he suggested we treat them with the utmost respect. That was fine by me; I was happy to watch them from the other end of the beach.

Nick was not going to be intimidated by some old seals dressed up in fur coats – at least not at first. He wanted a close-up photograph. With his Australian bravado, he marched up to the watching seals. The two males were some 8 or 9ft long, and by Tony's estimate weighted about 600lb apiece. The biggest made eye contact with Nick, who swears he saw the seal lick its lips before letting out a gigantic roar. Without breaking his stride, Nick did a 180-degree turn, and beat a reasonably dignified retreat.

We decided to try to cross over to the other side of the island, where the main colony of seals were said to live. The beach was fringed with the tussock grass which used to cover all the islands before man introduced cattle, horses and sheep, and allowed them to run wild. From a distance the grass looked pretty much like any unkempt meadow, with the grass growing in little tufts. When we came close, however, we found that it was more than 6ft tall, and one could easily walk between the tufts. Feeling a bit like Gulliver in the land of the giants, we set off along the paths between the gigantic tufts of grass.

Tony explained that the paths had been made by the seals, and we should make a noise so as not to surprise one. Nick was elected as the bravest, and certainly the noisiest, and was sent on ahead, armed with a dinghy paddle. At first he started shouting a warning to any hidden seals, 'I'm bad. Don't mess with me. I'm bad.' After the first little rustle of the leaves, however, his chant became 'I'm scared, you don't need to mess with me.'

He retreated to the back of the line. We took a vote on who was dispensable enough to be put at the front. We could not do without the cook, so Lana was safe. We would need the doctor if anybody did get bitten, so Tony off the hook. Chris already had his ticket to fly out from Punta Arenas, so he could not risk it. Only Jeff could prevent complete mayhem from developing in the engine room. Nobody, however, seemed to feel the skipper was needed at all, so I found myself unanimously voted to the front of the line.

It was unnerving poking along through the giant tufts of grass, expecting at any moment to be attacked by an enormous seal.

Lana and the tussock grass of Kidney Island. We were very wary of meeting a fur seal in among the grass.

Whether it was Nick's continuing noise that did the trick, or just that no seals wanted to use the path at that time, however, we safely crossed to the other side without even a glimpse of a seal.

It was worth the adrenalin. We found ourselves at the top of a rocky ledge, overlooking a whole family of seals, about 15 or 20ft below us. There were three little pups, looking friendly and fluffy, with the mother and maybe her sister lying beside them. They were all being watched over by big, ugly father. We did not try to get close, but satisfied ourselves with watching them from the cliff top.

The way back through the grass was not nearly so traumatic, at least not for me, as Jeff went first. Going back never seems to take as long as getting there anyway. Back on the beach, we found that the two big male seals had moved much nearer to the dinghy. I wondered whether they were going to give us problems as we tried to drag the dinghy back into the water. I had recently read an account of some people who had visited the Antarctic, and had left their black rubber dinghy pulled up on a beach. A big, myopic fur seal had spotted it, not recognised it for what it was, and tried to make love to it. When it failed to respond to his amorous advances, he had bitten it. After it burst, he had ripped it to shreds, leaving the people stranded on the beach with an over-sexed, frustrated seal. We were luckier. We got to the dinghy and although we got ugly looks and a few growls as we dragged it back down the beach, the seals did not try to eat us, and the dinghy retained its virginity.

Back in Stanley, the *Biscoe* had moved off the dock to let *Monsunen* back to her normal spot. As we came into the harbour George very kindly waved for us to come back alongside him.

The Boss finally arrived at lunchtime the next day. I went out to the new and enormous airport at Mount Pleasant to meet him. Before they were allowed to leave the airport, all the new arrivals had to sit through a short lecture about the danger of mines, and they were each given a mine map.

He wanted to sail the next morning, but the wind was howling out of the north-west, effectively pinning us to *Monsunen*'s side. So although he would have happily had us set off to sea, fortunately we could not move the boat with the wind pressing her so hard against the *Monsunen*. We took him on a tour of the harbour area, showing him some of the old wrecks, but he showed only a cursory interest; he was anxious to be off.

That evening we told him about our bank statement, and the missing pay. He was a bit flustered, but explained that he was reorganising his financial affairs, and since he had lost track of how many standing order payments were being made from his various accounts, he had stopped them all! He promised to sort it all out when he got back, and assured us that we would be paid. When we told Jeff, he decided that he had better contact his bank and see if his pay was arriving. It turned out it was not. The only crew receiving any money were Nick, Chris and now Tony, as Lana paid them on board, from petty cash.

The wind eased a little that evening, so we moved out to anchor, so that we would not be pinned on again if the wind freshened in the morning.

Freshen it did. It was so fresh it was howling again. It was blowing over 30 knots, but that was not going to stop the Boss, so off we set. I suggested that we go to Kidney Island again. I knew that the anchorage there would be snug in the north-wester. That was not far enough away for the Boss, however, he wanted to get to Salvador, halfway along the north coast of East Falkland. He scorned the radio forecast of strong gales and extremely rough seas, and insisted that *Thalassi* could take it. Perhaps she could, but I was less than sure that the mast or the crew could!

It was not too bad in the lee of the land, but when we turned the corner and felt the full strength of the gale, it was awful. There must have been a good current against us, because after three hours of hard sailing, bashing and crashing to windward, we had only made about 8 miles. As tactfully as I could, I pointed out to the Boss that there was no chance of getting to Salvador before dark – at the present rate of progress it would be about lunch time the next day. Reluctantly he agreed to let me turn round and run back and look for another anchorage for the night. Volunteer Beach was the nearest anchorage that would give us reasonable protection, but even that was a couple of hours away.

It turned out to be a snug enough anchorage, but we could not go ashore as the beach was shown as one that was mined. It cannot have been too thickly mined, however, because on the beach there was a big fur seal, which weighed a lot more than a person. If he did not set the mines off then nor would we, but nobody, not even Nick, wanted to take that chance.

We watched the fur seal stalking a big goose. It looked rather like a big cat, sneaking along, low to the ground. When it was about 15 or 20ft away, it pounced. The speed was amazing for such a big beast. It caught the goose totally by surprise. After catching it, the seal batted it about, just like a cat toying with a little bird or a mouse, before finally settling down to eat it. I vowed not to get within 20ft of a hungry fur seal!

Fortunately the wind eased again during the night, and we traversed the north coast the next day without too much trouble. By mid-afternoon, we were anchored in San Carlos Water. This is a good-sized bay off Falkland Sound, which is the strait that separates the two main islands. We were struck with another pang of homesickness. With the cool misty weather, rolling green hills and rugged, rocky shore, we could just as easily be anchored off our house in west Cork, Ireland.

San Carlos was where the main British assault force landed to retake the islands. Several ships were sunk in the sound, and many men died in the landing. We went ashore at the settlement, and walked up to visit the stone-walled cemetery, where many of them lay. It was terribly moving. We saw the grave of Colonel H. Jones, who led the assault. What was most upsetting were the graves of some of the young soldiers. Many were still teenagers when they died. On most of the graves were personal letters sent out by parents, brothers, sisters and sometimes wives and children. It was not just the cold wind that made my eyes water. It was sad. We asked ourselves, why?

The British Cemetery at San Carlos, where, amongst others, Col 'H' Jones is buried. It is very moving to read the personal family messages affixed to many of the graves of the young soldiers.

After a few quiet moments in the cemetery, we walked over to the nearby farm. Sheep shearing was in full swing, and we were invited into the shed to watch. Each farm has its own shearing shed, but in most cases the actual work is done by a group of itinerants who travel from farm to farm. Some come from as far away as Scotland or New

Zealand for the seasonal work. They use electric clippers, and it is incredible how quickly they remove each fleece. It was funny to see the bemused, newly shorn sheep emerge from the shed, shivering in the cool breeze. The foreman showed us how the wool is sorted by grade and then, using a very old manual press, squeezed into bales of some 500lb each, ready for George to collect with the *Monsunen*.

Over the next few days we made our way steadily west. The weather was like the little girl with the curl. When it was good, it was very very good, and when it was bad it was bloody awful.

We had a very pleasant sail to Keppel Island, then had to hole up there for an extra day while the next depression rattled up from Cape Horn. While we were at Keppel Island, we went to another penguin colony. This time they were gentoos. Again they were there in their thousands, living in apparent harmony with hundreds of ducks.

Perhaps the most exciting wildlife encounter, however, was our first visit to an albatross colony on Saunders Island. Saunders is quite a large island, but it is farmed by a single family. The farmers, David and Susan, had few enough visitors, and were proud to show us their island and its wildlife. They invited us all up to the house for tea, then we piled into two ex-army Land Rovers and they drove us over to the western side of the island.

Along the cliff tops was a colony of albatrosses. The young were some three months old, and already about the size of a full-grown chicken. They were covered in a fluffy grey down, and it would still be several weeks before they would be able to fly. Until that time they were destined to sit on their nests, being fed by their parents. The nests are curious pedestal-shaped structures, about 12in high. They seem to be built of seaweed and grass, cemented together by mud or perhaps the albatross's own droppings. One chick stands purposefully on each pedestal. As a parent swoops in to land beside the nest, the chick starts clacking its beak. The parent sticks its own beak far down the chick's gullet and regurgitates the food for it.

The chicks showed no fear of us. If we went very close to them they would start clacking their beaks, not from fear but, I think because they were hoping for us to regurgitate some food for them. Not even the adult birds were frightened of us. If we sat quietly beside a nest, one of the parents would often come swooping in, to land within inches of us and proceed to feed the chick. I think we were more wary of them than they were of us. At least to begin with, it was a little unnerving to make eye contact with such big birds at such close range. Their curved beaks are at least 4 or 5in long, and they were often pointed in our direction, from perhaps 1ft away. Never once, however, did they show the slightest sign of aggression, or

Many of the albatross nests were perched on the edge of the cliffs. While this was precarious for the young, it made it easier for the parents, who just had to step off the cliff to be airborne. Even parents with their young were happy to let us get as close as we wanted to.

indeed of fear.

When the parents want to take off, they nonchalantly stroll over to the edge of the cliff and step off into space. Just by spreading their wings, they soar away in the air currents blowing up the cliff. They do not give even a single flap with their wings. It is totally effortless.

Far below us, on the lower portions of the cliff, we could see our fourth kind of penguins, the comical little rockhoppers. It was so funny to watch them pop out of the water like small missiles, to land unerringly on a rock with a sort of 'Who me?' expression.

Leaving Saunders Island, we had our first look at krill, the shrimp-like creatures that abound in the southern ocean and form a major link in the food chain that supports all the wild life. We caught them in a very un-Darwinian way. As we were getting ready to hoist the anchor, the ever-vigilant Jeff spotted that the engine was running a little hotter than normal. He stopped it to investigate, and found the filter for the cooling water intake was blocked with half a bucketful of krill. I was surprised at how big they were; for some reason I had imagined them to be some microscopic form of plankton, but they were the size of small shrimp. The Boss wanted Lana to boil them up for lunch, but I persuaded Jeff to 'accidently' dump them, as we had no idea how long they had been in the filter. They were well and truely dead, and some might have been there for a day or two.

At each island we visited, we received an equally warm welcome ashore. On these outer islands, the people rarely get into Stanley, and generally their only visitors are George on the *Monsunen* or the other

Chris makes his first, slightly wary encounter with the Carcass Island Sea Elephants.

supply ship, the *Forest*. A few of the farms have bulldozed out an airstrip, and some of them offer R and R accommodtion to the soldiers from Mount Pleasant. Without exception, they seemed pleased to see visitors, and took a proprietorial interest in showing us 'their' wildlife.

Rob on Carcass Island took us to see his sea elephants. What monsters they were. The males can exceed 20ft in length, and more than 7000lb in weight, but it is not just the size that has given them their name. The males have a curiously shaped nose, remarkably like a somewhat shortened elephant's trunk.

He showed us several sea elephants on a beach, stretched out in the sun. Then he took us along a path through some tussock grass to where a family group of half a dozen were lying. Rob told us that they were ashore for moulting, which they do annually at the end of the breeding season. They were snuggled together in a muddy little hollow, sighing, burping and making smells in total satisfaction. I told Nick that with the noises and smells they were making, they reminded me of him relaxing after a big meal. He did not think it was funny.

We could get pretty much as close to them as we wanted, for as long as we could stand the smell. The biggest, and presumably the oldest, male was a bit protective, however. If anybody ventured a little bit too close, he would growl and burp until we retreated. Despite their bad breath (from both ends), their mouths looked pink, clean and soft. They had big, weepy-looking eyes which Lana found appealing.

In the area around the sea elephants, there were literally thousands of seabirds. Rob identified some of them for us. He pointed out kelp and dolphin gulls, heron, black-browed albatross, kelp and upland geese, more Magellanic penguins and, flying amongst them all, cariacara hawks. There were not just one or two of each species, but, with the exception of the hawks, hundreds if not thousands. As we walked along the northern point of Carcass Island we could easily imagine that we had stepped into Hitchcock's movie, *The Birds*. There were birds everywhere, and the noise was quite deafening.

My favourite island was West Point. Roddy and Lillian, the owners, were as welcoming as everybody else, and we were soon invited up to the house for the obligatory cup of tea. Lillian is a keen gardener and, against all odds, she has cultivated a wonderful rose garden in a sunken, well-screened area that Roddy has built for her. The whole farm is spick and span, and very well organised.

Roddy drove us across to their albatross colony. It was even more extensive than the one on Saunders. There were hundreds of fluffy

Compared to the King penguins, the Rockhoppers looked decidely scruffy, but they provided an endless source of entertainment, watching them literally hopping up and down the steep rocky cliffs.

grey chicks, all clacking their beaks as we walked past them. Once more there were Rockhopper penguins living below the colony. None was swimming, so we could not watch them doing their trick of popping up out of the water, but we did see them hopping up surprisingly steep cliffs. They seem to be unable to waddle like the Gentoos or Magellanics; they appear to hop everywhere they go. These penguins have a distinctive fringe of spiky yellow feathers over their bright orange eyes. We graded them better dressed than the scruffy Magellanics, but nowhere near as smart as the kings or even the Gentoos, who were voted into second place.

As we made our way back to the boat, Roddy gave Lana two enormous cabbages, and three lettuces which were nearly as big. All were fresh from the garden, and Lana was munching away on the lettuce before she was even out of the dinghy. In the bay, Tony identified our first oystercatchers for us. They were poking about on the beach with their long red chisel-shaped beaks.

Our departure from West Point was slightly delayed by another bucketful of krill in the filter, and an enormous ball of kelp round the anchor. When the anchor came up, it was lost from sight in a tangle of kelp some 4 or 5ft across. Nick was lowered over the side with the bread knife, and it took him several minutes to cut away the rubbery kelp so that we could stow the anchor.

Our last Falkland stop was to be at New Island, at the western tip of the group. This island is privately owned, and is being kept as a nature reserve. The owners were away in Stanley, but we managed to get permission by radio to explore it. Next to the landing spot, I was excited to find a Jarvis brace winch, still in working order. This winch is what revolutionised the last days of commercial sail, and allowed the ships to sail with much reduced crew. It consists of a pair of conical drums, which haul in the brace from one side of a sail's yard while letting out the other. The geometry of the thing is very subtle, since the rate at which the rope is hauled in varies as the sail swings round during a tack or gybe. Here was one, bolted to the end of a concrete ramp, used now for hauling dinghies out of the water. What ignominy.

Nobody else shared my interest or enthusiasm, and I was soon escorted off to the next penguin colony. I have to say that this was one of the best. We were able to walk right down among the rockhoppers, which were so thick on the ground in places that we had to be careful not to tread on them. Sometimes it was even necessary to push them gently aside to gain a foothold.

During our last day at New Island, we made our preparations for the passage to Cape Horn. We took off the large jib and stowed it below, leaving the smaller Number 2 jib in place. The storm jib and trysail came out of their stowage, and I got the crew to try hoisting each in turn. It was easy enough in the quiet calm of a sheltered anchorage, but I hoped that we would not have to set them in a Cape Horn storm.

After we had finished our chores, Chris and Tony dared each other into going for a swim. The water temperature was just 9 degrees above freezing. It was funny watching their reactions as they hit the water: I would say their swim should be entered in the *Guinness Book of Records* as the world's shortest. We did not think it was possible for two people to come up the ladder at the same time.

Lana baked an extra supply of bread and cooked a giant pot of stew. It all went into the freezer ready in case conditions became too rough to cook.

I was sad to be leaving the Falklands. We had only scratched the surface of this wonderful cruising ground, but at least we had done better than Darwin. How could he have missed so much?

It was time to visit new places. As Darwin had said a 150 years before, Cape Horn was now to be the gateway to further adventures.

Chapter 12

Cape Horn

As *Beagle* was making her way south into Le Maire Strait, Fitzroy chose to hug the shore of Tierra del Fuego, trying to gain some shelter from the endless westerly gales. In his journal, Darwin described the days as cold, gloomy and gusty. Off to the east they could see the forbidding sight of Staten Island, with its inhospitable rocky shoreline and snow-capped mountains.

Despite the bad weather, and another bout of seasickness, Darwin was thrilled to be visiting Tierra del Fuego. He was looking forward to some serious exploring of what he described as 'a country never before traversed by Europeans'.

Tierra del Fuego was discovered by Magellan in 1520, when he sailed through the strait which is named after him. It is a large island, over 28,000 square miles. To the north it is bounded by the Straits of Magellan, and to the south by the Beagle Channel. For the 300 years from its discovery to the beginning of the *Beagle*'s survey, it was rarely visited, and little was known of the land or the people who lived there.

In 1881, forty-eight years after Darwin's visit, the territory was divided between Chile and Argentina, with Chile getting the western two-thirds. The remaining islands to the south were arbitrarily allocated to the two countries at the same time. Nobody seemed to care much until oil was discovered in 1945. Ever since then, who owns what has been a serious bone of contention between Chile and Argentina.

Of course Darwin could not know anything of this, nor did he know that Tierra del Fuego's highest peak would be named after him. Mount Darwin is 7999ft high. If only we had had the time, I would have loved to go up and put another rock on top to make it up to 8000ft.

Working their way down the Fuegan coast, always on the lookout for new anchorages, Captain Fitzroy spotted a good sheltered bay, so they pulled in for the night. The bay was almost completely surrounded by comparatively low, rounded mountains. The slopes were thickly wooded, with the trees coming right down to the water's edge. The landscape was like nothing Darwin had seen before, and he was hoping to be able to explore it.

That night a gale sprang up. Heavy squalls came down from the mountains, making the *Beagle* tug at her anchor chain. They could see huge waves running past the entrance, but their bay stayed calm enough. Everybody was glad to be at anchor – it was not a night to be at sea. They named the anchorage Good Success Bay.

When they first sailed into the bay, a group of Fuegans had stood on the point watching them, waving their ragged capes and shouting. As soon as the wind began to ease in the morning, Captain Fitzroy sent a group ashore to talk to them. Darwin went of course, together with the three Fuegans they had on board.

To Darwin's disappointment they could not communicate at all. The three Fuegans from the ship could understand those on land no better than anybody else. To Darwin's ear their language was a barely articulate series of grunts. Captain Cook, on his visit, described it as sounding like a man clearing his throat.

This seems to be the first time that Darwin took much of an interest in the three Fuegans on board the *Beagle* – at least it is the first time he mentions them in his journal. It is surprising to me that he seems to have largely ignored them until then, especially as it was ostensibly to take them home that the voyage was being undertaken at all.

All three of them had become reasonably good at speaking and understanding English, but the girl, Fuegia Basket, was the linguist of the trio. Not only was her English the best, but she had picked up a fair smattering of Spanish and Portuguese on their voyage south. The younger man, Jemmy Button, who had been swopped for a pearl button, was the favourite with the crew. He was almost always cheerful and laughing. When Darwin was seasick, he would come to visit him, saying 'Poor, poor fellow', while at the same time laughing at him, as he could not believe that a bit of rough water could make somebody ill.

Jemmy was short, thick and fat, yet exceedingly vain. He wore his hair very short, and loved to study himself in a mirror. He almost always wore gloves, and would be very irritated if his highly polished shoes got scuffed.

The surviving adult was called York Minster, not after the cathedral itself, but after a large rock near his home, which in 1768 had reminded a homesick Captain Cook of it. He was a short but powerful man, who tended to be a bit reserved, even taciturn.

Despite the fact that all three were fairly good at English, Darwin had found it quite difficult to get information from them about the

way they had lived before coming on the *Beagle*. Sometimes it seemed to him as if the Fuegans thought in a different way to the Europeans, and they were often overwhelmed by the apparent complexity of what Darwin took to be a simple question. He did manage to understand that the living was difficult, and times could be very hard. Jemmy described how, in periods of famine, they killed the old women of the family by suffocating them to death in the smoke of a fire, and ate them. When Darwin asked him why they did not kill and eat the dogs, Jemmy looked at him in utter astonishment. He explained, as if to a child, 'Doggies catch otters. Old women, no.'

So despite his contacts with these three, Darwin was ill prepared to meet the Fuegans on the beach. He thought that they seemed 'like troubled spirits from another world'. They were a 'curious and interesting spectacle'. The only clothing they wore was a cape of guanaco skin, worn with the woolly side out. The guanaco is an animal that looks a bit like a llama. It used to be very common in much of South America, but it has been hunted for its skin almost to the point of extinction.

The Fuegan faces were painted with red, white and black stripes. The remainder of their skin was a reddish, coppery colour. They looked very fierce, and Darwin said that he could not believe 'how wide is the difference between savage and civilised man. It is greater than that between wild and domesticated animals.'

He and Fitzroy had another of their long philosophical discussions, and agreed that these people must be of a different species to themselves, and surely lacked the same high potential. Fitzroy refused to believe that he could be even remotely related to the Fuegans. This time Lieutenant Sullivan took the more sympathetic view, and suggested that the Fuegans were victims of the harsh surroundings in which they found themselves, and were perhaps just adapting to them. Darwin and Fitzroy remained unconvinced.

The Fuegans certainly seemed to have adapted to the cold. The crew of *Beagle* were to see naked mothers suckling bare children, apparently oblivious to the snow falling on their bodies. Most of the Fuegans wore just the cape, which sometimes, as a concession to a particularly cold wind, might be swivelled round and worn on the windward side of their bodies.

Fitzroy was anxious to press on and return Jemmy, Fuegia and York to their own territory, west of Cape Horn. They sailed south in gentle conditions, and rounded the Horn on Christmas Eve, which was a calm, bright evening. They had an almost unprecedented easterly breeze.

Captain Fitzroy felt a bit smug, the crew were all congratulating

themselves on an easy rounding of the Cape, and Darwin wondered what all the fuss was about Cape Horn. Their thoughts were an hour or two premature. Before they could reach an anchorage, the easterly wind vanished and a gale sprang up from the west. They were unceremoniously driven back past Cape Horn. It now looked as forbidding as its reputation. Low, black clouds scudded along and enormous waves broke against the ominous black rocks, throwing spray over the cliffs which are more than 200ft high. Rain and hail was mixed in with the icy cold spray.

Our landfall on Cape Horn itself. Nick and Chris were disappointed not to be rounding in a gale, but the rest of us were happy to take advantage of the brief spell of good weather.

They ran back into the lee of the land, and were fortunate to make an anchorage in a snug little cove in time for Christmas dinner. They dropped three anchors and rode out the gale without any further problems.

It was New Year's Eve before the wind abated and they could sail again. While they were waiting, Darwin tried to explore the area around the bay, but with limited success. Almost all the trees were a kind of beech, with unusual brownish yellow leaves, which Darwin says made the place look gloomy. He soon found that it was not going to be easy to explore, as the underbrush was extremely thick and virtually impenetrable. The only progress he could make was by crawling up the bed of a stream – what devotion to duty!

When *Beagle* set sail again, the wind was still in the west, and quite strong, but they made reasonably good progress. At least Fitzroy thought it was reasonable; Darwin was in the grip of seasickness yet again, and felt it was anything but reasonable.

They weathered the Horn again, and were within a couple of miles of the anchorage at Waterman Island, where York Minster lived, when the wind increased considerably. They took in sail and reefed as the wind got up, until they were down to just the topsails with five reefs in each. They kept beating, but could not make the final few miles. Slowly and inexorably they lost ground, and were swept back past Cape Horn again.

The gale increased to a full storm. Fitzroy reckoned it was the strongest that he had ever seen. They stowed and secured the top-sails and set the storm trysail, close reefed, and the forestaysail. Under this rig they lay virtually hove to for two days.

The ship was labouring in the huge seas. The noise of her creaking and groaning could be heard even over the shriek of the wind. The crew were getting tired. Everything they owned was wet, and there was no way to dry their clothes. Even their bunks were wet, and at the end of each watch they turned in 'full standing', without even bothering to get out of their wet oilskins.

Unperturbed by it all were the albatrosses. Even at the height of the storm, Fitzroy recorded that they were swooping and circling around the ship. Darwin was past caring.

One wave, bigger than all the rest, came roaring out of the mist. It stopped the *Beagle* dead in the water. Before she could gather way enough to answer the helm, a second wave hit her. That threw her round, beam on to the waves. The next one broke right over the struggling ship, and pressed her down until the lee bulwarks were several feet under water. One of the whale-boats, which was stowed on deck, filled with water and was swept away.

The two men on the wheel did not need to hear the command to put the helm down to run before the wind. They knew that if another wave hit them now, the ship would probably give up the struggle. It seemed an eternity before she answered her helm and began to turn. Slowly, ever so slowly, she began to turn and come back upright. The water was streaming off her decks in torrents. She was going to live to sail another day.

That turned out to be the last fury of the storm. It was almost as if the wind had tried its best, failed, and had now given up. The wind dropped quite quickly, and despite the large sea that was still running, they crowded on sail, and set off westwards once more.

Cape Horn was passed for the fifth time. This time, Captain Fitzroy decided not to try and go west to Waterman; instead he ducked in under False Cape Horn, and anchored in a small but very deep bay. They anchored in 47 fathoms (282ft) of water. The extra weight of the chain, reaching down to those depths, caused it to run out so fast that sparks flew off the new patent windlass. It was going to be a good test for the windlass to recover all that chain.

At last they were anchored west of Cape Horn. They had made good 30 miles to the west after twenty-four uninterrupted days of cruel beating.

We were hoping for a leisurely breakfast followed by an unhurried departure from New Island, for our attempt on Cape Horn, but we had reckoned without the Boss's impatience. He could not sleep, whether from excitement or fear we did not know. Before dawn he was pacing the deck, banging on cabin doors, anxious to go. He was not even interested in waiting for a proper breakfast. We had to make do with a rushed snack before hoisting the anchor at first light.

We stood out into a blustery south-westerly Force 7 – 30 knots of wind, right on the nose. Not a happy prospect. All day we crashed along. Lana had the worst of it, trying to cook a hot lunch to make up for the abbreviated breakfast. Things were flying off the cooker and going everywhere. Even Nick, with his cast-iron stomach, was off his food.

I was nervous. My confidence in the mast was close to zero. I gave strict orders to all the crew that I was to be called before shaking out any reefs, or at the slightest suggestion of an increase in wind, or if anybody saw an approaching squall. If it was like this now, on what really looked like quite a 'nice' day, what would it be like off the Horn if we were caught?

Dinner was not much easier than lunch had been. Chris was complaining because it was too rough to run the dishwasher, and he had been seconded to help clean up in the galley.

Fortunately the wind eased as darkness fell – just about the time Lana finished stowing the galley, it fell away to almost nothing. I did not hesitate or consult the Boss. On went the engine. I did not want to hang around. We rolled up the jib and motorsailed through the night, with just the reefed mainsail set. With the engine's help, we could lay our course, and we made excellent, if rather uncomfortable, progress. By early morning we were passing down the east coast of Staten Island.

We could have followed *Beagle*, and we would have saved a few miles by going through the Le Maire Strait, between Staten Island and the mainland. But that was Argentinian water, and we had been advised that a British-flag vessel bound from the Falklands would not be welcome in Argentina. Rather than risk a diplomatic incident, I decided to stay outside the island.

We were close enough to see the iron-bound shore that Darwin had described. It looked very forbidding, guarding the snow-covered mountains. A couple of months later, in Chile, we met an old man who was in his nineties. He had been shipwrecked there as a boy. He had sailed from Hamburg on a ship in the nitrate trade. They had been caught off the Horn and swept back to be wrecked on the south side of the island. He had swum ashore, and vowed never to go to sea again. He stayed in Chile for the next seventy-five years. Having seen the waves breaking on those cliffs, even on a gentle day such as we had, I can only think he must have been exceptionally strong or very lucky.

The wind stayed fairly light, and crept slowly round to the north. The barometer was rising and on the weather map the nearest depression was still well west of the Cape. I was not tempted to stop the engine, however. Our big jib was below decks, so we would not be able to set enough sail in the light wind to keep up our speed. We were making good progress as we were, and the good weather would not last long.

By dawn we were some 80 miles off the Horn. The wind was still light, about 10–15 knots, and it had gone right to the north. The Boss was now becoming anxious that it would be dark when we came to pass the Horn. As far as he was concerned, that would not do at all – he had not come all that way to go past it in the dark. He wanted me to slow down and wait until the next morning.

I did some sums and talked to Jeff. We reckoned that if we increased the revs a bit, and increased the pitch of the propeller a little more, we could probably get there late afternoon, in time for the Boss to get his photographs. Jeff shared my feelings. The sooner we got into a secure anchorage the better. The longer we stayed out, the more likely we were to be clobbered.

We shook out one reef from the main, and set the jib. Together with the help from the engine we were flying along, averaging close to 10 knots. Cape Horn was abeam at tea-time, and Lana opened the obligatory bottle of champagne.

The bleak and barren landscape was pretty much as we expected. We already knew that Cape Horn itself is a fairly nondescript little island, but what did surprise us was the miserable little lighthouse. We had expected a monumental stone tower at the very least, but instead found a very rusty, insubstantial structure, built right down on the beach on the south-eastern shore. We closed to within about 200yd of the cliffs, and spoke to the navy lookout on the VHF. He invited us ashore. It would have been calm enough to land on the beach with the dinghy, and that would certainly have been a exciting thing to do, but darkness would soon be approaching, and we still had to find an anchorage for the night. The Boss was insisting that we anchor somewhere to the west of the Horn for the night, so we could round it again the next day.

These islands are no place to be poking around in the dark – in fact they are no place to be poking around at all. In my opinion they are a place to visit if you must, before going north quickly, into more sheltered waters.

We found a promising-looking bay on the eastern side of Hermite Island. It would shelter us from the existing north wind, and from the westerly which must surely come soon. The barometer was still high, but it was already beginning its descent. On the weather fax a row of low-pressure systems were lining up across the Pacific, waiting their turn to give us a blast. The bay was deep, but nowhere near as deep as the 47 fathoms where *Beagle* had lain. We dropped the anchor in about 18 fathoms and let out all the chain. We dropped a second anchor as well, and despite a bit of complaining from the boys, we brought a third anchor up from below, together with its rode, and got it ready in case we had to drop it in a hurry.

By the time we were all cleared away, it was getting dark. Cape Horn looked as if it was crouching in wait for us. We went below and found that Lana had supper ready on the table for us. We had rounded Cape Horn – hard to believe, really.

Heading into Hermite Island for the night. I found it intimidating to be anchored for the night in sight of Cape Horn.

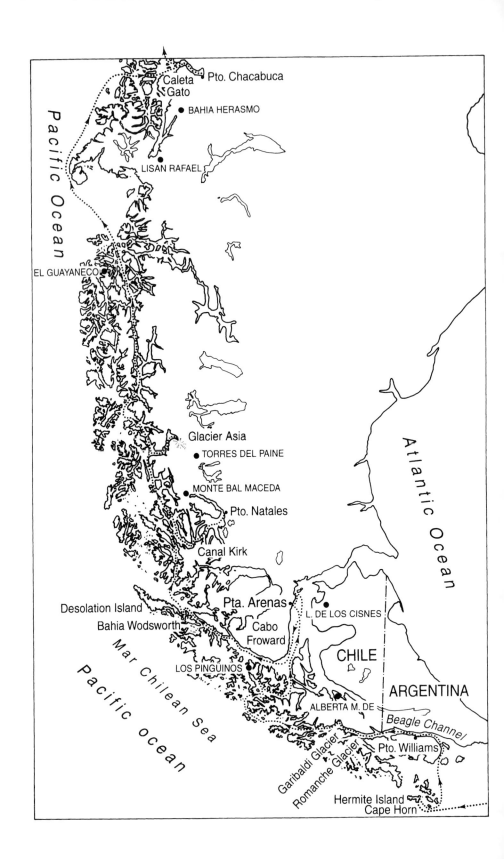

Chapter 13

Tierra del Fuego and the Beagle Channel

Fitzroy was anxious to get the three Fuegans home, but after the twenty-four days it had taken them to weather the Horn, he was not anxious for *Beagle* to leave the anchorage. He decided to mount an expedition westward through the Beagle Channel, using the yawl and three whale-boats. They could take the Fuegans home and survey the channel at the same time.

The carpenter fitted a temporary wood and canvas deck on the yawl, which they loaded with supplies for the expedition. Although it could sail quite well, it was too big and ungainly to row when there was no wind or the wind was ahead. When that happened, the three whale-boats would have to tow it.

Twenty-four crew from the *Beagle* set off, including Darwin and Fitzroy. Then there were the three Fuegans, and Mathews, a missionary who was hoping to convert the natives to Christianity. With all the necessary provisions, the four boats were heavily laden. They were open and offered no protection from the elements for the crews, but they did carry tents for shelter at night.

Darwin and Fitzroy were in the yawl. Despite the fact that it was the biggest of the four, it was carrying the most cargo, so it was pretty cramped for the occupants. All the crew were pleased to be ashore each night, if only to stretch their legs.

Fitzroy decided to begin his exploration by running back downwind to enter the Beagle Channel at the eastern end. This, I think, was in itself something of an act of faith, considering the struggle that *Beagle* had endured to get as far west as she had. It would seem to me that they ran a significant risk of not being able to beat back to the ship. Fitzroy, however, obviously weighed up the odds and decided that they would manage.

After leaving the ship, they sailed eastwards through the islands to get to the Beagle Channel itself. They found a snug little cove for their first night's stop. Darwin paints an idyllic picture of the place. Imagine a small bay, surrounded by low hills, with the four boats anchored off the beach. The water is glassy calm. Trees are growing right to the water's edge and actually overhanging the beach in places. Their tarpaulin tents are suspended over crossed oars, and in front of each a campfire is burning. The smoke is drifting up through the trees, curling up into the wooded valley.

Darwin, and one assumes the others, were supremely content. It had been an easy day, followed by a pleasant evening and a good night's sleep. Unfortunately, that campsite was not typical. Their first night was to be one of the few peaceful ones they were to pass on the entire expedition.

The Beagle Channel runs more or less directly east–west, with a fork towards the western end. The prevailing wind, of course is from the west, so it usually comes howling down the length of the channel, which is about 120 miles long and a fairly uniform 2 miles wide. It was likely to be a tough beat for the boats to make their westing.

As they entered the channel proper, conditions were still mild, and they enjoyed some more pleasant sailing. The channel reminded Darwin of the valley of Loch Ness, which he had visited on several of his trips to Scotland. It was easy sailing, augmented by a bit of rowing when the wind dropped light.

Parts of the channel are so straight that the water disappears over the horizon, between the lines of fringing mountains. Most of the mountains bordering the channel are over 3000ft, rising straight up from the water. The lower parts of the slopes are covered in the same dusky-coloured beech trees that Darwin had seen in the east. They exist only below about 1400 or 1500ft. Above that height there are no trees, and the cut-off line is remarkably sharp and well defined. As Darwin commented, it looks just like the high tide mark on a beach.

It was not long before they came across the first group of Indians. Like those they had met on the east coast, these were naked, with long straggly hair. They had perhaps never seen white men before, and their surprise at seeing four boats go sailing by could not have been greater had they seen ghosts. They waved, yelled and shook the sticks they were carrying.

At night the sailors could see fires burning on virtually every point. Were the fires for warmth, for cooking, or for passing along the word that these strange apparitions were coming? Earlier explorers had witnessed the same phenomenon, and hence the name they had given the island, Tierra del Fuego – Land of the Fire.

That night, a group of Fuegans approached the expedition's camp. Fitzroy was not sure whether their overtures were hostile or not, so he passed out gifts to try and encourage them to be friendly. The most popular item was red tape, which the Indians tied round their heads. Jemmy was visibly embarrassed by these people. He kept reassuring Fitzroy that his own tribe was better. He was to be proved woefully wrong.

Fitzroy was concerned that the Fuegans, as a race, were hard to intimidate. They seemed unable to grasp that guns were dangerous. Even when one of the sailors shot a bird or animal, the Indians seemed unable to accept that the bang from the gun was connected with the demise of the distant creature, since they were not able to see anything pass between the two.

As the boats progressed westward, they passed into an area of neutral territory between Jemmy's tribe and their neighbours. Jemmy himself was well aware of the strength of the expedition. He knew exactly what the guns were capable of, but he had still been very nervous about landing in his neighbours' territory. The respect each had for the other's fierceness was perhaps indicated by the broad no man's land which separated the two tribes.

The expedition stopped for one night close to the beginning of Jemmy's tribe's territory. They were to the west of Navarino Island and found a sheltered bay where a peaceful family of Fuegans were living. After a short period of mutual uncertainty, they shared the camp peacefully. *Beagle*'s crew set up their tents and lit their fires. They handed out some biscuits to the Fuegans, who after a nervous nibble or two gulped them down. Despite being clothed as warmly as the Royal Navy knew how, the men from *Beagle* had to sit close to the fires to try to keep warm. It was a chilly autumnal evening. In contrast, the naked Fuegans were sitting well back from the fire, and Darwin was surprised to see perspiration streaming off them from the roasting they considered they were getting.

As the expedition progressed ever further west, Jemmy began to recognise landmarks. They finally met up with his tribe at the settlement called Woollya.

His father had died while he had been away, but his mother and brothers came to meet him. He had been gone for five years, and Darwin expected a certain amount of excitement at the reunion. He was disappointed, however. He says that the meeting was as interesting as that between a horse turned out into a field when he joins an old companion. There was no display of affection at all. His mother stared at Jemmy for a moment, and then returned to attend to her canoe. Perhaps she was worried that she was going to have to return the button she had received in payment for him.

It transpired that Jemmy, never a gifted linguist, had forgotten most of his own language. Darwin found it rather pathetic listening to him trying to converse with his brother first in English, then in Spanish, and becoming angry when nobody could understand him.

The women of the tribe paid more attention to Fuegia than they did to Jemmy, even though she was not from their tribe. York, who had firm designs on Fuegia by this time, decided that they might settle right there. There was a reasonable amount of flat land next to the settlement, which is a rare enough commodity in this mountainous area.

Mathews the missionary had been casting around for a place to set up his mission, and decided that Woollya would suit him too. So the *Beagle's* crew set to work. They built three wigwams, dug two gardens on the flat land, and planted seeds enough to give the whole tribe food in the spring.

Although Fitzroy and the men had given the Fuegans many presents, it seemed that they always wanted more. The first word that a Fuegan would utter on meeting a stranger was *yammerschooner*. This, York explained, meant 'Give me.'

There were some 120 members of the tribe living in and around Woollya. The women worked hard, doing all the domestic chores, while the men lounged around watching and *yammerschooner*-ing. The whole tribe was fascinated, and most of them came to watch, when any of the crew washed themselves in the little stream that bordered the camp. Like the gauchos in Argentina, they had never seen such a curious thing before.

It was all very peaceful and relaxed. Darwin and one or two of the officers took long walks in the bush surrounding the camp. Everything seemed fine and friendly, until one day Fitzroy noticed that all the women and children had vanished. Neither York nor Jemmy knew why. Fitzroy became very nervous. He wanted to avoid a confrontation because he knew that his men would kill many of the Fuegans if it came to a fight. He decided to move his camp that night, to another bay a mile or two down the channel. Mathews, however, decided to stay put.

The night passed uneventfully, and when they returned to visit Mathews the next day, all was well with him too. Fitzroy therefore decided to leave him there and carry on with the survey. He sent the yawl and one of the whale-boats back to the *Beagle*, and carried on west with the two remaining whale-boats.

That day was hot and sunny enough to cause some sunburn among the crew. Beagle Channel was looking at its best, with the brilliant white snow outlining the mountains against the deep blue sky. The water between the mountains was almost as blue as the sky. A group of whales swam, puffing and spouting, ahead of them. The light wind meant that the sailing was pleasant, and Darwin was not the only one to wish that it would always be so.

They sailed all day and just before dark found a good campsite. It was a beach of well-rounded pebbles. Rather to his surprise, Darwin found that that was one of the most comfortable nights he spent on the whole expedition. Peat was cold and damp to sleep on, while rocks were usually jagged and sharp. He did not like camping on a sandy beach, as sand always got into the food and into his bedding. He discovered that a sleeping bag on a pebble beach was heaven at the end of a long day in an open boat.

Even though they were moving away from the settled areas, they kept a watch all night. Darwin took the watch from midnight to 1 a.m., and there was just the occasional distant bark of a dog to remind him that they were not alone on the planet.

Their luck, and the good weather, held the next day too, and they passed the fork in the channel. Fitzroy decided to explore the northern arm first. The mountains on the northern shore, that is on Tierra del Fuego itself, towered some 4000ft above them, and several peaks were considerably higher. The tops of all of the mountains were permanently covered with snow, and all along the shore were streams and waterfalls fed by the melting snows, plunging down through the woods.

After a mile or two they came to their first glaciers. They found several of them reaching right down to the water. Darwin was surprised at their blue colour, as we were when we got there. He described it as beryl-like. The contrast between the blue ice of the glaciers and the white snow above is striking.

They stopped for lunch on the shore opposite a big glacier. From Darwin's description of the place, it seems to have been the Romanche Glacier. They pulled the boats up onto the beach and settled down to eat lunch. While they ate, they admired the ice cliff facing them on the other side of the channel. A few small bits of ice broke free and splashed down into the water. They were hoping to see some bigger pieces fall in, and their wish was fulfilled with a vengeance. Suddenly, with a crack like a cannon shot, a great section of ice fell off the face. The gigantic splash it made sent a large wave racing across the channel towards them. Everybody dashed to save the boats. One seaman reached the water just as the first wave arrived and was tumbled about in the breakers, although fortunately he was not hurt. The boats took a bit of a pounding, but were fortunately not holed. Fitzroy was shaken. All their provisions and weapons were in the boats, and if they had lost them they would surely have died. They were more than 100 miles from the ship, and of course since radios were yet to be invented, they had no way of summoning help.

Just before the wave came, Darwin had been prowling about the beach. He had found some boulders that appeared to have been

The Romanche Glacier, with meltwater running off from under the ice. All the glaciers are retreating, and we have seen photos only about fifteen years old, of the glacier reaching right down into the water.

moved recently, and he had been wondering who or what could have moved them. Now he knew.

At the western end of the Beagle Channel, they found many desolate, uninhabited islands. The weather had turned more characteristically miserable. In many places the coast was too steep and rugged to find room for the tents, and they would have to row extra miles in the dark searching for a campsite. One night, the only place they could find to sleep was on top of two big boulders. When the tide came in, their perch became smaller and smaller, until they had to move back into the boats.

158

The furthest west they got was Stewart Island, about 150 miles from the ship. Finally even Fitzroy had had enough, and they turned round and headed back.

With the wind behind them the going was easier and quicker. They sailed back along the southern arm of the channel, and soon arrived back at the settlement at Woollya, where Mathews told a sorry tale. He had been systematically robbed of everything he possessed, and then several times threatened with violence. One group had tried to keep him awake for several consecutive nights by making loud noises beside his head whenever he lay down.

Darwin felt sure that they had arrived just in time to save Mathews's life and Fitzroy decided that he should not stay, but should return to the ship with them. Mathews did not protest too much. Jemmy was sad to see what was happening. After five years of civilisation, he had come to enjoy some of the habits he had acquired. Now he was finding them impossible to keep. Even his own brother had robbed him of some of his clothes.

Rather than go all the way back to the eastern end of the channel, which would leave them with a long beat back to the ship, Fitzroy decided to go to the west of Navarino Island and take the outside route downwind to the ship. Although they had used a lot of their supplies, the whale-boats were still low in the water. Darwin does not dwell on the passage, but says that it was a rough and dangerous voyage – surely an understatement. He makes no mention of seasickness, so perhaps he could handle the motion of the small boat better than the ship itself.

After 300 miles and twenty days in open boats, they were all pleased to get back to the comparative comforts of the *Beagle* once more. Fitzroy and his officers spent a couple of weeks surveying the area around the anchorage, then after waiting for yet another gale to pass, they retreated to the Falklands for one of the recurring refits and then sailed back north to Montevideo for the worst of the winter.

They returned the following summer, 1843. *Beagle* once again anchored near the eastern end of the Beagle Channel. Perhaps it was the memory of the thrashing they had taken the previous year, but Fitzroy decided to try to beat westwards down the channel with the *Beagle* rather than face the Horn again. It would be hard enough to do this with a modern yacht, but with a ship such as the *Beagle* I would have considered it impossible. Since a square-rigger is not very efficient when going to windward, they would end up sailing about 3 or 4 miles for every 1 mile made good. They would have to zigzag up the channel against the wind, and at every tack there would be a tremendous amount of pulling and hauling for the whole crew, as the

heavy yards had to be swung round and the sails trimmed.

On the rare days when the wind went light, Fitzroy ordered the crew to launch the whale-boats, and with ten men rowing in each, they towed the ship. We were spoilt. A touch of a button, and with a roar of the Mercedes we could do an effortless 9 knots, under the same conditions. Sailing or rowing, it was exhausting work for them, but they managed to get the *Beagle* up the channel to Woollya. They were escorted for the last few miles by a dozen canoes. The Indians had no understanding of why the *Beagle* was tacking, and so followed her every zigzag instead of just paddling a direct course up the middle of the channel.

On board the ship, Darwin felt more comfortable, physically and psychologically, than he did ashore. He felt that not even the boldest Fuegan would try and attack something as big as the *Beagle*.

When they reached Woollya, the place looked deserted, but then a canoe appeared. It was Jemmy, although to begin with nobody recognised the thin, gaunt, naked savage with the long scraggly hair. They had left him plump, clean and well dressed. He was obviously ashamed of the way he looked, and most of the time he kept his back to the ship. Fitzroy invited him on board and gave him a big meal. Jemmy told them that he had lost all his possessions, but had gained a wife. Fitzroy offered to take him back to England, but he declined. This was where his wife was and where his life lay.

He told them that he had relearned quite a lot of his old language, but when they eventually met his wife, and some other tribe members, Darwin and Fitzroy were amused to hear that they all had a smattering of pidgen English. York and Fuegia had left the settlement. York had built a canoe, and they had last been seen paddling westwards.

As the crew of the *Beagle* said goodbye for the last time, and sailed southwards out towards the open sea, Jemmy lit a signal fire in farewell. *Beagle* headed back to the Falklands yet again, and that was the last time she would be in the channel to which she gave her name.

We kept an anchor watch through the night, but did not have even one squall. It turned out to be a snug, calm anchorage, but I did not sleep well. An overactive imagination had offered various scenarios of what a 100-knot squall would do to us. At the first sign of dawn I got up, and when a very gentle tap of the barometer resulted in the needle jumping markedly downwards, I sent Nick to wake everybody. For once I was as impatient as the Boss to get moving. The wind was back in the west, and it did not take a meteorologist to forecast that we were in for a blow.

We had a quick breakfast and then recovered both anchors. Left to my own devices, I would have stayed in the lee of Isla Hoste, and passed between it and Navarino to get into the Beagle Channel. But that would not do for the Boss. We had to 'round the Horn' again. I suppose Nick and Chris were pleased enough. They had been disappointed to motor round on a sunny day. At least now we had a bit more breeze, about 30 knots, and the passing rain squalls made the Horn look a bit more fearsome. As we sailed past for the second time, the Boss got enough photographs of the Horn looking tempestuous to satisfy him.

We turned north to pass Lennox Island, and entered the Beagle Channel east of Navarino. This was the route Fitzroy had chosen for the boats to get into the channel. Once we were in the lee of Navarino, I began to feel a bit more relaxed. We entered the Beagle Channel at lunch-time, and started motoring against the moderate west wind towards Puerto Williams.

I had automatically assumed that we would be stopping there if only to enter Chile officially, but as we got closer, the Boss told us that he had been there on a previous trip, and in his opinion it was not worth stopping. He wanted to keep going. We had a small mutiny. I wanted to do the right thing with Costumes and Intimidation, and Lana was keen to see if there was any fresh food. The boys were anxious to have a run ashore and Jeff was hoping to top up the fuel tanks. When the Boss found that he had no support he backed down, and we anchored for the night in a well-sheltered bay close to the west of the town.

The bad weather passed in the night, and the next day dawned as what they would call in Maine a 'sparkler'. There is no other word to describe it. The clear, deep blue sky, the brilliant white snow on the mountains and the bright red roofs of the buildings ashore were all in happy contrast with each other.

By 6.30 the Boss was pacing to and fro, anxious to get ashore. He had suddenly decided that he had to make a phone call, and when we found that the surrounding high mountains made it impossible to do so by radio, he was in a rush to get ashore to find a telephone. Lana managed to persuade him that nothing would be open at 6.30, and that we should at least have breakfast before going in. As it was we were ashore by 8, only to be told that nothing opened until 10. So we had time to explore a bit before starting what turned out to be the rather lengthy process of clearing into Chile.

Puerto Williams is a very small settlement. It claims to be the southernmost town in the world. I would not question latitude I but I wonder whether it deserves the status of a town. It is really little more than a naval base. The navy rules the southern part of Chile, mainly because there are no roads or railways, so everything moves by ship. Puerto Williams really only exists because of the navy and their perceived need to maintain a presence on the island of Navarino. The islands to the south of the Beagle Channel all nominally belong to Chile, a claim that has long been disputed by Argentina, which controls the eastern section of Tierra del Fuego. Each country jealously patrols its shore of the Beagle Channel, and the gunboats seem to be almost glaring at each other as they pass. Politics and the British flag kept us from the Argentinian side, but there was more than enough to see in Chilean waters.

Puerto Williams – the southernmost town in the world. We made our official entry into Chile here.

The Chilean entry procedures were long and complicated, but they were completed, I thought, in a friendly manner. The Boss finished his phone call and was anxious to go. The navy Commandant offered to allow us to come into their dock for fuel, and knowing that the Boss liked to go everywhere at 10 knots, and that the next settlement was Punta Arenas, almost 300 miles away, I insisted that we took the time to top up the tanks. I felt that it would be a mistake to pass up the opportunity of a fill-up, especially in an area such as this, where the chances are few and far between.

The Boss was almost apoplectic by the time we got under way at about 2.30. He reckoned that we had wasted a day, and was determined to reach the Romanche Glacier that afternoon. As the glacier still lay some 65 miles to the west, we were going to have to burn a fair amount of our newly purchased fuel to get there before dark.

We had been under way almost an hour when the radio burst into life. It was the Port Captain from Puerto Williams. Evidently I had omitted to get somebody to stamp one of the many papers I had been given. They wanted us to come back. I thought the Boss was going to die – he was so angry he looked as if he was about to have a heart attack. He was determined to ignore them and carry on. I was even more determined to play by their rules. It was we who would be left trying to sort out the mess, possibly long after the Boss had flown out from Punta Arenas. So we did a U-turn, and as we got close to Puerto Williams, the boys put the dinghy over and I zoomed in to get the required stamp on the necessary bit of paper.

We did not get to the Romanche that day, but we did find an excellent anchorage for the night. It was a little cove off the channel, completely surrounded by trees. We had the place to ourselves, with no sign that anybody had ever been there before. Although the weather was looking settled for once, we lay to two anchors and ran a rope ashore to one of the trees. This was to become our Patagonian routine; whenever we could, we ran a rope or two ashore in addition to setting at least two anchors. We knew the weather could change in a flash, and I did not want to be dragging round some little anchorage in the dark if a big squall came.

Our little bay was so quiet, it was almost spooky, and we found ourselves talking in whispers. We were already probably 25 or 30 miles from the nearest people, and about to move further away. Although we were close to where Jemmy had been returned home, there were no signs of any Indian settlements. Sadly it seems that all the Indians have either died or moved to the towns. While we were in south-western Patagonia, we often went 100 miles or more without seeing a house, a boat, a navigational aid or even a puff of smoke.

We seemed to have the world to ourselves.

We were blessed with another spectacular dawn. Although we probably had our fair share of bad weather, we did have a number of truly superb days. This was going to one of them. The water in the Beagle Channel was like glass, reflecting the snow-capped mountains that climbed straight up out of the water. The pale dawn sky was tinged with green and pink. It was almost overwhelming.

We carried on up the channel, arriving at the fork that Darwin and Fitzroy had struggled to reach in their open boats. What had taken them almost two weeks, we had done in a day and a half. We passed the mountain which is now named after Darwin.

Every few hundred yards along that part of the Beagle Channel, there is a waterfall tumbling over the sheer cliffs and splashing into the channel below. Glaciers are visible in the distance, winding their way down the mountains from the snow cap, but seeing them from afar had not prepared us for meeting one face to face as it were. It was a bit of a shock, therefore, when we came up to the Romanche Glacier, which empties, if that is the right word, directly into the Beagle Channel.

Although we had all read that glaciers are blue, none of us had expected them to be quite so blue. The colour almost matched *Thalassi*'s topsides. There was some ice in the water in front of the glacier, and remembering what had happened to Darwin and company here, we did not linger close in front of the glacier for long – not that it was the Boss's habit to linger anywhere for long.

All too soon he was ready to press on to the next one. I was anxious to find an anchorage for the night, but the Boss was determined to 'do' another glacier first. He wanted to visit Garibaldi, and assured me that he had been there before, and that there was an excellent anchorage right beside the glacier.

What could I say? We motored up the long fjord, through everincreasing ice. Obviously Garibaldi glacier was a lot more active than Romanche. We had to pick our way round the larger bits of ice, many of which were the size of a car, with a few bigger, house-sized pieces mixed in with them. Because of the ice, our progress was slow, and dusk was creeping up on us by the time we got to the head of the fjord. We would have to anchor soon, but as we got closer to the end, the Boss became increasingly vague about where this safe, secure anchorage lay. His previous trip had been seven years before, and now he admitted that nothing looked familiar, and he was beginning to wonder if we were even up the same fjord that he had been thinking of.

All fjords tend to be deep. Most of the Beagle Channel is between

400 and 500ft deep. Canal Messier is reported to be an astonishing 4000ft. Although the fjord at Garibaldi was nothing like that deep, we were struggling to find anywhere less than 100ft. It was too late to go back through the ice to the Beagle Channel; like it or not, we were there for the night, and just had to make the best of it.

After doing a fairly comprehensive survey, we found a spot on the north side. It was a little indentation, not big enough to pass for a bay, and it was still over 100ft deep, but that would have to do us. There were a couple of stunted trees ashore that we could tie on to, so we layed our main anchor towards the face of the glacier and ran a line ashore to the strongest-looking tree.

We were much too close to the face of the glacier for safety. If a big piece of ice came off we could have been in trouble from the waves. During the night, as the temperature dropped, a katabatic wind started up. The cold air dropped down from the snow plain, and came howling out through the fjord where we were anchored. It was unnerving seeing the creaking rope vanishing into the dark and knowing that it was tied to a rather questionable tree. The anchor was not doing much – every time I tried to put a bit more weight on it it dragged, and if we pulled much more we would pull it home. So it was all down to the tree. As we listened to the waves on the rocks behind us it was an anxious night, and Lana and I stayed on deck for most of it.

As soon as the sun rose enough to warm things up, the katabatic effect was lost and the wind dropped. It was the third sunny day in a row. The Boss had slept through the night, and was convinced that it had been a snug enough anchorage. He took the boys off in the dinghy to poke around the glacier, and I went to sleep while Jeff kept an eye on things.

Chris brought back a piece of glacier ice and made an interesting discovery. The ice was probably several thousand years old, and it was so hard and compressed that it would hardly melt in a drink. One lump would suffice for at least three drinks. A piece he left in the cockpit for several days also refused to melt, despite an air temperature well above freezing.

Once their exploration was over the Boss was ready to go, so we picked our way back through the ice, down to the Beagle Channel. He had picked out a spot off Burnt Island, in Canal O'Brien, where he wanted to spend the night.

I should explain that the Patagonian 'canals' are not in any way man-made, or even man-improved. They are an intricate network of inter-connecting fjords, and are, for the most part, as natural as the day God made them. The term simply derives from the Spanish for channel.

Canal O'Brien is at the western end of the Beagle Channel. When he made it his planned destination, the Boss had not reckoned on the westerly gale that was now howling down the length of the channel. *Thalassi*'s 200 horse-power kept us moving into the teeth of the gale, but only slowly. After about 20 miles or so, even the Boss had had enough. We spotted a reasonably sheltered-looking cove, and pulled in for the night.

On the chart, only the main channels have soundings marked to show the depth of water. Whenever we left these main thoroughfares, we were on our own. The big dinghy was fitted with a depth sounder, and we often sent it ahead to investigate for us. Before anchoring, we always sounded around the bay to check depths, either from the dinghy or by circling round with *Thalassi*. I wanted to be sure that there were no hidden rocks for us to swing on to if the wind changed or the tide dropped.

As we were getting ready to anchor in our unnamed, possibly unsurveyed bay, we did the usual circuit, checking the depths. The centre of the bay was about 150ft deep, but there was a handy little shelf to the north, with only about 30ft on it. That is where I tried to anchor. We had four attempts, all to no avail; the anchor dragged every time. It was getting dark, so we were more or less committed to staying in that bay for the night. More in frustration than any real hope of success, I dropped the anchor right in the middle of the bay. It was 148ft deep where we let go. Normally we like to put out chain at least five times the depth of water, but here it was far too deep for that – we had little more than twice the depth. Much to my surprise the anchor held at the first go. Once the main anchor was dug in, we let the second one go, and it too held.

Eventually after a few similar episodes, we realised that in these rocky little bays, it was best not to look for a shallow spot because they were invariably rocky. If we dropped in the deepest part, we always found good holding. Whatever silt found its way into these bays migrated to the lowest point, and however rocky a bay was, there was always a pocket of good sand or mud in the deepest part. If ever I venture back in these waters, the main anchor will have at least 500ft of chain – more if there is room to stow it.

We kept an anchor watch, just to be sure that we did not drag in the night. Squalls were rattling down off the hills all night long; the spell of fine weather had broken.

The wind was still howling when we left the next morning. In the Beagle Channel it was a steady 40 knots. I was glad we were not in an open boat with Captain Fitzroy. On board *Thalassi*, whoever was off watch was able to get warm and dry, sitting in front of an electric fire. I was able to do almost all my navigating from the comfort of the chart table, using the satellite navigator and the radar to identify each headland or island as it loomed out of the rain. The person actually on watch did get wet, but at the end of the watch they could throw their clothes in the tumble drier, so they were dry to put on before the next one.

Although it was not too uncomfortable, it was not much fun. We felt we were missing all the scenery, but the Boss had his schedule. We finally reached Burnt Island, our target from the previous day, and as it was getting late, we called a halt. We were getting towards the western end of the channel, and it was becoming much more exposed, and noticeably rougher. We anchored in Caleta Ancha, off Burnt Island.

There were a few stunted trees growing down by the water, and after a bit of searching the boys managed to find one big enough to be worth tying to. Since it did not look any too strong, they also found a large rock, round which they passed a chain to make a second, rather stronger securing point. With two anchors down and two lines ashore, I felt reasonably happy for the night, but we still kept a watch, just in case.

The wind did not let up all night, but early the next morning the Boss was making his usual 'let's go' noises. Lana expressed what everybody else was feeling. She had been watching the wind-speed indicator hovering close to 50 knots and said, 'It'd be really stupid to go out there now.' The Boss knew better than to argue with the cook. But after lunch, he had another go at encouraging us to leave. Although the wind had eased, it was still gusting up to 40 knots. It was also bucketing down with rain, and the visibility was about 20yd. The looks the crew gave him were enough to persuade him to stay put until the next day.

I think he would have gone crazy if we had had to stay another day, but fortunately the gale blew itself out in the night and we were able to get under way for Punta Arenas, which is about halfway along the Magellan Straits. To get into the strait we had to duck out into the open Pacific for a few miles. Even though the wind was down, there was still a big sea running. I thanked my lucky stars that we had not tried to come out there in 50 knots of wind. The coast was so exposed, so windswept, that there were no trees, indeed nothing growing at all. The granite cliffs have been polished smooth by the perpetual onslaught of wind and waves from the westerly gales. Even on this relatively calm day, the spray from the waves was being thrown 100ft or more up the cliffs – not a place to be shipwrecked.

We managed to sneak round the corner into the south-western

entrance to the Magellan Straits before the wind could get up again, and within a few miles we were back in the shelter of the islands and canals again. I had plotted a route which followed the main channel up to Punta Arenas. This seemed to be the obvious way to go, but the Boss had other ideas. He had been studying the chart and had spotted a narrow little canal that wound its way between two islands. It would admittedly save us 3 or 4 miles on our 60-mile passage, but no soundings were shown on the chart for that canal, nor was it mentioned in the pilot as an alternative route. The Boss, however, was anxious to press on after the delay, and determined to reach Punta Arenas that night. He was sure it would save us some time, and insisted that we take his short cut.

We turned into the canal, and within a mile or two the cliffs began to close in on us from each side. I slowed right down, in case it suddenly became shallow as well as narrow. We had gone about 12 miles up the canal when our way was blocked by a series of rapids. Fortunately the water was flowing towards us so it was easy to stop, just stemming the tide while the Boss was summoned to study the situation. To my amazement he said that we should just motor against the stream, and go up the rapids. At first I thought he was joking, but he was serious. Before I would even agree to try, we put the dinghy over and Nick and Chris went to reconnoitre.

From on board *Thalassi*, we could see the dinghy bucking and bouncing as they drove up through the rapids. We hardly needed their report when they came back. 'No bloody chance, mate,' said Nick, as they started to hoist the dinghy back on board. 'It's deep enough all right, but that sucker's running at 20 knots.'

Since *Thalassi*'s best speed under power is a little over 10 knots, we did not have to argue any more. There was no hope of us going against 20 knots, so we turned round and retraced our steps back to the main channel.

Because of the time we had wasted it was a race to reach Punta Arenas before dark. Jeff turned up the wick on the engine, and we set the jib and mainsail. By motorsailing as hard as we could, we got there just at dusk, and anchored off the town for the night, to a collective 'Phew' from the crew.

Chapter 14

The Straits of Magellan and Northwards

After her visit to the Falklands, and the trip back to Uruguay, *Beagle* returned to Patagonia for the last time. On this occasion she sailed into the eastern end of the Straits of Magellan; no more attempts on Cape Horn for Captain Fitzroy.

Having managed to beat through the Beagle Channel to Woollya, he was confident that he could manage to get *Beagle* through the Straits of Magellan. Although much of the strait is wider than the Beagle Channel, which would let them sail longer tacks when beating, there are a couple of narrow parts where the tide roars through at 8 knots or more. Despite the fact that *Thalassi* was a lot easier to handle than the *Beagle*, I would not have fancied trying it without being able to use the engine.

Their first anchorage was at Cape Gregory, where they met a group of the fabled Patagonian giants. Darwin was a little disappointed to find that they were not really giants. They were certainly taller than the likes of Jemmy's people, but far from the size he had imagined. Most of them, including the women, were around 6ft, with a few slightly taller. The way they dressed made them look taller. They wore full-length sweeping capes made of guanaco skin, and had long, flowing hair. Over the years, they had had numerous contacts with the European seal hunters who regularly worked in this area, and many of the them had at least a smattering of English. Darwin found them to be friendly and classified them as being at least 'half civilised'.

In contrast, when they later anchored off the settlement at Port Famine, they were once again pestered by Fuegans, all of whom were *yammerschooner*-ing. It got to the point where Fitzroy ordered the ship's guns to be fired to intimidate them. The guns were aimed low, and when the shots splashed into the water, the Indians threw rocks in retaliation. The fact that the ship was about ½ mile away did not seem to deter them. If the 'rocks' from the ship could all but reach them, then surely their rocks would reach the ship.

On their first visit to Port Famine, Darwin had ventured ashore to climb the nearby Mount Tarn. At 2600ft, it is the highest mountain in that locality. He and a couple of officers set off at 4 a.m. to try to reach the peak. As soon as they passed the high tide mark, however, they found themselves struggling through almost impenetrable forest. No landmarks were visible through the trees, so they had to lay a course with Darwin's trusty compass. After a couple of hours, they had made only 100yd or so. At that rate there would be no chance of reaching the summit that day. They almost gave up, but then they stumbled, literally, into a ravine. The going was still tough, but at least they could go a little faster.

The wind that had been whistling through the trees did not penetrate into the ravine and it was deathly calm. It was so cold, damp and gloomy, that not even fungi, moss or ferns could grow there. The bottom of the ravine was filled with a tangle of fallen and rotting tree trunks which they had to climb over and under. When Darwin, pausing for breath, leaned against one tree, the whole thing disintegrated and fell down, it was so rotten.

By way of the ravine, they finally reached the treeline. A row or two of stunted trees was the demarcation line, and above this, the ridge was bare rock. From there it was an easy walk to the summit. From the top they had a good view down the strait, and across the fjords and inlets. To the north lay row after row of snow-capped mountains separated by deep dark valleys.

The wind was bitingly cold, so despite the view they did not linger. They went down much quicker than they came up, because, as Darwin pointed out, every time they fell, it was in the right direction.

Most of the trees were beech, some of gigantic proportions. Darwin measured the girth of one as 13ft. Many of them had big lumps of fungus growing on them. Darwin found that one type grew only on a particular species of beech tree, and another type of tree was host to an altogether different kind of fungus. There was never a mixing of the two. The Fuegans ate this fungus in large quantities. Indeed it was about the only vegetable that they did eat.

There were few animals, and even fewer birds for him to study, so for once Darwin focused his attention on the sea and the tidal zones. He became interested in the kelp, the long rubbery strands of seaweed that fringed every rocky area here, just as it had in the Falklands. He managed to pull up one strand that was over 350ft long, and felt sure that there must be longer strands in even deeper water. He speculated that kelp is probably the longest plant on earth.

Along the shoreline, he spent hours pulling up kelp plants and shaking out the creatures that were living among the fronds. There were several kinds of shellfish, which he discovered were collected and eaten by the Fuegans. In fact these and the fungus formed the major part of their diet. In the kelp, he also found crabs, cuttlefish, starfish and sea urchins. Growing on the fronds themselves were a variety of coral-like polyps. He decided that there was more life to be found in the kelp than in any terrestrial forest.

Fitzroy wanted to leave the Straits of Magellan by the newly reported Magdalen Channel, which lay to the south of the more usual route. The weather did not treat them kindly, and Darwin was disappointed to be missing so much of the scenery in the overcast and foggy conditions. He caught tantalising glimpses of blue glaciers, high, rugged peaks and spectacular waterfalls. *Beagle* anchored one night in thick weather near Mount Sarmiento, but its 7000ft peak remained hidden in clouds that reached down almost to the water. On the beach they could see the remains of a long-deserted wigwam, a reminder that people did visit the area, although they had not seen any settlements for many miles. Early the next morning, the clouds parted long enough for them to see the whole mountain. Above the treeline it was completely covered in snow. On its flanks were several big glaciers, which Darwin described as 'frozen Niagaras'.

HMS Beagle *in the Straits of Magellan – Mount Sarmiento in the background.*

After a long day, *Beagle* reached the western end of the strait just before dark. It was too late to navigate their way out through the mass of islands, and the water was too deep to anchor. One small cove offered a possible anchorage, but Fitzroy decided to give that to the *Adventure*, which was following close behind them. *Beagle* would stand off for the night. Winter had arrived, and there were fourteen hours of darkness to suffer through.

There was an area of about 4 square miles in which it was safe to sail. During those fourteen hours, they criss-crossed it in every direction. Fitzroy decided to keep a good press of sail on the ship, and keep her moving. She was much more manoeuvrable when sailing at a reasonable speed than when sailing slowly or hove to. He also felt that the crew would be more alert working the ship than if she herself seemed half asleep.

For the first part of the night they had to beat hard, just to hold their own against the incoming flood tide. Later, when the tide turned, they had to bear away and run back east, as the ebb tide tried to draw them out into the offshore islands. It also rained almost all night, and squall after squall came racing in from the west. To sail to and fro for fourteen hours, in such confined water, with no lighthouses or buoys for bearings, knowing that a winter gale could arrive at any moment, must have given Fitzroy more than one grey hair.

Darwin noted the night's activities in his journal, but did not seem to be concerned. What impressed him more, as they sailed out at dawn, was an area they passed called the Milky Way. This is an area of shoals, reefs and jagged rocks, where the sea always breaks white. He said, 'One sight would be enough to make a landsman dream for a week about shipwrecks, perils and death.'

Beagle got safely clear of the land, and turned north. That was to be their last sight of Patagonia.

Punta Arenas is the capital of southern Chile. Darwin did not visit the town for the simple reason that it did not exist when he was in the area. It was to be another fifteen years before the first settlement was established there, in 1849. As steamships began to reach and pass through the strait, Punta Arenas became an important coaling station, and it rapidly increased in size and importance. It is now a city of over 100,000 people.

The Boss was ashore almost at first light, trying to meet a friend from his previous visit, and to organise his flight out. It was also time for Chris to fly back to reality, so he too was off visiting the travel agents. For the rest of us, there were plenty of chores to do on board the boat. We hoped to get our chance to explore the town once the Boss was on the aeroplane.

He was gone all day, and arrived back in the evening with his friend Julio, Julio's brother Jorge, and their respective wives. Julio runs a TV and radio repair shop and a small coast radio station to enable ships to make telephone calls by radio. His brother Jorge is a dentist. He rather reminded us of Wacko the film-maker.

It was a bit difficult for us to entertain them unannounced. Lana had not been shopping for three weeks, and provisions were getting low. The Boss, living as he does in a hotel, could never grasp the logistics of trying to feed unexpected guests.

During the course of the evening's conversation, the Boss let us in on the next stage of the plan. We were to go to Puerto Natales, about 100 miles to the north-west, to pick up some Chilean guests to whom he had given the use of *Thalassi*. The chart showed that our route would involve some 300 miles of twisting and turning channels, yet the Boss had decided we could do it in two days, regardless of what the weather might be. He thought I was being very pessimistic when I expressed some doubts.

The Boss and Chris were both booked to fly out the next afternoon. In the morning we hired a pick-up truck and started on the provisioning. Driving in Punta Arenas was very strange at first. Every street in the town is one way, with alternate streets going in opposite directions. There is no two-way traffic anywhere in the town. Later we were to discover that this was by no means unique to Punta Arenas; many towns in Chile have a similar system. Indeed, Chile seemed to us to be a land of one-way streets.

Jorge took the Boss to the airport in his car, while Chris came with Lana and me in the pick-up. They had both checked in, and we were sitting in the lounge waiting for their flight to be called, when the Boss dropped one of his bombshells. Quite casually he mentioned that Julio and his 'family' would be moving on board the next day to sail to Puerto Natales with us.

This was our twenty-fourth day in succession with the Boss, and while some of it had been fun, we were physically and emotionally exhausted. Lana and I had been looking forward to at least a day to ourselves. We looked open-mouthed at each other and at him. He seemed oblivious. For once even Lana was struck dumb. I stood up and said, 'We'd better get busy then.' We walked out of the airport without another word. When we broke the news to the others, I thought for a moment that we were about to be left crewless.

Julio had told them about Mother Teresa's bar, grill and whore-house, and they were determined to visit it – just for the food, they assured us. They were unanimous that they were going nowhere until they had paid their respects to Mother Teresa.

The breeze was picking up, and the anchorage off the town is not very well protected. I cannot understand why the main dock was built where it was, in a totally exposed position. We moved the boat a mile or so up the coast, to anchor in a well-sheltered little bay, surely a better place for them to have built the port. Lana drove the truck round to meet us.

We split into two teams for the evening's entertainment. I did not want to leave the boat on her own, so Lana and I went out first and had a nice, peaceful dinner ashore in one of the hotels. By the time we got back, the second contingent was all spruced up and ready to make their foray. We did not ask where they got to, but it was the wee small hours before they returned.

The next day Julio came down and told us that it would be just him and his brother sailing with us. Neither wife could go. That was better than we had feared. We had imagined four adults and a clutch of kids. What was even better news was that they could not leave until the next day, so we had a day's reprieve.

We needed the extra time. Jeff was tasked with locating fuel, and failed to find anybody who would deliver it. In the end he found or borrowed a couple of 50-gallon drums; we took the boat alongside the dock and ran a shuttle service with the trusty pick-up. It was easy enough, but it took a lot of time, syphoning each drumful into *Thalassi*'s tank.

I set about trying to sort out Costumes and Intimidation. It was not easy to get permission to put Chilenos onto our crew list. Eventually I had to get Julio to come and help. He sorted it out fairly quickly, and I suspect a little money changed hands.

Lana seconded Nick to the grocery shop and the market. They came back with the pick-up sagging on its springs. Not knowing when the next chance would come, Lana had done some serious shopping.

She and I managed to squeeze in a quick trip down to the naval shipyard. The hulk of a big iron sailing ship was lying on the beach, forming a breakwater for the little patrol boats. She was the *City of Glasgow*, the ship that Stanley had chartered to search for Dr Livingstone in Africa in 1871. On a later trip round the Horn, she had fallen into the trap of visiting the Falklands for repairs. Like so many of the others, she had been condemned; and had lain there for a

The wreck of the City of Glasgow *in Punta Arenas. This is the ship that Stanley chartered to try to bring back Doctor Livingstone from Africa. We were allowed to board the wreck, but not allowed to photograph it for 'security reasons'.*

number of years before somebody had tried to salvage her. I believe that her new owners were hoping to tow her to California, but as they were passing Punta Arenas a gale arrived. The towline snapped, she was swept ashore and there she lay, condemned for a second time.

We received permission to board her, but the puzzled navy people could not understand why we would be interested in a wreck. Although we tried to explain in our phrasebook Spanish, they thought we were on some clandestine mission. They let us on board, but forbade us to take any photographs. She was largely intact, with a fair amount of her deck gear still there. It would have been an interesting project to record it all, but bureaucracy and the Boss's schedule precluded it.

175

We got Julio and Jorge settled aboard, and bade adieu to Punta Arenas. It was a beautiful, sunny, windless day, another sparkler. As we rounded Cape Froward, the southernmost point on the South American mainland, we decided it looked much more as Cape Horn should have done – a big, bold headland with a large cross on top. Julio told us that the cross is regularly blown down, but somebody always goes back up to install another.

An effortless 113 miles were reeled off, and we found a reasonable enough little bay in which to anchor for the night. We were hoping that it was all going to be that easy, but of course it was not. The next day dawned wet and windy – back to normal! We made an early start, mainly because Julio woke us all up yelling for his brother – he had seen a flying saucer. I got up to investigate, and found that he had in fact seen Venus, which appeared to move past his hatch as the boat swung at her anchor in the breeze.

By the time it was light we had breakfasted and were ready to leave. Outside the shelter of our little bay it was a bit ugly – damp and drizzly and blowing about 30 knots on the nose. Thank goodness we did not have to beat, tacking to and fro as the *Beagle* had been forced to do. The engine pushed us easily into the wind, but as we approached the end of the strait, it became a bit rough. *Thalassi* started to slam into the waves and take heavy water on deck.

By late afternoon we had reached the aptly named Desolation Island, a forbidding piece of land. Even the trees looked as if they were huddling down to try and escape the perpetual wind. On the chart, we spotted a very promising-looking inlet on the island, called Bahia Wodsworth. It is a fairly long, twisting fjord, and the twists and turns promised us complete shelter from the swell. When we reached the inner end, we found a perfect little pool just big enough for *Thalassi* to anchor in.

There was not room for her to swing if the wind changed, so we dropped the anchors at the entrance of the pool, then as I turned and backed down, Nick and Tony ran two lines ashore with the dinghy. We were completely landlocked, surrounded by tree-covered hills around 1500ft high. The bay was so small that not even the squalls could reach us; it was glassy calm. What a contrast to what we had been suffering outside. A spectacular waterfall poured over the cliff, to crash onto the beach close on our port side. It was a truly beautiful spot, with no sign of habitation. In fact there was probably nobody within 60 or 70 miles of us that night. It was a privilege to be there.

Jeff and I decided that there must be a good-sized lake at the top of the cliffs to feed such a waterfall. We thought we would pop up and take a look before dark. However, what looked like a few bushes

The superbly sheltered anchorage at Bahia Wodsworth at Desolation Island.
Thalassi *well secured with two anchors down and a line ashore, our typical*
Patagonian anchoring routine.

on the hills turned out to be virtually impenetrable jungle. From the
boat it was impossible to judge the size of the trees ashore; there was
nothing to give a sense of scale. We struggled through the undergrowth for an hour, much as Darwin had done near Port Famine. We
had gone only a small fraction of the distance by the time dusk
approached. Neither of us fancied being caught in the jungle after
dark, so we gave up and headed back to the boat.

Back on board, we found Tony engaged in a chess match with

Julio. During his winter in the Antarctic, Tony had played many chess games via the radio, mainly with Russians wintering at another base. In those games they had made just one move a day, so they had had plenty of time to think about it. It was a bit of a novelty for Tony to have a 'live' opponent, and he felt a bit rushed, not having twenty-four hours to consider each move.

Jeff and I had hoped to make another attempt on the waterfall at first light the next morning, but when we woke, the rain was pouring down, so we had a long and lazy breakfast instead.

From Desolation Island our route took us across the Straits of Magellan for the last time, before entering the smaller and generally more sheltered canals that go northwards. The canal that leads up to Puerto Natales is Canal Kirk. It has a formidable reputation, and we received several warnings to treat it with respect. The problem is that Puerto Natales is in a gigantic shallow bay. The enclosed area is perhaps a couple of hundred square miles, and the only connection to the open sea is Canal Kirk. As the tide rises and falls, a prodigious amount of water must pass through the canal. To make matters worse, there is a very narrow section, and here the current regularly exceeds 15 knots. The Port Captain in Punta Arenas had told us to attempt the passage only at slack water, and then only if it was not too windy. The narrows are called Angostura Kirk, but we renamed them Angustia Kirk – *angustia* being Spanish for grief!

When we left Desolation Island, we were reminded just how sheltered our anchorage had been. As soon as we stuck our nose outside into the Magellan Straits, we found it was blowing 30, gusting 40 knots. It was rough enough as we crossed the strait, and we were all glad to get into the comparative shelter of the canal on the north side. We passed the wreck of a big freighter. It had been tossed up on the land, almost clear of the water. I did not want even to imagine the conditions that could have done that. *Angustia*.

As we approached the entrance to Canal Kirk, the wind increased and heavy squalls came funnelling down out of the mountains. These sudden bursts of cold wind dropping out of the mountains are called 'williwaws'. As they raced across the canal towards us, they picked up the surface of the water. An area, in some cases the size of a football field would suddenly lift up in the air, to be blown away as spray. What would happen to us if we were in the middle of one of these mini-tornados? Luckily we did not find out, but trying to avoid them kept things interesting for us.

The Admiralty tide tables are a bit vague for this area, but as near as I could tell, slack water at the narrows was at 2.30 p.m. As we approached the narrows, I tried calling the Port Captain at Puerto

Natales for confirmation. Nobody answered my calls, so Julio called up his own radio station, and got them to telephone the Port Captain for us. There seemed to be a bit of hesitation, before he finally told us that he thought it would be about 5 p.m. He did not say it with any degree of conviction, however, so I decided to stick with the earlier time. If we were too early we could wait, but if we missed it, there would be a 15-knot current against us, and we would have no chance of pushing through against that.

As soon as we turned the corner into Canal Kirk itself, we seemed to leave the williwaws behind, much to my relief. We were still a mile or two from the narrows when Julio spotted a fishing boat. We went over to ask them for a bit of local knowledge. As we pulled alongside, Julio saw bags of scallops in the boat, and immediately started bartering for some. It was only after he had made his deal that I was able to remind him to ask for the fishermen's advice about the narrows. For a six-pack of beer and half a case of Coke, Julio got a sack of scallops, a bucket of mussels and the suggestion that we would be all right to pass through the narrows right away.

There was a bend in the canal just before the narrows, and even as we came round the corner, the current, which was pushing us along, increased dramatically. We had probably already passed the point of no return, as the current was already going faster than we could, and we could neither turn round nor stop. Ready or not, we were on our way through the narrows.

The narrows really *are* narrow, and just to complicate things, there is a big rock in the middle of the channel at the tightest part. There are range markers showing that the rock should be left to port. As we passed it, we could see a waterfall ahead. The drop was probably only a foot or so, but as we raced up to it, it looked like the brink of Niagara Falls itself.

I kept our speed through the water at about 6 or 7 knots, to make it easy to steer. With the speed of the current and our speed through the water, we were doing close to 20 knots over the ground. It all happened very quickly, so I did not have to hold my breath for too long. *Thalassi* was squirted out of the narrows into the wide bay which leads up to Puerto Natales. Although the wind was howling again, it was a relief to escape from the confines of Canal Kirk.

For once we actually had a following breeze, so we set the jib and a bit of mainsail and sailed up the bay to Puerto Natales. The closer we got to it, the stronger the wind became, until it was blowing a steady 45 knots. The Port Captain must have spotted us, because he called us on the radio to say that the port was closed because of the bad weather. It did not really affect us, as I would not want to tie up to their rather exposed dock in that wind anyway.

We anchored in the lee of a low bank to the west of the town, and were perfectly snug. The wind was howling in the rigging, but on deck everything was relatively calm. Julio called his wife on the radio to find out how best to cook the scallops and mussels. While Julio was relaying instructions to Lana in the galley, Jorge kept us all amused by making us guess which singer or actor he was trying to impersonate. He had quite a repertoire, which increased with each drink he took. It was a pleasant evening, rounded off by an excellent meal of fresh seafood. What could be nicer?

Julio and Jorge were to leave us here, and we were to await the next visitors. The Boss had given the use of *Thalassi* to a gentleman called Klaus, from Santiago, in the hopes that he would ask the Boss's boatyard to build him a similar boat. Julio had offered to help with the logistics of getting Klaus and his friend to Puerto Natales to join us, and also offered to take all our exposed film back to Punta Arenas, get it developed, and send it back with Klaus. Both offers were eagerly accepted. Nick took him and Jorge ashore the next morning to catch the one and only bus back to Punta Arenas, and came back looking like a drowned rat. It was still pretty rough.

Julio and Jorge had been good if exhausting company, and we needed some quiet time, to get ourselves ready for the next visitors. The day was declared a no-work day, so we explored the little town, and ate ashore to give the cook a break.

Puerto Natales is a real frontier town. It looked like something out of the Wild West – slightly ramshackle, clapboard buildings lining unsurfaced roads. Jeff, Tony and Nick rather lost interest when they failed to find a single bar. The town appeared to be dry.

We had a couple of days to get organised before Klaus was due to arrive, or so we thought. When the wind dropped we brought the boat in to the dock for the usual routine of topping up the fuel again – the never-ending quest. This time Jeff had managed to find a tanker which would deliver right to the door. Apart from the fact that the nozzle on the tanker's hose was about twice as big as our filler, the operation went quite smoothly, and we were soon back at anchor.

Lana visited every shop in town and bought what provisions she could. She had just arrived back on board when the VHF radio crackled to life, and we heard the unmistakable sound of Julio's voice. We knew that he must be close, because that radio has a range of only 20 miles or so. What on earth was he doing back here, when our guests were due the next day?

I went in with the dinghy to meet him. He had met Klaus and his friend, another Jorge, at the airport. Rather than leave them in a hotel for the night, he had decided to help by driving them 150 miles to deliver them to us, albeit a day early. A big panic ensued. Since we were not expecting the guests until the next day, their cabins were not ready for them. And as it was getting dark, we could not send Julio off to drive back; he would have to stay the night too.

Lana's consternation was softened a little by getting all her photographs back, plus a new batch of mail, and a great big box of chocolates from Julio and his brother, addressed to their 'fair lady'. She managed to rustle up a scratch meal for eight – no small feat, since we had been planning to have a 'last supper' ashore for the crew before the guests came. It was a rather hectic start to Klaus's visit.

Chapter 15

Torres del Paine and North from Patagonia

Having once negotiated the dreaded Canal Kirk, it no longer held the terror that it had the first time, but we still gave it a healthy dose of respect. After we had waved goodbye to Julio again, we safely negotiated the narrows at slack water, more by luck than tide tables.

The plan was to take Klaus and Jorge to Puerto Aysen, some 500 miles to the north as the condor flies. However, the zigzags and little detours would probably add at least another hundred, so we had quite a distance to cover. The Boss had told us we would be doing it in a week, which would have been hectic. Fortunately he had also told us that the most important thing was to give them a good time, in the hope that Klaus would buy a boat.

Both Klaus and Jorge were delightfully laid back, and seemed more than happy to do the trip at a slower pace. They were both interested in exploring, and Klaus especially was an absolute fount of local knowledge. He knew one of the admirals in the southern Fleet, and on Klaus's chart he had marked all their secret fuel dumps in the area we would be crossing. Apparently the navy has established dozens of 'secret' bases where their submarines and patrol boats can refuel in the event of war with Argentina. Klaus had been given *carte blanche* to raid these supplies if we needed to. We never had to, but it was reassuring to know that extra fuel was available. This was but a small example of the doors that Klaus was able to open for us. Nick and Tony took to calling him 'Mr Chile', not entirely flippantly.

A couple of calls on the radio rearranged their flight schedules, to give us a more realistic timetable for the passage. The only real pressure for them to get back came from Jorge's wife, who was intensely jealous that she was not able to leave her travel agency business long enough to join us.

It was Klaus's opinion that the best area to explore was around the extensive national park, Torres del Paine. When we heard the words 'national park', we pictured hot-dog stands, souvenir stalls and tourist day-trip boats, but there was none of that. We saw the occasional fisherman, but otherwise we had the park, and sometimes it seemed the world, to ourselves.

We did 81 miles the first day, and 89 the second, which brought us to the edge of where Klaus reckoned the good part started. We stopped for the night in the aptly named Puerto Bueno. It was very *bueno* indeed, with good holding for the anchor, pretty scenery and hundreds of wild flowers ashore. Despite its name, it was like no other port we have been into. It was as nature had designed it, and it did not look as if anybody had ever been there before us. So we learned that the term *puerto* on the chart did not necessarily mean that there was any settlement there, but that it was likely to be a good anchorage. Jorge gained points with the cook by collecting a large bunch of wild flowers for her.

The next morning found us well into glacier country. There were at least a dozen coming down the mountains on the mainland side, all shining that strange, almost iridescent blue. There were several pieces of ice floating by, broken off from glaciers that came right to the water's edge. We turned into the entrance of Estero Peel, and immediately found much more ice in the water. By the amount, we guessed that there must be a more active glacier in this fjord. There was a bit of a dog-leg to the fjord, and as soon as we came round the bend, we could see two glaciers coming down at the end.

We often found it impossible to judge distances in Patagonia. I am not sure if this was because on a good day the air was very clear because there is no haze-making pollution, or whether it was just because there were no man-made objects to give us a sense of scale. Whatever the reason, we regularly underestimated distances, usually by a factor of two or more. So when we sighted the two glaciers, Jeff got everybody to guess how far away the nearest one was. The estimates varied from a low of 1 mile to a high of 3. He measured the distance on the radar, and found it to be almost 10 miles. It took us a couple of hours to cover that 10 miles, dodging lumps of ice along the way. We anchored in Caleta Amelia just as Lana announced that lunch was ready.

Klaus and Jorge were happy enough to spend the afternoon exploring the area. If the Boss had been with us, we would have had to do another three glaciers before tea time. Klaus chose a beach in front of the northern glacier to visit. This was much the smaller of the two glaciers, but it finished right on the beach. Jeff and I decided to go for the big one. Jeff had an ambition to stand on a big glacier, and this one seemed to be only a mile or so up the valley. We would have done well to remember our distance-judging efforts of the morning.

The expedition to the little glacier was the popular one, perhaps because it was less energetic. Jeff and I had no takers for ours. The others dropped us off at the beach near 'our' glacier *en route* to theirs. We took a portable radio so that we could call for a pick-up when we arrived back. Just as we were landing, a guanaco appeared on the beach. It was very shy, and after it realised we were coming ashore, it ran off. That was one of only three of these small deer-like animals that we saw in all the time we were in Chile.

One of only two guanacos that we saw. They used to be plentiful but have almost been killed off for their meat and skin. This one watched us land on the beach for our assault on 'Jeff's' glacier.

The first part of our expedition went smoothly enough. We walked up the valley floor, which consisted of gravel that had been crushed by the glacier. All the glaciers in that area are retreating, and where we were walking would have been under at least 100ft of ice a few years before. We could see great gouges in the cliffs on either side of the valley, where the ice had scraped by.

The first snag we came to was the river. Because it was summer, there was a steady flow of melt-water coming off the glacier. The river did a big zigzag from the cliff on one side of the valley to the one on the other. There was no way round it. The cliffs were too sheer to climb. We could either cross the river or go all the way back down to the beach and look for another route. Ever a man of action, Jeff pulled off his jeans and waded across. The water was just about at freezing point – an hour or two previously it had been ice. The river was just shallow enough for Jeff to avoid getting his underpants wet, but when I followed him over, I discovered that even on tip-toes, my legs were about 6in shorter than his – a rather crucial six inches from my perspective. I got no sympathy from Jeff.

All went well for the next couple of miles. It was easy walking on the valley floor, although we were beginning to realise that we had been hopelessly optimistic about the distance. Eventually we reached the face of the glacier – or at least we almost did. At the bottom of the face was a big pool of water, stretching right across from one cliff to the other. It was too deep to wade across, and far too cold to swim in.

We were disappointed, but not yet totally thwarted. We had passed a section of the cliff that had fallen into the valley. It was only ½ mile back, so perhaps we could climb up there to get up out of the valley, and reach the glacier from above. We hurried back, and sure enough, we managed to scramble up to the top of the cliff without too much serious climbing. There was not much vegetation along the cliff top, so we were able to walk back to the area of the glacier fairly easily. Now the problem was to get down to the ice itself. We were a good 100ft above it, but having come this far, Jeff was determined to walk on the thing.

After a couple of false starts, we found a route down, and finally reached the glacier itself. Because it was melting, the surface was fairly smooth. There was a surprising amount of dirt embedded in the surface – we were rather surprised that the whole thing looked rather grubby. As the ice melts, any dirt trapped in it is left on the surface. Because this glacier is hardly moving at all, the dirt we saw could have been hundreds, even thousands of years old.

We walked about on it quite casually, until we found our first

Looking down onto the glacier that Jeff was determined to walk on.

crevasse. Down on hands and knees, we peeped cautiously over the edge. The crack was quite long, but only a foot or so across. It really did look bottomless, going down and down into inky blue darkness. That did it for me. I decided I had seen enough and headed straight back to terra firma.

The climb back up to the cliff was a bit of a struggle, but we managed it. I was very keen to avoid the river on the way back, so we stayed out of the valley and made our way back along the cliff tops. A mile or so from the glacier, we came to a patch of very fine gravel, almost like coarse sand. Right across the middle of it was a row of gigantic footprints, each about 25 per cent bigger than Jeff's size eleven, and not quite the right shape to fit a shoe. I have always been sceptical about the tales of 'yetis' and 'bigfoots'. But having come across those footprints in the wilds of Patagonia, I must now at least concede the possibility that they exist. Whatever had made them was very much bigger than us, and we hoped that we would not meet it face to face on the way back.

Having gone further than we had anticipated, we had a small race against the darkness to get back to the beach. It was almost a dead heat. Nick came to pick us up, just in time for a hot shower and a good dinner. The others had enjoyed their less strenuous expedition, and everybody was happy. It had been an excellent day.

The weather became better and better. A rare but welcome high came and sat over Patagonia, and we were blessed with three perfect days for exploring glaciers. There was no wind to blow the ice about, the sun was warm all day and the sky was the clearest blue it is possible to imagine.

The best glacier was Glacier Asia – at least that was what it was called on the Chilean charts. The British had it down as Calvo, but the Chileans placed Calvo further south. Whatever it is called, it is spectacular. It was the most active glacier we found, and there was so much ice cooling the water, that the open stretch in the approaches was starting to skin over with ice. We met some fishermen who warned us that it would freeze solid for the winter with the next cold spell. *Thalassi* was breaking ice all the way up the fjord. Remembering what had happened to the *Beagle's* crew, when they ate lunch too close to a glacier, I stopped the boat about ½ mile short of the face and I turned her round to face the way out before the ice

The mysterious footprints we found on our way back from the glacier. Do these belong to a yeti type creature? Not even Darwin saw one of those, but many people attest that such a creature lives here. Having seen the footprint, I am prepared to believe it.

Near Glacier Asia there was so much ice in the water that it was often hard to see a way through. Often we had somebody up the mast looking for the best way. We could break the thinner ice, but I did not want to hit any of the big lumps.

we had broken could freeze again. The water was about 300ft deep, but we did not need to anchor; *Thalassi* was held quite snugly in the ice.

The glacier itself is huge – a little over ½ mile across the face. Doing a bit of a Fitzroy, we calculated the height of the face by taking a sextant angle and measuring the distance off with the radar. It was 375ft above the water, give or take an inch or two. If the ice went down to the floor of the fjord, it could well be over 600ft thick in total – a lot of ice. The northern side was the most active. A steady stream of bits were falling off. Every now and then a larger piece, about the size of a car, would come crashing and splashing down.

We had heard that noise can sometimes start an ice fall, so Nick, always happy to make a noise, started hooting away with *Thalassi*'s foghorn. There was no noticeable reaction. Ever since Brazil, Jeff had been trying to teach me to play the bugle, so we got our bugles out and blew as hard as we could. There were a few rumbles, but no splash. Lana thought she would show us how to do it. She took my bugle and gave a rather off-key toot. Instantly, a piece the size of a house fell in. Jeff and I were convinced that we had loosened it for her.

Jorge was anxious to get closer. I did not want to risk puncturing the inflatable on some ice, so we launched the fibreglass pulling boat, and Tony, Nick, Jorge and Jeff tried to paddle it to the shore. They did not get more than about 6ft; the ice was too thick to let them row or even paddle effectively, but it was also much too unstable to walk on. We decided to see how the outboard would cope. I passed it down to Jeff, and he fired it up. It pushed the boat along quite well. Most of the time there was clear water under the stern of the boat, but if any bits of ice got in the way, the motor worked like a blender making pina coladas, and ground it up with no apparent difficulty, or harm to the engine.

There was a big rounded rock close up to the ice face, towards the southern edge. Jeff landed the others there and came back for Lana and me. That part of the glacier was not nearly so active as the northern side, but there were enough big pieces of ice lying about from previous falls to make us more than a little wary.

The glacier was always making a noise, sometimes a gentle creaking noise, at other times a rumble like distant thunder. Then a sudden crack and an avalanche would come roaring down the face. It was almost as if it were alive.

We reluctantly left it to go and look for a safer anchorage for the night. We found one of the best ever, off Estero Calvo. It was an almost totally landlocked little bay which we shared with a camp of fishermen. A very large rock in the middle of the entrance ensured perfect shelter once we were inside, but made the entrance itself very narrow. *Thalassi* had only 3 or 4ft to spare on either side as we squeezed gently in. Once inside there was plenty of room to anchor, with a couple of lines ashore to stop us swinging. No ice could get in and bother us in the night, and even if the wind came, we would be perfectly sheltered.

The fishermen came over to see us. They had built a camp on the beach and had two boats from which they went diving for scallops. Their diving technique was somewhat unorthodox. For air they used motor-driven spray-paint compressors connected to a length of garden hose, with a scuba second-stage regulator on the end of it. They were diving under the ice, in considerably more than 100ft, and

Nick trying to develop a new sport, which he called Windberging.

staying down for much of the day. Nobody had told them it could not be done, nor that they should all have died from the bends years ago. They had not even heard of decompression.

Klaus proved to be as adept at striking a bargain as Julio had been. The fishermen traded an enormous sack of scallops for two bottles of wine, a packet of Jeff's cigarettes and one of Nick's rude magazines. Klaus and Jorge spent most of the next day cleaning what looked to me like a lifetime's supply of scallops.

We were almost settled down for the evening when something happened that I had not bargained for. An extra big lump of ice had floated across the fjord and stopped right in the entrance of our little bay. There was immediate panic. As pretty and snug as the bay was, none of us fancied staying there for the approaching winter. If the tide went out and left the iceberg stranded there, or if a cold snap froze it in place, we could find ourselves in what a friend of ours would describe as 'Dicky's meadow'.

190

The others looked at me as though I was mad when I said that we should go and move it before it got stuck. Tony was trying to work out how many tons it might weigh, and by the time Jeff and I had launched the big dinghy, he was into the thousands. Lana, Jeff and I motored the dinghy over to the unwelcome iceberg. We put the bows against its side, and started pushing with all the 55 horse-power that the outboard could muster. For a while it looked like a hopeless task, but then we realised that it was moving – only slowly, but it was moving. Lana scrambled up onto the top to tell us which way to steer, and we kept pushing for about ten minutes or so. By this time we had moved it about 50yd, which I hoped would be far enough for it not to come back. We recovered Lana and retired back on board.

The scallop fishermen of Estero Calvo, with their supply boat.

From *Thalassi* we watched the iceberg. Although it was barely moving fast enough to see, it had enough momentum to keep it moving against the general flow of all the smaller ones, knocking them out of the way. We watched it until it was too dark to see, by which time it had gone at least a mile down the fjord. It may have taken us a long time to get it moving, but it was not going to be easily stopped.

Three sunny days among the glaciers must have used up our ration of good weather. It soon returned to normal, but it was time to move on anyway. I could easily spend a whole summer just in that one area, walking, exploring and glacier spotting, but even Klaus's laid-back schedule was ticking by. We set off northwards once more. Even though the canals here were basically running north to south, the wind always seemed to be on the nose and we had to motor a lot.

Lana in command of the iceberg that we had to move because it was blocking our way out from the anchorage. She guided our efforts, telling us which way to push the berg clear with the dinghy.

Our regret at leaving the glaciers was tempered a little by finding a wonderful anchorage off the Paso Brassey. The weather was cold and rainy, and as Darwin had said, we were missing a lot of the scenery. Fortunately the rain stopped as we approached our chosen anchorage, a perfectly landlocked circular little bay at the end of its very own tiny canal. There were no soundings on the chart, so we did not know whether the approach would be deep enough for us. We launched the big dinghy, and Lana, Tony and Nick went ahead, doing a rapid survey for depth. They zigzagged to and fro across the channel, telling me on the radio where the deepest water lay.

The channel was very narrow, only about twice as wide as the boat, with steep, rocky cliffs on either side. It made a dog-leg about halfway along, which made things very tight. The dinghy team had done a good job checking depths, and assured me that there was plenty of water right up to the cliff, but none of them had looked up above. As we came round the corner, I was horrified to see a tree sticking out over the water. It was growing on the top of the cliff, but there was a big branch sticking out into the middle of the channel, just about level with the upper spreaders. Almost on the end of the branch, there was a large bird's nest. I could not see how we could miss it, but a big push with the bow thrutcher got the main mast round it. Then I swung the stern as far over to port as I dared, and the mizzen rigging just brushed by the nest. Had the branch been a foot longer, there would have been a homeless bird or two that night.

Our effort was rewarded by a superb anchorage, as snug as can be imagined. There were high hills all around, usually a sign of nightly williwaws, but the bay was so small that they passed over the top of us. The water was completely calm. A waterfall at the head of the bay was pouring over a cliff that was more than 400ft high. The anchorage was given eleven out of ten. The chart gave it a Spanish name, but we logged it as Bird's Nest Bay, and that is what we will always remember it as.

Jeff and I were getting beckoning signals from the waterfall, saying 'Come and climb me', but unfortunately, once more we had to press on.

In the Canal Messier, the main north–south route, we had a reminder not to become complacent. The water was consistently between 200 and 300ft deep, and we were chugging along quite happily, watching the scenery go by. In the distance we spotted a ship – the first we had seen since leaving Puerto Natales. It took a long time for us to reach it; it seemed to have stopped right in the centre of the channel. As we got closer, we could see that it was a wreck. It had run up onto a rock, right in mid-channel. The rock must stick up like a spike, in water over 200ft deep. 'MV *Leonides*' had ended her days there, and if she had not been marking that rock, it might have been us instead of her that hit it.

The dreaded Golfo de Penas lay ahead. The well-named Gulf of Pains has a fearsome reputation. It is a bay some 70 miles across, wide open to the west winds of the Roaring Forties. A sailing ship such as the *Beagle* could easily be embayed in heavy weather, unable to beat out past either headland, eventually to be swept ashore on to the jagged rocks.

On the northern headland, Taito Peninsula, the Indians had a portage, an area where they could carry their canoes over a narrow neck of land. Using this, and the smallest canals, they only had to be in exposed water for 10 or 15 miles. Obviously we could not follow their route, so we had to go outside for about 170 miles before we could get back in behind the next chain of islands. A hundred and seventy miles of lee shore in the Roaring Forties did not sound like much fun.

Nick was still feeling that he had been robbed of a Cape Horn gale. Tony said he would be interested in seeing the big waves he had read about. He seemed to forget that to see them he would have to feel them. Jeff was with the rest of us   fingers, toes, arms and legs crossed that we would have an easy passage.

The weather map showed a small high-pressure ridge building, which should give us light winds, so we made a dash for it. The wind stayed light through the night, but there was still quite a big sea running. Poor Klaus lost his dinner, I came close and even Nick refused second helpings. But it was probably due as much to anticipation of what might have been as to the waves themselves. Once again the Forties failed to roar, and as far as I was concerned, that was perfect. We found a sheltered little cove in time for tea, followed by a good night's sleep.

North of the gulf, the terrain and the weather were noticeably softer. There were many more trees, growing on low, rolling hills. For the first time in a long while, there were no snow-capped mountains in sight, and when the sun came out, it was warm enough to sit out on deck. We had a couple of easy days, sailing in sheltered waters. The weather was being gentle, and we had less than 100 miles to go to Puerto Aisen, where Klaus and Jorge would leave us, and three days to do it in.

Klaus was determined to make the most of the last few days. In one small bay, in among the Chonos Islands, he led Jorge, Tony, Nick and Jeff on a little expedition to reach a waterfall that we could see from the boat. Jeff told us later that the going was pretty tough, with

The wreck of the MV Leonides, in Canal Messier. It might just as easily have been us that hit this pinnacle of rock which was not shown on our chart. If I ever go back, we will have a forward-looking echo sounder to spot such dangers.

very dense undergrowth. Klaus was undeterred, however, and pressed on in the lead. He led them, one might say, up a gum tree. It was not really a gum tree, it was actually a dead beech tree, but he got everybody up it. It was a very big tree which had fallen over. In the thick undergrowth it afforded a handy path, so he scrambled up onto it, and walked along the trunk. The vegetation was so thick that he did not realise that the tree had not fallen all the way down. When

The anchorage at Caleta Gato, or Pussycat Bay as Jorge not quite literally translated it.

they got to where the branches made it difficult to continue, and Klaus was about to jump off the trunk, they suddenly realised that they were about 30ft off the ground!

Back on terra firma, he decided to take them along the bank of the river. His luck was still out. Part of the bank collapsed, and Klaus fell headlong into the river. Jeff was stripping off to go in after him, with visions of what might happen to us if we drowned one of Chile's most important industrialists. But while he was still teetering on the brink, he realised that Klaus was all right, and laughing his head off. Klaus thought it was a huge joke and swam back to the boat, leaving the others to struggle back through the jungle.

Our last night with Klaus was spent in Caleta Gato, 'Pussycat Bay' in Jorge's not quite literal translation. It had rained most of the day on the way there, but in the late afternoon the weather cleared up. The bay was quite a bit bigger than most of those we had been wriggling into, but it was just as well sheltered. Tree-covered hills surrounded us once again.

Klaus wanted one last expedition. He had been here a couple of years previously, and remembered a lone fisherman who lived nearby. The fisherman lived by catching *centollo*, gigantic crabs, and shipping them off by a cargo boat that kept a monthly schedule. He thought that if we could find the fisherman, we might be able to have crabs for dinner. Jeff said his nerves could not stand keeping an eye on Klaus for another of his expeditions, so Lana, Tony and I went with him and Jorge.

The harbour at Chacabucco, which is the port that serves Puerto Aisen, which is too silted up to be a port. We dropped-off Klaus and Jorge here, and fuelled up for our passage north.

Klaus found the camp without any problems, but it was deserted. The wooden house was open and obviously abandoned, although there were a few home-made tools lying about in a workshop beside the house. The garden was running amok: everything was over-grown, and obviously nobody had tended it for several months. It was so sad. Somebody had put in an enormous amount of work to clear the area, plant a garden and build the house. Now it had all been left, and the jungle would soon reclaim it. Lana and I were suffering from a real dose of melancholy when Klaus started yelling.

He was down on his hands and knees, scrabbling about with something. He had discovered potatoes, lots and lots of potatoes, and he was digging them up. He said they would only go to seed if we did not take them. Feeling a bit guilty, even though it was all but certain that the place had been abandoned for good, we joined him. We dug up as many potatoes as would fit in Tony's hat. Lana cast around the overgrown garden with a more culinary eye. She soon found carrots, cabbages, a clump of chives and a little bush of thyme. Then she found a patch of lettuce which unfortunately was just about to go to seed. We had more fresh vegetables than we had seen since Punta Arenas, and we had a very big and very healthy meal that night.

The next day, April Fool's Day as it happened, we dropped off Klaus and Jorge. Although Aisen is termed a *puerto*, it has become so badly silted as to be effectively closed, so we anchored off Chacabucco, letting them complete their trip by taxi. They promised that they would see us again when we got close to Santiago, which was still the best part of 1000 miles north. We looked forward to it; they were both fun people and had been good shipmates.

Chapter 16

Patagonia to Valparaiso

After *Beagle* stood out to sea from the Magellan Straits, they ran into some awful weather. Although it was unwelcome it should not have been entirely unexpected, since it was by now the middle of winter. I would not have liked that at all. Apart from the added risk of bad weather, the winter days are very short, and the nights correspondingly long. A gale by day is infinitely less frightening than one at night, when the helmsman cannot see the waves coming.

Leaving the Milky Way and the coast of Patagonia behind them, they had to beat to windward to get themselves off the lee shore. Poor Darwin succumbed to the seasickness once more. For more than two weeks he made no entries in his journal, and for much of that time lay flat out in his hammock.

It took them eighteen days to make good the 800 miles to Chiloe. Because they were beating and tacking, the distance they actually sailed was a lot more than that, and every mile of it was hard going. The crew were cold, wet and miserable. Every squall or increase in wind sent them aloft to reef or furl the sails. Rain and spray wet their clothes, and with no heating and little ventilation below decks, there was no chance to dry them. The clothes actually began to rot.

I wonder how long our crew would have lasted under those conditions. Nick liked to put his socks in the tumble drier as he came off watch so that he always had warm, dry ones to put on for the next one. Jeff usually managed to organise generating time while he was off watch so that he could keep the electric fan heater running in his cabin while he slept. I think only Tony might have coped. He seemed oblivious to the cold. I do not know whether it was because of his Irish ancestry or the past winter in the Antarctic, but he never once complained about being cold. In fact he was becoming worried about how he would handle the heat when we got further north.

The day before the *Beagle* reached the island of Chiloe, one of the crew died. Darwin does not say whether it was an accident, illness or just plain fatigue, but the entry in his journal expresses his feelings. He writes: 'It is an awful and solemn sound, that splash of the waters over the body of an old shipmate.'

When they reached Chiloe, they anchored off the town they called San Carlos. From Darwin's description, I think it must be the present day Quellon. The schooner *Adventure* caught up with them a couple of days later. Her passage north had been no easier; although she sailed to windward better than the *Beagle* did, she was considerably smaller and suffered even more in the bad weather.

Both ships lay anchored off the port for two weeks, and Darwin was soon fit enough to take some walks ashore. He enjoyed beating his own path through the lush vegetation, which reminded him of Brazil. During that first visit, he spent much of his time studying his geology books. His mind was struggling to cope with the almost unbelievably long epochs that are suggested in geological history, compared to the relatively short periods that people, and indeed all animals and plants, have existed.

They sailed north from Chiloe in easy conditions. As they arrived in Valparaiso, Darwin reports that after the rigours of Patagonia, the climate felt quite delightful. They arrived in the dark, and when Darwin got up in the morning, he marvelled at the view. The soil was very red, contrasting starkly with the whitewashed houses and their tiled roofs. It reminded him very much of Santa Cruz in Tenerife, where the health authorities had denied them permission to land what now seemed like a lifetime before. The sky was blue, with not a cloud to be seen. The atmosphere felt wonderfully dry, and he says 'all nature seemed sparkling with life'. One gets the feeling that he was glad to have stopped sailing for a while.

Fitzroy's plan was to spend several months in Valparaiso, doing the inevitable refit on the ship and bringing all their survey records up to date. Darwin was looking forward to using that period to sort out his own collection, and hopefully to ship the next lot of samples back to England.

Darwin describes Valparaiso as consisting of a long straggling street running along the beach, joined by houses built on either side of ravines running down from the low hills. What would he make of it now? It has expanded to house over 300,000 people, and a series of funicular railways, elevators and zigzag roads connect the original lower parts of the city with the various levels that have been built above it in the hills.

When he got ashore, Darwin was delighted to find a group of English-speaking academics, with whom he was able to have long and involved discussions. He was also excited to receive a batch of mail with up-to-date news of England, which had taken less than eighteen months to reach them. In the mail was a letter from

Henslow, praising him for the collection that he had sent from Montevideo. It seemed to Darwin that all was well with the world.

By coincidence he found that one of his school friends from England was now living in Valparaiso, and he arranged to move in with him for the duration of *Beagle*'s stay. He was happy to escape the confines and routines of the ship for a few weeks.

If all was well with Darwin, the reverse seemed to be the case with Fitzroy. He had worked himself up into a state of nervous tension, and had opted out of all the official functions and shore duties, sending Lieutenant Wickham in his place. Fitzroy spent all his time plotting and planning what to do next, and his schemes were becoming more grandiose by the day. He started to talk of a return to Tierra del Fuego, to survey the coast of western Patagonia, all of Chile and Peru. Then on their way across the Pacific he thought they might well survey New Zealand as well as the Pacific islands themselves. Whatever his officers felt, naval protocol prevented them from commenting. Darwin began to worry that the voyage would go on for ever, but he comforted himself with the thought that since the ship was made of wood and iron, it could not last for ever, so the voyage would have to end eventually.

Fitzroy's plans took a severe blow when he got word from the Admiralty that they would not authorise the purchase or even the hire of the schooner *Adventure*. This was not only a blow to his plans, but to his pride and his pocket as well. So far he had paid all of the *Adventure*'s expenses himself.

Darwin considered leaving the *Beagle* then and there, but his fascination, almost obsession, with the geology of Chile made him stay. He knew he was unlikely to return, and he could not bring himself to leave without taking a look at the geology of central Chile and Peru.

Eventually Fitzroy got a grip of himself, but his attitude was permanently changed. Perhaps even he was becoming a little homesick. He wrote that he could no longer bear the thought of such a long separation from his country, yet he had always made light of being away for long periods, and had shown little compassion for those who were homesick. After his change of heart, he announced that they would complete their survey of Chiloe and the Chonos Islands, then sail north to Peru. From there they would cross the Pacific and head for home. Everybody was relieved about that. The mood among the officers improved at once.

Just before they left Valparaiso, Fitzroy and Darwin had another of their rows. All the officers had been well entertained ashore, and Fitzroy was grumbling about having to throw a reciprocal party on board before they left. Darwin suggested that if it was such a problem for him, then perhaps it was best forgotten. Fitzroy roared at Darwin that he had always thought him to be a man to take favours without feeling the obligation to repay them. Darwin left without saying a word, and went to stay with his friend ashore. When he returned a few days later, Fitzroy received him cordially, and the matter was never referred to again. It was probably just another example of the pressures brought about by close living. We can sympathise.

Adventure was discharged, and *Beagle* returned south to survey Chiloe and the Chonos Islands. When they reached Chiloe, *Beagle* once more lay anchored off San Carlos. While they were there, on a rare clear day, Darwin watched Mount Osorno and two other mainland volcanoes smoking.

A month or so later, they had grandstand seats for an eruption of Osorno. It happened at night, and *Beagle*'s lookout, who first spotted it, thought it was a star rising. The light became steadily brighter, until it was obvious that it was something other than a star. Suddenly flames and lava shot up into the air. Even though the volcano was more than 70 miles away, they could see the streams of red-hot lava running down the side of the mountain. Darwin was fascinated to find out later that several other volcanoes, some as far away as 3000 miles, had all erupted at exactly the same instant.

Witnessing the eruption increased his geological interest still further, while the damp, drizzly weather dampened, literally and metaphorically, his biological ardour. He decided that Chiloe's climate, which he described as being detestable in the winter, is only a little better in the summer.

Fitzroy wanted to survey the whole coast of the island. It is quite large, over 90 miles long and about 30 broad, so he decided that he would take the *Beagle* down the exposed west coast, while Sullivan could survey the sheltered east coast from one of the whale-boats.

Darwin chose to go with the whale-boat. He rode overland to join them at the north end of the island, where they were to start the survey. He found that, because the ground was so damp and boggy, a wooden road had been built from squared-off logs. Because the forest was so difficult to clear, only one road had been built. Boats were the main form of transport for both people and goods, even when going from one part of the island to another.

The climate is the main reason why the islanders found it so hard to clear the forest. The regular and almost continual rain prevented them from burning areas of trees, either for road building or for agriculture. After felling, the trees all had to be cut up into small pieces and carried away. The soil is certainly very fertile, which is why the

The island of Chiloe – after the rugged barren south, the patchwork fields of Chiloe looked soft and inviting. Where we found fields, Darwin had found almost impenetrable forest.

trees grow in such abundance, but the climate makes it virtually impossible to grow anything which needs the sun for ripening. The staples for the locals were potatoes, pigs and of course fish. Little fruit, and almost no grains were being grown.

Once Darwin joined the whale-boat, they worked their way south along the length of the island, camping on the beach each night. They aroused considerable curiosity. Strangers were rare enough on the island, and several people approached them, asking if they were soldiers who had come to liberate the island from the patriot government of Chile. Chiloe had been one of the last strongholds of Spanish Imperialism, and Spain had relinquished control of the island only eight years before.

Darwin was fascinated to find that most of the inhabitants of the island wore home-knitted garments, a tradition that continues to this day. They not only wear knitted sweaters, but often knitted hats and ponchos as well.

The survey team paid a visit to Castro, which is now the capital of the island. Darwin called it a forlorn and deserted place. Under Spanish rule it had obviously been a bigger, more important town, because they could still see the quadrangular arrangement of disused Spanish streets. In the remains of the plaza, and indeed on many of the roads, a fine green turf had grown, and where the *señoritas* had once paraded their charms, sheep now grazed.

Darwin visited the wooden church, and describes it as having 'a picturesque and venerable aspect', but they found the whole town to be very poor. Because none of the 200 inhabitants could afford a watch or a clock, an old man, who was said to have a good sense of time, was employed to ring the hours on the church bell by guess-

Inside the wooden church at Castro, on Chiloe. This was where Darwin found a man paid to guess the time and ring the bell, as nobody had a clock.

work. I have no doubt that Darwin will have timed him, but unfortunately he does not record whether the chimes were accurately rung or not.

As they worked their way south, Darwin was intently studying the rock formations. He concluded that granite was the 'fundamental rock' of the world; at that time it formed the deepest layer of the earth's crust that man had been able to penetrate.

When the whale-boat crew rejoined *Beagle* at the southern end of the island, Darwin went ashore where some of the officers were taking bearings for the survey. He saw a fox, of a species which is unique to this area and extremely rare. It was so engrossed in watching the surveyors that Darwin was able to creep up behind it, and whack it on the head with his geological hammer. It eventually ended up stuffed and mounted back in London. It did not seem to worry Darwin that he had killed one of the last of the species, perhaps contributing to its extinction.

He accompanied the survey team in an attempt to reach the summit of one of the hills. They ran into the same problem as Klaus had. The trees were so densely packed and tangled together that he reckoned they sometimes went ten minutes or more without touching the ground. At one stage they found themselves so far above the ground that some of the seamen, in jest, started calling out the soundings.

They also explored and tried to survey the Chonos Islands. It was not easy: the weather stayed bad almost the whole time. One day, while they were anchored in the Chonos, they had one particularly strong gale which Darwin felt was worthy of Cape Horn. The water was white with flying spray, and sheets of dark rain drove past them. At the height of the storm, the sun peeped out through a brief break in the clouds, and they saw a very bright rainbow. As they stood on deck looking at it, the wind picked up enough spray from the sea to complete the rainbow's circle.

Christmas came and went, and was recorded by Darwin as a dreary occasion. For one so young he was rapidly becoming a bit of a curmudgeon. A couple of days after Christmas they discovered a new harbour, which of course had to be surveyed. Much to their surprise, they saw a man on the beach, waving furiously. A boat was sent ashore, and they found a group of six men who had run away from an American whaler. They had absconded with one of the ship's boats, but had lost it in a storm and were now marooned. It was their greatest good fortune that *Beagle* had stumbled upon them; otherwise they would certainly have perished.

The new year, 1835, was ushered in with yet another gale. The weather obviously intended to start as it meant to go on. Darwin was looking forward to leaving this coast before the end of the year, and wrote that he was looking forward to crossing the Pacific, 'where a blue sky above tells one there is a Heaven – a something beyond the clouds above our heads'.

The survey of the Chonos continued with difficulty, as gale after gale swept through. Darwin made a few sorties ashore, and on one of them discovered a lot of wild potatoes. The potato as we know it is derived from those which the Spanish explorers found growing in several areas of South America. It is thought that the Indians in some areas have been cultivating potatoes since before the time of Christ. Darwin dug up some of them and was a little disappointed that when they were cooked, they were not as good as the home-grown ones he was used to. He found them a bit watery and almost completely tasteless.

He did not find many animals to study. There were a lot of seals, which always seemed surprised to see visitors, and he also saw several sea-otters and a capybara, a creature that looks like a large rat.

When the survey of the islands was finished, they headed north again for the last time. They stopped briefly in Chiloe once more, then anchored close to Valdivia, on the mainland. When he rode inland to the town itself, Darwin discovered that it was almost awash in apples. The trees virtually engulfed the town, and everywhere he went, there were apples. The soil and climate were so suitable for the fruit that a branch cut off a tree would root, sprout and even sometimes bear fruit if it was just stuck in the ground.

He spent a few nights there, and commented that his first night ashore was often a bit restless, as he was not used to the tickling and biting of the fleas. Although *Beagle*, like all ships of her time, was infested with rats, the fleas seem to have been kept under control. I wonder whether rats eat fleas?

While he was ashore, Darwin experienced an earthquake at first hand. He was sitting in the forest, taking a breather, when the ground began to shake. He leaped to his feet and found that he could stand, although the swaying of the ground made him feel giddy, almost like being back at sea. The trees swayed and the leaves whispered. He found the experience more interesting than frightening. Fitzroy and some of the officers were in Valdivia where not many of the wooden buildings fell down. As the houses shook, however, the planks creaked and groaned, and people came running outside in terror. It was the general panic that made it seem more frightening there than out in the forest where Darwin was.

On their way back north, they found that Concepción and

Talcahuano had been all but levelled. A tidal wave had come roaring through Talcahuano to complete what the quake itself had started. The wave reached a height of 23ft above high water, and when it receded, little more than a single row of bricks remained where the houses once stood. A schooner had been thrown up into the ruins of the fort, and left 200yd from the sea. When he saw the damage, Darwin tried to visualise the effect that such an earthquake would have on London. It was beyond his imagining.

The earthquake heightened his geological interest. He saw that the land around Talcahuano had risen by 2 or 3ft above the sea, and at an island a few miles north, rocks that they had recently surveyed as being under water now stood 10ft clear. It was fine to theorise about geological upheavals, but to see it happen at first hand was fantastically exciting. In Concepción, he studied the way in which walls had fallen. He noticed that the walls running along the line of the shock wave had often stood intact, while those running across the line, had almost invariably fallen. He may have felt a little guilty that his compassion for the inhabitants had been overshadowed by his geological interest. He wrote that this was the most exciting thing he had seen since leaving England.

Back in Valparaiso they had a final refit, to get the *Beagle* ready for crossing the Pacific.

The last word we had received from the Boss had been for us to get to Talcahuano as soon as possible after dropping Klaus. We did the usual fuelling and provisioning, and started north. We were coming to the part of Chile that Klaus knew best, and before he left he went through the charts with us and marked on a few suggested stops.

On the first day, we covered an easy 58 miles and stopped in a long narrow bay called Puerto Amparo. Perhaps it was the low grassy hills that reminded Tony of his native Ireland, but something inspired him to try his luck at fishing. 'This looks like grand salmon country,' he said as he, Nick and Jeff went off in the dinghy to try and capture supper.

While they were gone, two fishermen stopped by *Thalassi*. They wanted to trade fish for cigarettes. I stole a packet from Jeff's supply, and got two big, ready-cleaned hake in return. When the boys came back empty-handed, I rather smugly showed them what I had 'caught'.

Our next anchorage was rated a 'do not miss' by Klaus. It was a little bay about halfway up a long fjord. At the head of the fjord was a little town called Puyuguapi – pronounced as near as we could get it as 'pooyoowappy'. The bay where he had told us to stop was a small fishing resort. Normally we shy away from known resorts, but we were glad we had heeded Klaus's advice on this one.

The hotel was a very low-key little place. It was in the process of closing down for the winter, so there were no guests. When they did have guests, the resort's speciality was to fly them to the lakes, high in the mountains, in a small float plane. This way their guests could fish otherwise inaccessible lakes. But, although most people came to Puyuguapi for the fishing, what Klaus had told us to investigate were the hot springs.

There were three pools at different levels down the side of the hill. The lowest was the hottest – too hot for any of us to get into. The middle one was a small swimming pool, but our favourite was the top one, a little rock pool set into a grotto-like cave. It was just big enough for the five of us to get into. It was very hot, but just bearable if one eased in gently. Once in, it felt wonderful. Across the fjord were the last of the snow capped mountains, just visible through the trees from the pool. Lana had had the foresight to pack a cooler full of beers and Cokes. To lie in the steaming water, sipping a cold drink, surrounded by dripping ferns and flowers, gazing across the fjord at the snowy mountains was just about the most sybaritic experience one could imagine. Wonderful.

Afterwards, five wrinkled prunes finally staggered back to the boat, to face another bombshell – a message saying that an engineer from the boatyard, José was arriving to join us the next morning, in Chacabuco. The Boss had arranged for him to come and sail with us for ten days so that he would see what problems still existed with the boat and hopefully learn from our experiences when building the next one. That was fine, except that the Boss had forgotten to tell us, and we had left Chacabuco two days previously. We were now over 120 miles away, and there was no way we could get back there in time for José's arrival.

I tried calling the boatyard in Spain, but it was Friday night and the place was closed for the weekend. I called Julio, back in Punta Arenas, and asked him to help us sort things out. He got Klaus involved, and we managed to get a message to Santiago airport, where José would have to change planes *en route* to Chacabuco. Julio had discovered that there was a bus from Chacabuco to Puyuguapi,

In the hot springs at Puyuguapi. To soak in the hot pools while looking across at the snow covered mountains was wonderful.

so I decided that we would stay put and let José come to us. It would be much quicker than for us to sail south to collect him and then have to come all the way north again to resume our journey to Talcahuano. At least that is what we thought, but that was before we had experienced Chilean public transport. In the meantime, we reconciled ourselves to having to spend another day in the hot pools, waiting for José and the Chacabuco bus to reach us. Life can be so trying!

The bus was due to arrive late the following afternoon, so after soaking the day away, we dinghied into town to look for José. There was no bus, no José. A policeman saw us wandering around, and asked us if we were looking for José. When we said we were, he told us that the bus (there was only the one it seems) had broken an axle and would not be running for several days. Somehow the policeman had found out that José was coming by boat, and would arrive the next morning on the Chacabuco ferry.

When José did eventually arrive, he was almost out on his feet, having been travelling for about four days. He did not seem to be in any state to sail so, out of consideration to him, another lazy day at the hot pools was forced upon us. By the time we left the following morning, we must have been the cleanest crew of yachties ever to set sail!

We made 88 miles in very light winds that day, to reach Tictoc Bay. Klaus had promised us some resident killer whales there, but it was not to be. We cruised around searching the bay, but all we found was two groups of sea-lions. Compared with their Falkland cousins, they were wimps. They dived into the water without even a growl as soon as the dinghy came anywhere near them.

It was Lana's birthday the next day. Nick undertook to get up early (a serious sacrifice for him) and to cook breakfast. He insisted that Lana was served hers in bed. By the time the resulting mayhem in the galley was cleaned up, we were a bit late getting underway, so I decided to make a fairly short hop of about 50 miles, to the southern end of Chiloe, *Beagle*'s landfall after her eighteen-day passage up from the south.

It was a grey and rainy day. It was not a howler, but the wind was fresh enough as we crossed the open Golfo Corcovado. Poor José was looking distinctly green; he had not found his sealegs yet.

About halfway across the gap, Lana went into our cabin to fetch something, and found hydraulic oil pouring out of the deckhead, all over her bunk and a fair number of her clothes. Happy birthday! Jeff and I started to take down the panelling to see where the oil was coming from. Lana went up into the cockpit and we could hear her roaring at poor José: 'You built the stupid boat, so you go and stop the oil pouring onto my bunk.'

José came down and took a brief look, then hastily retreated, preferring to face Lana's wrath rather than the smell of hydraulic oil in the bouncing cabin. Meanwhile Jeff and I were getting close to losing our breakfasts, which Nick had laboured over for so long. The heavy motion and the stink of the oil were a powerful combination. We traced the leak to the seal under one of the hydraulic winches. There was nothing we could do about it until we stopped. No more oil would come out if we did not use that winch, but there was plenty of oil still to be cleaned up.

Lana had another go at José. She gave him a bucket and some paper towel and sent him back down to help. 'It's the boatyard's fault that all my things are covered in oil – the least you can do is help them clean it up.' He appeared dutifully at the cabin door, clutching his roll of paper towel and bucket. He took a look and a sniff at what was going on, and a moment later his breakfast was in the bucket. Lana finally relented, and he was allowed to retreat before he made a bigger mess for us to clean up.

No sooner was our cabin back in reasonable order than Jeff found that the stern gland was leaking again, even worse than before. We hove to for a while so that Jeff could tighten his makeshift lashings. José was openly relieved that Jeff did not make him go into the engine-room bilge to take a look. We were hoping to haul the boat in Talcahuano and replace the whole gland, so Jeff contented himself with grumbling at poor José all the way to Chiloe.

By the time we got into the lee of the island, everybody had had enough. We anchored in the first sheltered spot we came to, off the town of Quellon. Nick and Tony were sent ashore to try and find a restaurant where we could take the cook out for a birthday dinner. They did well, and a nice meal ashore put everybody in better spirits.

Quellon is a sleepy little town that still has a fair amount of horse-drawn traffic. The green hills, the scattered cultivated fields and the damp drizzly weather reminded us of Ireland. The invention of the chain saw has resulted in the demise of a fair amount of Darwin's dense forest. There are now quite big areas patchworked with fields, and a network of roads cover the island.

When we got to Castro, about halfway up the east side of the island, we found it to be bigger and a bit more bustling than Quellon. The houses along the waterfront are all built on stilts, with water lapping around them at high tide. Almost all the buildings, including the big church that Darwin visited, are wooden. Most of the houses and shops seem to be made of some kind of pine, but the church appears to be built of cedar.

I am not sure whether the church we saw is a new one, or the original one which has been refurbished, but it is all in extremely good condition. The inside is spectacular – all vaulted ceilings and arches. Everything is of wood, even the massive pillars, which are built in sections and reach up to the high ceiling. The whole church smells like a cigar box. I was somewhat surprised to see four confessionals, each of them a two-seater. The people of Castro must be either very sinful or very pious.

There is still a thriving woollen industry in Chiloe. Many of the locals wear home-knitted garments. Lana received a sweater from me and a knitted poncho from the boys for her birthday.

From Castro, we coast-hopped up to the north end of the island. It seemed that every mile we went, the land became more and more cultivated. Big tracts of forest had been cleared, to be replaced by cultivated fields.

From the north end of Chiloe to Talcahuano is about 300 miles. There are no more off-lying islands or sheltered canals, so I decided to do it in one shot. It was getting close to the time when José was due to fly out anyway, and he did not relish another journey by Chilean public transport – he was anxious that we deliver him to Talcahuano itself in good time for his flight. On the second night out, we crossed the fortieth parallel – we had escaped the forties without getting seriously roared at.

A couple of hours before dawn, Tony spotted a red flare off to the east. Jeff, who was on watch with him, came to wake me. On the radar we could see a small echo about 5 miles away. We motored over to investigate. As we came close, we could see that it was a small fishing boat, in total darkness. Although Jeff's Spanish is quite good, we decided to roust out José, and let him do the talking.

I was distinctly nervous about going too close to an unknown vessel in the dark. We had read about pirate attacks and dope smugglers who steal yachts. Were we being set up? I am basically opposed to guns on boats, and I was not happy when I had found that the Boss had four guns and several thousands rounds of ammunition on board. On this occasion, however, it gave me some comfort to have his .45 revolver in my pocket.

The crew of the fishing boat told José that they could not start their engine, and had flattened their battery in the process of trying. They asked us for a tow. I really did not want to tow them the 50 or 60 miles to port, so we used the radio and managed to raise another vessel in their fleet. He agreed to come and do the tow. We gave them our position and turned on our deck lights so that they could find us. We stood by, a discreet distance off, until the second boat came into sight, and then continued on our interrupted journey northwards.

Klaus had warned us that Talcahuano could hardly be considered the garden of Chile, but we were entirely unprepared for the dirt, pollution and general squalor of the place. The little town that Darwin described is gone forever. Talcahuano is now a city of over 250,000 people, and Chile's main naval port. The anchorage close to town is dirty and extremely smelly. Ashore there is a fish-processing plant and a slaughterhouse, and neither of them appear to be too careful about what they allow to run into the water. As we walked past the slaughterhouse, there was a row of big vultures sitting on the fence, licking their beaks, waiting for lunch. The fish plant was even more depressing – great truckloads of fish being tipped into the grinder to make fertiliser.

Costumes and Intimidation took a good part of the day, then we walked up to the big shipyard, where the Boss had assured us that we would be able to haul the boat. It was well past time to renew the anti-fouling paint on the bottom, and we had to do something about the now permanently leaking stern gland. It turned out that the yard had no equipment for lifting yachts, and never had had. All they could offer was to put us into the dry dock for big ships. If we went in with another ship, then we would have to stay as long as it did, which might be anything from a week to a month. If we went in alone, the charge would be the same as for a big cargo ship. When we sent the Boss the quote for that, the telex almost smoked with his reply. The gist was that we were to haul the boat elsewhere, but he offered no further suggestions as to where.

We waved goodbye to José, and hoped that he would not have to suffer another four days' travelling to get home. If the twenty-five-page report (that he took back with him) helped the yard improve their product, then his journey would have been worthwhile.

Lana, in her foray ashore, had found a Chinese restaurant, and everybody was keen to go there for dinner. Since I did not want the boat to be left unattended, we went in shifts. Lana and I went first, and had a reasonable meal. The only problem we had was with the street children begging. They were pestering and jostling us, and I even caught one with his hand in my pocket. Threatening to break it off did not seem to worry him. We got back without being robbed, and then the boys set off. As usual, they took a radio and said they would call me when they were ready to be picked up. It would not be safe for them to leave the dinghy tied up ashore unattended; if our experience with the children was anything to go by, it would be stolen in a flash.

I settled down with a good book to await their call. Midnight came and went. By 2 a.m. I was feeling like an anxious parent, and by 4 a.m. we were downright worried. Had the radio broken down or been stolen? Were they stretched out bleeding in some gutter after being mugged? There was really not much we could do in the dark. I was not going to go wandering round town on my own looking for them. If it was a radio problem then surely they would think to go to the Port Captain or even a fishing boat, and use their radio? We decided to wait until 9 a.m. before taking action.

I was just finishing breakfast when a cheery sounding Jeff came on the radio, saying that they were ready to be picked up. I found three somewhat hungover but giggly crew standing on the dock. They started to tell me that they had decided to spend the night in a guest house that they had found. The guest house must have been very busy, because they had each had to share a bed with a total stranger – three girls as it happened. I was furious. It was the only time on the whole trip that I yelled at them, and all became a bit sheepish when they realised how cross I was. If they had called on the radio I would not have minded at all, but I had missed a night's sleep, and Lana and I had worried unnecessarily, just because they were to idle to call.

Back on board they all found jobs to do, and went straight to work. It must have hurt them not to be able to sneak off to bed, but to be fair to them, they did not try.

Luckily none of us bore grudges, and everything was back to normal the next day. Their night ashore was to come back to haunt them, though – but more of that later.

Our mail arrived, together with a replacement stern gland from the boatyard – unfortunately the wrong size. The other bit of bad news was that we still had not been paid. Nor had Jeff, and he was absolutely furious. 'The Boss's not going to get away with this,' he said. I do not think I have ever seen Jeff so angry. 'I'm going to get a writ put on the boat, so that we cannot move until he pays up.'

Lana, ever the practical one, tried to calm him down a bit. 'If we do get the boat arrested, then let's find somewhere nicer than Talcahuano to stay in.'

She and I had a family conference, and decided that we had had enough. We sent the Boss a telex giving him three months' notice to find a new crew, and in the meantime, asked him to bring Jeff's and our salaries up to date. We were feeling a bit as Fitzroy did when he heard that the Admiralty were not going to repay him for the *Adventure*'s expenses. He did not understand why he should have to pick up the bill for doing part of the Admiralty's survey, and we did not see why we should be subsidising a millionaire's yacht.

Since we were not going to haul the boat at the shipyard, there was no reason to linger in that smelly harbour. That morning, when I had gone into the cockpit, I had come face to face with two vultures, sitting on the mizzen boom and looking down the hatch. They are such ugly birds close up, especially as these looked as if they had just come from breakfast at the slaughterhouse. Vultures have no feathers on their heads or necks, so that if they stick their heads into some rotting carcass, there is nothing to catch and stop them pulling it back out. I went back below to tell the others so that they could come and look. 'I recognise them,' said Nick. 'They are the Boss's accountants who came to the boat in Spain.' After he had pointed it out, we all agreed that there was indeed a strong resemblance.

Klaus had given us an invitation to visit his yacht club at Algorrobo, about 15 or 20 miles south of Valparaiso. The plan had been to go there in three or four weeks' time, after our supposed haul and refit, but the vultures decided it. I went ashore to call Klaus, to ask if we could head up there at once, and do our bits of work in prettier, less smelly surroundings.

He seemed a little hesitant, and asked if we could delay for a couple a days. If we could wait until the weekend then he would be able to meet us there and guide us in. I did not want to be too pushy, but told him we had had enough of Talcahuano, and were going to leave that day regardless. I said we would be more than happy either to anchor outside the club's marina until the weekend or, if that became too exposed, to go up to Valparaiso for a day or two. Anything would be better than another night in Talcahuano.

We had a couple of hundred miles to go, so it was going to be an overnight journey. As we left the bay of Talcahuano, we ran into thick fog. There were all kinds of little fishing boats messing about, and some of them did not show up too well on the radar, so we set the foghorn going, hooting every two minutes. Fortunately the fog cleared enough a few miles offshore for us to turn it off, otherwise nobody would have got any sleep.

On the way up the coast, Jeff started teasing Tony unmercifully. 'You think you're a sailor now, just because you've done 2000 miles on the boat. You've been round Cape Horn (twice by the Boss's reckoning) but you've still got the real test to come.

Tony was looking a little nervous. 'What's that?'

'You've never been into a marina yet,' said Jeff with a self-satisfied smirk. 'That's really going to test your mettle.'

We found the club without difficulty. The marina was a very small artificial harbour, protected in part by a large rock – or perhaps I should call it a small island. On the rock/island was a colony of penguins. We thought we had left them far behind, but then realised that

215

the cold current which flows up the coast there is the same one which affects the climate of the Galapagos, and of course there are penguins there too.

I was about to anchor just north of the marina entrance, where it looked as if we would be sheltered from the swell, when somebody ashore spotted us. There was a lot of whistling, yelling and waving. They wanted us to go in. The entrance was very narrow – like Bird's Nest Bay all over again. They directed us along the end of the harbour, where it became apparent why Klaus wanted to delay us: they were building a floating dock specially for us to tie up to.

It turned out that when Klaus called it 'his' yacht club, he was not exaggerating. He was the founder and the main mover behind it. He had been planning to build a dock big enough for his dream ship, and our visit had brought that building forward. He told the club staff to build his dock now so that we could use it! They were mortified that it was not quite finished.

The club was a much nicer spot than where *Beagle* lay in Valparaiso, and infinitely better than Talcahuano. It turned out to be a great place to get our jobs done, and thanks to Klaus and Jorge, a good spot to do a bit of sightseeing from as well.

The vultures on the boom at Talcahuano.

Chapter 17

In and Around Valparaiso

During the *Beagle's* two stays in Valparaiso, Darwin managed to do a fair amount of exploring and collecting. On their first visit, he made a fairly serious foray into the foothills of the Andes. Along the way, he found several signs that many of the mountains had been under the sea at one time. There were old seashells at a height of over 1300 ft – not just one or two shells, but great banks of them, enough for the locals to burn them to make quicklime. He tried to imagine the forces that must have been involved to lift the whole range of mountains bodily upwards for over a 1000 ft.

On his various trips in the mountains he noticed a comparative lack of animals. He sought to explain this by saying that perhaps none had been 'created' since the land had risen up from the sea.

The dry climate suited Darwin well. He felt that the last of the Patagonian dampness was being driven from his bones. The prevailing summer winds are mostly offshore and very dry. It is usually only during the three months of the winter that any rain falls at all. The dry climate determines what vegetation can grow. Trees are few and far between, but he found many species of wild flowers. He had noticed that in a dry climate, plants often tend to have a stronger smell than those in damper regions. During the course of his walks, his clothes picked up the scents of plants he brushed against.

He visited the hot springs at Cauquenes, which are still used as mineral baths today. He measured their temperature, and pondered the puzzle that the water in the springs is not only hotter but more plentiful during the dry summer months. What he does not record is whether or not he enjoyed a soak, as we did in Puyuguapi.

Towards the end of his first expedition, he went down with a mystery illness. It laid him up for three weeks, and although he never did find out what it was, he blamed it for his subsequent bad health. It may just have been a bad case of 'traveller's tummy'. When visiting new places, we sometimes fall prey to some 'bug' to which the locals are completely immune. Curiously enough, in the cold dampness of Patagonia, none of us had so much as a chill, yet once we got to the kinder climate near Valparaiso we, like Darwin, all developed various ailments.

From *Beagle*'s anchorage off the city, they could see the Andes, and the peak of Aconcagua. This is the highest peak in the Andes, indeed in the western hemisphere. By a series of triangulations, the *Beagle's* officers measured it to be 23,000 ft. That is remarkably close to the figure 22,834 ft that today's cartographers have arrived at.

One can begin to understand just how narrow the country of Chile is when one realises that from the coast one can see Aconcagua, which is well within Argentina's borders.

If Darwin perhaps looked wistfully at the mountain, he must have accepted that it was beyond their resources to climb it. It was to be another fifty years before a serious attempt was made, and it was not until 1897 that it was first climbed, by Matthias Zurbriggan. Even though Darwin did not climb Aconcagua, he did make a trip high into the mountains, to cross to the Argentinian plains. He travelled first to Santiago, Chile's capital, but did not linger, preferring to spend his time in the mountains. He had two local companions, and a train of eleven mules.

He was fascinated by the way one mule, termed the *madrina*, or godmother, controlled the group. Wherever she went, the others followed, like obedient children. Her sole task was to lead the troop; she was never ridden, nor did she carry a load. The *madrina* wore a small bell, and when it was time to get under way in the mornings, all that was required was to find her and ring her bell, and the troop would form up in line astern. On level ground each mule could carry more than 400 lb of cargo, but on a mountainous route this was reduced to around 300 lb. Of the ten mules they took, not counting the *madrina*, six were intended for riding, and four for carrying goods. They were rotated in their tasks during the expedition.

Because it was late in the year, and there was a risk that they might be snowed in somewhere, they took extra food with them.

As they made their way up the valleys into the mountains, Darwin studied the shingle terraces that they passed. It occurred to him that the shingle looked exactly the same as the material which a mountain stream deposits when it is suddenly checked in its course by flowing into a lake or the sea. Finally it dawned on him that perhaps these banks had been formed in exactly that way, as the mountains were slowly thrust upwards. The banks would have formed first near the head of the valley, at what was then sea level. As the mountains rose, successive banks would form lower down.

This was radical thinking, because until that time the popular view was that the mountains had been formed by some vast cataclysmic upthrust, not a comparatively gentle, slow rising. The further he went, however, the more signs he saw and the more convinced he became that his theory was correct.

They crossed the ridge at about 14,000 ft, and even the mules were finding it difficult to breathe. They would stop every 50 yd for a few seconds to catch their breath. Then they would restart of their own accord, such willing beasts were they. Darwin says he felt a slight tightness across his head and chest, and likened the feeling to that of leaving a warm room and going outside to run on a frosty day. The Chilenos called the feeling *puna*, and did not understand that it was related to altitude and the air becoming thinner. They thought that wherever there was snow there was *puna*, and they were convinced that the only cure was to eat a lot of onions. Darwin found that the best cure for him was finding fossil seashells at the top of the ridge – he was so excited that he completely forgot about the *puna*.

The other effect that the altitude had was on the cooking. They carried a big iron pot in which they boiled their potatoes on a camp-fire. Because of the reduced pressure, the water boiled at a much lower temperature than at sea level – just the opposite to a pressure cooker. The boiling point is reduced by 1 degree Fahrenheit for every 500 ft of altitude. So at 14,000 ft, the water was boiling at 184 degrees Fahrenheit, or about 84 degrees Celsius. Despite leaving the pot on the fire all night, with the potatoes boiling all the time, they were still too hard to eat in the morning. Darwin overheard his two companions discussing the matter. He knew that they both firmly believed in *puna*, and now he heard them say that the pot, which had been newly purchased for the expedition, was cursed. It had obviously decided not to cook the potatoes.

After their potatoless breakfast, they carried on over the ridge and began their descent to the plains of Argentina. Darwin was at once struck by the difference in vegetation between the two sides of the mountain chain. He found similar differences between the animals, and concluded that the mountains had been there, as an impassable barrier, longer than the animals and plants had existed.

As they reached the valley floor, they came to an outpost, where an officer and three soldiers were stationed to check passports. So Costumes and Intimidation were in full operation even then. One of the men was a pure-blooded pampas Indian. His job was to track anybody trying to sneak past the outpost. The officer in charge told Darwin that a few years before, somebody had tried to get past them by taking a long detour over a nearby mountain. The Indian, by chance, crossed his track. He was able to follow the track over dry and stony ground for a whole day before finding the fugitive hiding in a gully. It strikes me the Customs could use more agents like him

today to catch the drug smugglers and illegal immigrants.

When Darwin and his companions eventually arrived back at Valparaiso after some three weeks in the mountains, they found that the *Beagle* was almost ready to continue her voyage northwards. Darwin wanted to investigate the geology of the land further north. Fitzroy agreed that he could go overland, and be picked up at Copiapo, about 420 miles north of Valparaiso.

For transportation Darwin bought four horses and two mules, for the princely sum of £25. At the end of his journey, he sold them for £23. Since rain was so infrequent, they usually slept under the stars, so all in all, it turned out to be a cheap journey for him. He set off along the coast, accompanied by one of the guides from the mountain trip. They had not gone many miles north before the few remaining trees gave way to scrubland. He found the coast road more or less barren, and singularly uninteresting. He took a few detours inland to visit one of the gold-mining areas, and to do a bit of geological work.

They reached Coquimbo and had a brief rendezvous with the *Beagle*. Fitzroy came ashore to dine with Darwin at the guesthouse where he had taken a room. The meal ended in chaos, as another earth tremor shook the house. The locals all fled in panic, anticipating the worst. As it happened it was a mild tremor, and no damage was done.

Darwin went to examine the shingle terraces above the town. They were narrow and fringe-like, rising one behind the other. On the highest, over 250 ft above the sea, he was delighted to find the shells of existing marine species. This strongly reinforced his theory about the land being slowly uplifted.

On another day he was taken into the foothills to visit a silver mine. The thing he found most remarkable about this trip was that the bedroom he stayed in at the silver mine had no fleas. Where he was staying in Coquimbo, there was a swarm of them. At the silver mine they were at about 3000 ft and it was a littler cooler, but not very much. Yet there was not a flea to be seen or felt. He was very curious to know why. Was it the altitude? Could fleas not get up to 3000 ft?

While they were in Coquimbo it rained for the first time for seven months. It was a light rain, and hardly seemed to wet the ground, yet to Darwin's amazement the whole area, which the day before had been as bare as the road, grew a green fuzz almost immediately. We have seen a similar thing in the West Indies, when the first rain of the season turned a brown hillside green overnight.

Darwin, his companion and the animals carried on northwards to Copiapo, which is on the edge of the Atacama Desert. This is the driest desert in the world, and rain has never been recorded in some parts. The Andes form a barrier for the north easterly trade winds, and the cold Humbolt Current makes a temperature inversion, holding cold, dry air close to the surface. It is no wonder that the words sterile and barren frequently occur in Darwin's account of the last part of the journey.

Beagle arrived at Copiapo soon after Darwin did. He sold the horses and mules and said goodbye to his riding companion. He seemed happy enough to be back on board the *Beagle* as she left to sail north the next day.

For the passage up the Peruvian coast, Lieutenant Wickham was temporarily in command. Fitzroy had heard that another naval ship, HMS *Challenger*, had gone aground south of Talcahuano, and had set off to organise her rescue. When he got there, he had a blazing row with the officer in charge, who was actually his superior. Fitzroy thought he was dragging his feet, and threatened him with court martial. He then proceeded to take control of the whole operation. Perhaps it was fortunate for him that the ship was safely refloated. The jaunt did him good, and he was in fine form when he eventually rejoined the *Beagle* in Callao, the port for Lima.

Darwin had not had such an exciting time. They stopped at the small town of Iquique, which was then in Peru, but is now well and truly inside Chile. He did not think much of the place. It is totally isolated by desert to the north and to the south, and he thought life there was no better than that on board a ship. Everything, including water and food, had to be brought in by boat. The town existed because of a saltpetre mine, which Darwin of course had to visit. These deposits of nitrates are what sparked the war between Chile and Peru in 1879. In the battle of Iquique, on 21 May, the Peruvians suffered the loss of their best battleship, the *Independencia*. This allowed the Chilean forces to land, and they eventually captured Lima. Under the terms of the peace treaty, the southern section of Peru, including all the nitrate beds, became part of Chile, which they are to this day.

The road to the mines was remarkable for the number of mule skeletons. The mules had all perished making the same trek, and now lay beside the road. Other than vultures, which were constantly circling above as if waiting for Darwin and his companions to join the mules, he saw neither bird, quadruped, reptile nor insect for the whole journey.

Darwin was happy enough to leave Iquique, and sail north to Callao. At least he was happy until they got out to sea. Strong following winds made the ship roll, and soon put Darwin back in his hammock. The weather was overcast for much of the time. When he

had been in the Atlantic, he had longed for the Pacific. Now he fondly remembered brilliant days, cool evenings, glorious skies and bright stars; the Atlantic had all the virtues.

Darwin did not think much of Callao either. The whole town was filthy, and he said that the inhabitants were drunken and depraved. He felt the whole country was on the brink of anarchy. From stories we heard from other yachts, it seems little has changed in the last 150 years.

Lima he liked, however. He said that the dark-eyed women, their tight gowns showing off their firm, full figures, were better to look at than all the churches and buildings in the city.

Although the ship was there for six weeks, awaiting the return of Captain Fitzroy, Darwin spent most of his time on board, writing up his diary and his geographical notes covering the preceding six months. He was anxious to get out into the Pacific proper. He wanted to visit a coral atoll. The current thinking was that the circular atolls only grew on the rims of submerged volcanic craters. Now Darwin began to wonder, if the whole of the South American continent was being slowly lifted up, as he had seen, what was to stop equally large areas of the seabed from sinking? If this was the case, then the reefs could easily be growing up around the edges of sinking mountains. We now know this to be the case. Before even seeing his first atoll, Darwin had solved the riddle, but he was anxious to go and see if he could find proof.

Fitzroy finally returned, full of the joys of life after his adventure. He went out and bought another schooner, and sent it back to Chile to continue the survey. The *Beagle* set off towards the Galapagos, taking Darwin towards his greatest discovery.

O ur stay in Algarrobo was a delight. The town is small, clean and prosperous. It is one of several popular coastal weekend destinations for people from Santiago, Chile's capital. It did not take Lana long to discover that there were numerous little restaurants within a few minute's walk of the marina.

Ajoining the marina compound was a tree-filled park, with a series of paths zigzagging through it. We instituted an evening get-fit jog, to try and get rid of some of the fat we had all gained from the general lack of physical activity. Spending so much time at sea had taken its toll on our waist-lines.

What really made our stay memorable – and pleasant – was the hospitality shown to us by Klaus and Jorge. Jorge brought his parents down to visit *Thalassi*. He gave them the tour of the boat, and then invited us all to go to his parents' weekend cottage for a barbecue lunch. Fortunately it was only a few miles away, because it was a squeeze to get everybody into two cars.

The weekend cottage turned out to be an old farm of about 200 acres. The original stone house had been most beautifully restored, and a section of the garden is now a dedicated barbecue area. There is not only the normal barbecue pit, but also a separate spit and a traditional Chilean stone oven. Tables and benches are arranged in the shade of big, droopy flowering trees. Pisco sours, Chile's national drink, which the crew were managing to drink all too easily, were followed by an excellent lunch of grilled sausages, steaks and a variety of vegetables. Everybody ate too much.

Jorge told us the tale of how his grandfather, whom he brought to visit the boat later, had swum ashore on Staten Island after being shipwrecked seventy-five years before. He had forsaken the sea and his native Germany, and had chosen to settle in Chile. He had started making and mending things, and this had slowly grown into the steel construction company that Jorge and his father now ran.

While we were trying to digest the lunch, Jorge showed us the rest of the farm. The only part that was run with any commercial sense was a big barn with some 300 angora rabbits which were being bred for their wool. The rest of the land was slowly being turned into an enormous garden. He told us that his mother had already planted over 20,000 trees and shrubs.

At the end of the tour, Jorge's father asked if any of us played golf. Tony and Nick both fancied themselves as golfers. 'Is there a course nearby?' asked Tony.

Jorge's father gave him a slightly puzzled look. 'We have one,' he said. He sounded as if he thought everybody had their own golf course at their weekend cottage.

We walked beyond the trees behind the barbecue area, and there was a fully fledged golf course. Jorge was a bit apologetic that it was only nine holes; they had not got round to building the second nine yet. The greens should have been called browns. In the dry climate short grass cannot survive, so the greens were hard-packed sand. Jorge said that when it rains in the winter, flowers spring up all over the greens, and they have to be cut.

Jeff, Lana and I are no good at golf; I find I can throw the ball further and straighter than I can hit it. So Jorge produced a couple of motorbikes for us so that we could tour the rest of the farm while he and his father soundly thrashed Nick and Tony. It was a fun day.

To complete a lazy weekend, Jorge arrived on Sunday morning to take us for a drive to Santiago. It took Darwin a whole day to reach the city by mule. An hour or so up the motorway in Jorge's car and we were there. Santiago has, of course, grown since Darwin passed through. It now has a population of some 4½ million.

Jorge took us to the main shopping area, and Lana was drooling. Fortunately for the bank balance, she did not get much encouragement to shop, being with five men. She was somewhat appeased when we stopped in a little café for a drink. For the first time since arriving in Chile, she was able to buy real coffee. Nescafé seems to be the national hot drink of Chile. If one asks for coffee, even in a fancy restaurant, one is given a cup of hot water, a spoon and a tin of Nescafé. Lana really likes her coffee. She bought three month's supply of coffee beans, and on the strength of that voted the whole expedition to Santiago worthwhile.

Jorge then took us on a walk through the old part of the city, pointing out the various buildings, and explaining where the action had occurred when Pinochet overthrew Allende. All over the city, but especially near the government buildings, there were soldiers to be seen, all with machine-guns dangling.

Once we had finished being tourists, he took us back to his apartment to meet his wife, Maresol, and her parents who were visiting them. We went out *en masse* for a Chinese meal, and ended up overeating yet again. After the meal, Jorge told us that they had decided to lend us their second car for the two weeks that we anticipated being in the marina, doing our repairs. It was very generous of him, and certainly made life much easier and more pleasant for us.

Our only worry was getting back to the marina from the centre of Santiago. Jorge escorted us to the outskirts of the city and, with Jeff at the helm, we set off down the motorway to the coast. We hit a small snag at the toll booths. The soldiers checked our papers and became very excited because Jeff did not have a Chilean driving licence. It took a bit of sweet talking, but eventually they let us continue, and we finally arrived back at the boat.

We now faced two weeks of pretty concentrated work, trying to get the boat in shape for the next part of the trip. The Boss came to see us, just for the day – he said he was too busy to stay longer. Klaus collected him at the airport and brought him down to the boat. He was a bit sour with us for having given notice, and concentrated on persuading Jeff to stay on. Like us, Jeff had not been paid for over four months, and he laid into the Boss saying that the money, and interest for the delay, had better be in his bank within seven days, or he would have the boat arrested. The Boss assured us that it was all an administrative error and that we would be paid at once.

With that out of the way, he gave us the new plan. Up until this point, we were supposed to be heading west across the Pacific. Now he wanted us to get back to Britain as soon as possible. His racing boat had been chosen to represent Spain in the Admiral's Cup races, and since the professional racing crew would not let him sail in any of the races, he wanted *Thalassi* back there so that he could at least watch. He promised us all a bonus if we got the boat back in time.

At first that sounded quite reasonable; Britain was about 8000 miles away, and the races started in approximately twelve weeks. After we had agreed it was possible, however, the Boss said that he was planning to meet us in Panama and again in the West Indies, for two small cruises. A week in each place would effectively give us just under ten weeks. The two weeks of planned work in Algarobo reduced it to eight. A thousand miles a week was still possible, but left no room for delays or bad weather. But having set the schedule, the Boss disappeared back to Spain.

When Tony heard about the new plan, he decided to leave, and fly back to Britain. He had been looking forward to visiting some of the Pacific islands, but a virtually non-stop sail to England did not appeal. We could hardly blame him. It did not appeal to us much either. However, we felt that we had to see it through to complete our obligations, and it was probably our only chance of getting our outstanding four months' pay. Tony agreed to stay long enough to help us prepare the boat for our long journey. We were very sorry to lose him. His personality, medical knowledge and helpful attitude were going to be missed.

We thought that if we made a big push with the work, we might get away a few days early. Our course north to Panama would take us close to the Galapagos, and the Boss had told me I should stop there, since Lana, Jeff and Nick had never been there. That would have been very generous of him, except that he had not allowed any time in the schedule for a stop. If we could shorten the refit without compromising the boat, there might be a few days for a little expedition. I had certainly enjoyed my previous visit there, and Lana was determined that we were not going to sail past without stopping.

Unfortunately the work schedule suffered somewhat as one by one we all fell sick. Tony was the first to go down. He contracted food poisoning from a little restaurant we visited. It is a poor situation when one's doctor is sick. He did not want anybody to tend him, and steadfastly refused to take any medication. He wanted to suffer alone, and heal in his own time.

He was just about back on his feet, when the boys' night out in Talcahuano came back to haunt them. One of the trio discovered that he had a small problem. He has begged, pleaded and threatened that he should remain anonymous so as not to spoil his future chances with the ladies, so let us just call him crew. He had contracted what might be termed a communicable disease, as a direct result of the night ashore. At first I laughed, but then I realised the seriousness of it. Of course the other two members of the trio started sweating and counting the days for the incubation period to pass. Were all three going down? It would have been poetic justice. I realised that it was not a laughing matter when said crew could hardly walk the next day. Obviously something had to be done. He could not go to sea in that state.

I did not feel that I could discuss the matter with our hosts. There we were, in Chile's fanciest yacht club, and one of our crew had the clap. I had the feeling that they would not be thrilled to know that. The next problem was that our Spanish dictionary was light on medical terms, and ignored all symptoms and organs below the waist. Then I had a brain wave. Valparaiso is a very big port, and since all too many sailors go down with various diseases of this ilk, I felt sure there must be a special clinic there. It was only a question of finding it.

We drove into Valparaiso, found the docks easily, and a parking place with difficulty. We walked down to the main gates of the docks – at least I did, my companion was hobbling along in a manner bound to invoke sympathy. At the gates was a young, machine-gun-toting guard. He watched us a little suspiciously as we approached him, my friend with his curious bow-legged gait. Surely the guard would know where to send us.

In our best fractured Spanish we told him that my friend had *un problema abajo* – a problem down below – and pointed a little south of his belt buckle. We needed a *clinica especial* to take care of the problem. Slowly his puzzled expression was replaced by a grin of comprehension. Yes, he knew where there was a special clinic that could take care of the problem. Leaving me to hold his machine-gun, he drew a complicated little map. At the end of the trail he marked, '*Clinica Especial*'. Feeling rather as if we had solved the last clue on a treasure hunt, we sallied, and hobbled, forth.

We eventually found the clinic, but found that our soldier had been deceived by my companion's curious walk. He had sent us to a foot doctor! Fortunately the foot doctor could speak good English and knew all the more graphic medical terms in both languages. He directed us to the right clinic.

It turned out to be a rather seedy little place, and I felt glad it was not me being treated. After the walk, however, crew was beyond caring, and collapsed into a grubby chair. They took care of him in short order, and within forty-eight hours he was pretty much back to normal. I kept a note of the address, in case either or both of the others went down with the same problem. Fortunately for all concerned they did not. The incubation period eventually passed, but they certainly sweated it out.

Next to go down was Lana. Perhaps foolishly, we went back to the same restaurant where Tony had been infected. He figured that it would be alright since he was the only one of the five of us to become ill, and we had all enjoyed the food. Again the rest of us were fine, but Lana was ill for about three days. To have the cook laid up with food poisoning severely cramped our culinary style. When we all took turns at trying to cook, we realised how much she had spoiled us over the previous months.

One of the most important boat jobs was to replace the stern gland. We had finally persuaded the yard in Spain to send us the right one; all that remained was to fit it. The gland is a waterproof seal that fits over the propeller shaft and the tube which it passes through. If the boat were out of the water, it would be an easy enough job. The propeller shaft is disconnected from the engine and slid back far enough to allow the old seal to be taken off and the new one put on – no problem.

Our problem was that there was nowhere that we could haul the boat. Jeff and I discussed whether we could change it in the water. At low tide *Thalassi*'s keel was almost touching the bottom, so I thought we would be safe enough to have a go. We did not know how much water would come in when we took the old seal off, but at least at low tide, if we did have a problem, the boat would not sink without a trace.

Jeff got the coupling, and the control gear for the variable pitch propeller disconnected. Before we could push the shaft back, however, somebody would have to go into the water to remove an anode off the shaft. It was a hot sunny day, so I was happy to jump in and have a go. I had forgotten about the Humboldt Current. The water was icy – it took my breath away. I could not dive down to touch the shaft, never mind work on it. Jeff called me a wimp, and put on his wet suit. With the benefit of this protection, he managed it with no problem. Before the tide rose, the new seal was in place. Hopefully that would be the end of a longstanding leak.

Finally the jobs were all ticked off the list. We waved goodbye to Tony, and did an enormous three-month food shop. Then it was my turn to be sick. I caught flu and postponed our departure. A day later, I was still feeling grim, but decided we should go anyway. To clear out from Chile we had to take the boat round to Valparaiso; Costumes and Intimidation had said I could not drive there, the boat had to come. Klaus and Jorge and an assortment of family and friends sailed round with us. When we got there, they came with me to help with officialdom.

The clearing was a long draw-out affair. They wanted to know our exact route along the coast, and I was told to call in with our position each day while we were in Chilean waters. It all seemed terribly complicated, but eventually it was all done. Nobody came out to the boat, so we probably could have got away with driving over, but at least Klaus, Jorge and friends had had a bit of a sail out of it. We were sorry to say goodbye to them; they had certainly made our stay memorable.

After an early night, we were ready to leave the next morning. We motored out of the bay after breakfast, and ran into thick fog and a stiff southerly breeze. We made sail, and headed straight out to sea, to get clear of all the fishing boats we could see on the radar. Fortunately, as before, the fog thinned a few miles offshore, and the visibility improved to about a couple of miles. We altered course to the north, and steered towards the Galapagos.

The *Beagle* made a pit-stop in Peru, and that would have been interesting for us, but we had heard horror stories from southbound yachts about boats being arrested, detained and fined on the flimsiest of pretexts. Peru has been going though a long period of civil unrest, and even if the Boss's timetable had been a little less demanding, I think we would have chosen to give it a miss.

We were just settling down into our seagoing routine, when we heard a call on the VHF radio: 'Northbound blue sailing yacht, this is Chilean warship calling you.' We were blue, and heading north, but we could not see any ship that could be calling us. On the radar the nearest vessel was about 10 miles away – much too far for them to be able to see us – so I ignored the call. The warship was persistent. In the end I called them back, said we were a northbound blue yacht and gave them our position. I explained that I did not think we were the vessel they were hailing, because we had no warship in sight.

The voice on the radio came right back to me at once. 'Yes it is you I am calling. What is your destination and last port?' After getting the answer, he asked more questions about the boat and about us. I gave him all the information, and then asked him where he was, as we still could not see a warship. He replied, 'Under the sea,' and signed off. We were being escorted from Chile by a submarine. What would

Captain Fitzroy have thought of that?

We thought afterwards that we should have turned on the big depth finder. In addition to the normal one *Thalassi* had a huge depth sounder with almost unlimited range. If we had turned it on, I felt sure that they would have been able to hear it, whereupon we could have said, 'Oh yes, we see you.' That would have given them as much to talk about as we had!

All day the breeze blew. In fact it picked up as the day progressed. We were roaring along, making excellent progress, averaging around 10 knots, but the motion was not very pleasant. The boat was rolling around in the following sea. I was still feeling grim, and had managed to pass the flu onto Lana, so neither of us was enjoying the sail at all.

There was nothing on the weather maps to show where the breeze was coming from, and the pilot chart showed the expected average wind to be about 10–15 knots. The wind ignored all the charts and forecasts, and stayed strong. It blew between 25 and 30 knots for four days. We were nearly half way to the Galapagos, well into the tropics once more, when it stopped. One moment it was blowing 30 knots, then the next, it was down to almost nothing. We started motoring, but the motion was still uncomfortable, as the swell continued to make us roll. It was another day of light winds before the motion eased enough to be called comfortable. The sun came out, Lana's flu started to get better, and Jeff had a birthday. Things were looking up.

The wind stayed light, and the engine ran for three days. Jeff and I started doing some calculations regarding the fuel. The Galapagos are close to 1000 miles from the Panama Canal, in an area renowned for light winds. I wanted to be certain that we had enough fuel to motor from the Galapagos to Panama if necessary. The Boss's schedule did not allow for us to become becalmed. I sent a telex to our agent in Britain, asking him to contact the Ecuadorian Embassy to find out whether fuel would be available to us anywhere in the islands. I knew from my previous visit that finding it would not be easy.

After three days of flat calm, we got a bit of wind. It tended to pick up a little during the day and die away at night. We sailed whenever we could, and motored when we had to, in order to keep our average speed above 7 knots.

One particular dark night, Lana called us up to watch a spectacular light show. The bioluminescence – sparkling plankton – shining in our wake was exceptionally bright. For some reason the plankton only switches its light on when it is disturbed by a wave or a wake. Our wake was a silver shining ribbon stretching to the horizon. Four dolphins had come to play around the boat, and each of them was leaving a shining zigzag trail through the water. They criss-crossed under the bows, weaving an intricate pattern of light. Lana wondered if they could see the sparkling trails they were making. Were they also enjoying the pattern?

Less than 50 miles short of the Galapagos, the engine broke down. At least, Lana heard it change note and stopped it so that we could investigate. It was 3.15 a.m. and there was not a breath of wind. It took Jeff about one minute to discover that the drive belt for the cooling water pump had snapped. As it came off, it had taken two more belts with it, so now the engine had no cooling water and the alternator was not charging the battery. Jeff devised a jury rig which was good enough to get us into port. To fix it properly would involve removing the hydraulic pump from the front of the engine, and that could wait until we were anchored.

We made our landfall on San Cristóbal, the easternmost island, just twelve days after leaving Valparaiso. We had averaged 181 miles per day, and were almost three days ahead of schedule!

Wreck Bay, San Cristóbal Island, our port of entry for the Galapagos. We were careful not to leave the dinghy in the water unattended, in case it became home to a sea-lion. Almost every unattended boat had its resident sea-lion.

Chapter 18

The Galapagos

Although it was his observation of the wildlife of the Galapagos which was to make Darwin famous, he concentrated on the geology first.

From his reading on board *Beagle*, he knew that there are ten main islands, five of which are rather larger than the others. In addition there are numerous smaller islands, some little larger than rocks poking up from the seabed. They straddle the equator, and are a little over 500 miles from the mainland of South America. They are owned by Ecuador.

All the islands are formed by volcanic rock, and all the larger ones are studded with craters, some of which are enormous, the rims rising in some cases more than 400 ft. The flanks of the big craters are peppered with smaller craters. Darwin estimated that there are approximately 2000 craters in the archipelago. He had hoped to find an active one to study, but although he saw wisps of smoke coming out from one or two, he could not find one that had bubbling lava in it, nor one that was spewing out rocks or even ash. It was a bit of a disappointment, but he did manage to study several of the dormant craters.

He found that there are two basic sorts of crater. Some are formed by jagged lava rocks, thrown up in jumbled heaps. The others are composed of finely layered material called tuff, which looks rather like sandstone. These were made by eruptions of volcanic mud, without any lava being present.

He examined twenty-eight of these tuff craters, and found that without exception, the southern sides were much lower, some even broken down altogether. This suggested to him that they had formed while standing in the sea, and that the waves and swells from the trade winds had eroded the sides. The fact that they were now above the sea was strong evidence that the land had risen up in a similar way to the places he had looked at on the mainland.

The Galapagos had a reputation among early navigators as being hard to find. Indeed one name often given to them was the Enchanted Islands, because on some days they seemed to have vanished. Ships would often sail to where the islands were supposed to be and search

for them in vain. The reason for this elusiveness is that near the islands the skies are often overcast. They are in the area known as the doldrums. This region, between the trade winds, often has grey and squally weather. If the sun and the stars were obscured by clouds, then the navigator could not take sextant sights to fix his position. Under these conditions he would have to rely on what is called dead reckoning, plotting the course and distance made good, and calculating where the ship had got to. Unfortunately, often there are also strong and variable currents near the islands, and these would upset the most careful of calculations. So it was not a case of the islands not being where they were supposed to be, but more that the ship was not where the navigator thought it was.

Beagle's passage over from the mainland was uneventful. Captain Fitzroy managed to make his landfall as planned, on Chatham Island. Although he was a consummate navigator, he must have been relieved when the island appeared over the horizon on cue.

Perhaps I should explain about the names of the islands. Each island has two names, one given to it by the early explorers and surveyors and the other which Ecuador has bestowed upon its possessions. I will use the old names throughout Darwin's narrative, and the modern ones in ours. To avoid confusion, the first time an island is mentioned, I will give both names.

Beagle anchored off Chatham Island, which is now called San Cristóbal, in the bay which has come to be called Wreck Bay. Darwin was soon ashore, but was disappointed with what he found. He said that nothing could be less inviting than the first appearance of the island. He found broken black lava thrown into waves, which were crossed by great fissures. Walking across it was very difficult. The only plants he could see was the occasional stunted, sunburnt brushwood, which showed little signs of life. Fitzroy described the landscape as 'fit for Pandemonium', while one of his officers compared it to the cultivated parts of Hell.

Undaunted, Darwin set off under the noonday sun to go collecting. The air felt like the blast from an oven. The sun quickly heats up the black lava to the point where it becomes uncomfortable to walk on, even when wearing thick boots. He soon discovered that the brushwood, which appeared lifeless from a short distance, was actually in full leaf, and in some cases even in flower. The leaves and flowers were extremely small so that not much water would be lost by evaporation. The commonest bush was a kind of acacia. The only other plant big enough to cast any shade at all was a big prickly cactus. He returned to the ship hot, sweaty and weary. Although he had been searching for botanical samples, he described the few that

he found as 'weeds, that would have better become the Antarctic than an equatorial flora'.

It rarely rains in the Galapagos, but the higher elevations are often shrouded in clouds. The lower parts of all the islands are for the most part dry and barren, but as Darwin was to find on later walks, above about 1000 ft, the clouds keep the climate damp and there is reasonably luxuriant vegetation, especially on the windward side. Moreover, many of the craters hold water, and in them the growth is as thick as in any jungle.

Darwin's second trip ashore on Chatham was a little more rewarding. He found an area where there were sixty miniature volcanos, each with its own little crater. These craters were formed by red slag, which appeared to have been cemented together. None of the cones was much over 50 ft high. The surface of the entire area was pierced like a sieve. The lava had been blown into bubbles just as it was setting, and this had left thousands of circular, steep-sided pits. The regular uniformity of the pits and the cones gave the area an artificial, man-made appearance. He remarked that it reminded him of the potteries of his native Staffordshire. Do we detect a twinge of homesickness?

On his way back to the ship, Darwin came across a pair of the giant tortoises after which the islands were named. They were quite big ones; each must have weighed at least 200 lb. Darwin was enthralled. One was eating a cactus plant, and as Darwin crept closer, it kept a beady eye on him but continued munching. The other proved to be more timid. As he came closer, it suddenly gave a hiss, and retracted everything into the safety of its shell. Darwin sat fascinated. The whole scene caught his imagination, with the big reptiles surrounded by the jet black jagged lava, the virtually leafless shrubs and the prickly cacti. It all seemed so primitive to him as to be antediluvian.

As he sat there quietly watching, he saw a few dull-coloured birds, which cared for him no more than they did for the tortoises. He in turn took little notice of them. Although it was these finches that were to make his reputation, for the moment it was the tortoises that held him enthralled.

Beagle spent a week at Chatham. Darwin explored and collected, Fitzroy and his men surveyed the shores of the island. At the end of the week, they sailed across to Charles Island, now called Santa Maria. It was, incidentally, not named after Darwin, but after the King of England. Like several of the others, it had long been visited on a regular basis by buccaneers and whalers, but only six years prior to *Beagle*'s visit, the first permanent settlement had been established. Some 300 people, whom Darwin describes as 'being of colour,' had

Wild tortoises – much more satisfying than seeing them in the zoo at the Darwin Institute. Our guide found them by following a trail of fresh droppings.

been sent out from Ecuador, mostly as punishment for political crimes. They were condemned to live in this remote spot for the rest of their lives.

Darwin set off almost at once to visit the settlement. He thought it strange that it was not on the coast, but over 4 miles inland, and at an altitude of 1000 ft. As he climbed up the steep rocky path, however the reasons for choosing the site became apparent; the higher he climbed, the greener the land became. When he finally reached the highest ridge, Darwin found a cooling southerly breeze and fairly big areas of cultivated land. Most of the fields were devoted to sweet potatoes and bananas.

The natural vegetation was mainly a mixture of ferns and coarse grasses. He puzzled over the fact that there were no palm trees, as he knew that Cocos Island, so named because of the abundance of coconut trees, was only about 350 miles to the north.

The villagers told him that there were wild goats and pigs roaming in the woods surrounding the settlement, but most of the locals preferred to kill tortoises for meat; they were easier to hunt than the swift goats and pigs. The numbers of tortoises had been greatly reduced by hunting, not just by the locals but also by visiting ships. Even so, there were still enough to provide a week's supply of meat for a family after an average day's hunting.

Sailors and buccaneers had long ago found that the tortoises could be kept on board their ships for long periods without food or water, and they were a convenient source of fresh meat in the days before refrigeration was invented. When the islands were first visited, a single ship might take as many as 700 tortoises. Even just a year or two before *Beagle*'s visit, the crew of a frigate managed to collect over 200 in a single day.

The Vice-governor of the settlement, a gentleman by the name of Lawson, talked to Darwin at length about the tortoises. He said that they differed so much from one island to another that he could tell at a glance where any tortoise came from. Darwin did not recognise the significance of these remarks for several days, and continued collecting specimens and mixing them with those collected on the other islands. Indeed, even when he did finally realise that there were specific differences between finches shot on the different islands, his own collection was hopelessly muddled. Fortunately Fitzroy had made his own collection of birds and, being methodical, he had noted where each had been caught. When they got back to England, Fitzroy's collection was used to help sort out Darwin's own, and prove that birds of the same type had evolved specific differences adapting to the local conditions found on each island.

Mr Lawson went on to tell Darwin that he had seen several tortoises so big that they required eight men to pick them up, and that one that size, when butchered, gave over 200 lb of edible meat.

Some tortoises live on islands where there is no standing water, or on the equally dry coastal plains of the bigger islands. The only moisture they take in is what they get by eating the succulent cactus.

Those tortoises that live in the higher, damper regions eat leaves, and they are very partial to a green lichen that hangs down from the trees. Despite their ability to survive long periods without it, the tortoises are actually very fond of water, and will often travel great distances to visit a small pond. Given the chance, a tortoise will drink vast quantities of water, and enjoy a long wallow in the mud. After spending three or four days drinking, they will return to their normal territory. Mr Lawson explained that after drinking, the tortoise's bladder is distended with fluid, and he thought that this is an extra store. After a period without drinking, the volume of fluid in the bladder decreases, and the fluid itself becomes less pure. He told Darwin that if the locals became thirsty down on the dry coastal plain, they would sometimes kill a tortoise to drink the contents of the bladder. Darwin, the devoted scientist, remembered that, and when he saw a tortoise killed, he tried drinking the fluid. He described it as being quite limpid, and with only a very slight bitter taste. I think I would have to be very thirsty indeed before I would want to drink tortoise urine!

The tortoises provided the inhabitants not only with meat, but also with oil, which they rendered from the fat. When they found a tortoise, it was common for the locals to cut a slit in the happless animal's skin, under its tail, to look inside the body. If there was a good layer of fat under the dorsal plate, then it was killed. If there was not much fat, it was actually freed, and the hunter looked for a better specimen. Mr Lawson assured Darwin that the slit soon healed.

From Charles Island they sailed for Albermarle Island. This is the largest in the group, and is now called Isabela. They sailed round its southern tip and beat up towards the channel between it and the smaller Narborough Island (Fernandina). As they neared the entrance to the channel, they ran out of wind, and lay becalmed for much of the day. Darwin spent almost the entire time on deck, gazing up at the peaks of the volcanoes which formed the two islands. The landscape was bleak – streams of naked, black lava, which had flowed over the rims of the great cauldrons to spread over miles of the coast.

Eruptions had been known on both these islands, and as they crept slowly up the coast of Albermarle, Darwin became very excited when he spotted a wisp of smoke curling out of the top of one of the craters. Although he had watched the eruption of Aconcagua in Chile, he wanted to get close to an active, bubbling crater.

Beagle finally reached her anchorage. The bay that Fitzroy chose was actually a flooded volcanic crater called Bank's Cove. It was one of the tuff craters, whose south-western side had been so eroded as to let the sea flood it.

Early next morning Darwin set off exploring. It was not enough for him that the ship was anchored in a crater, he had to climb up to another one. The crater he found was almost a mile across, and some 500 ft below the rim was a lake, in the centre of which, forming a little island, was a perfect miniature volcano. It was a very hot day.

The Galapagos

The black lava was almost too hot to touch, and Darwin was very thirsty. The clear blue lake looked very appealing, and he swiftly scrambled down the cindery slope into the crater, expecting to drink his fill. When he finally reached the bottom, he found that the water was saltier than the sea.

On his way back to the ship, he paused to study some of the giant lizards, or iguanas, for which the islands are well know. He soon spotted that there are two types: a purely land sort that lives in burrows, and a marine kind, which seems equally at home on the shore or in the water. During their stay on Albermarle, he spent considerable time watching these marine iguanas, which are unique to the Galapagos. He caught several and opened up their stomachs to see what they had been eating. He found minced seaweed; they appeared to be purely vegetarian in their diet.

The marine species have flattened tails and webbed feet to help them swim, whereas the land-based ones have rounded tails and clawed feet. The preferred food of the terrestrial ones is cactus, the pricklier the better, it seems. The marine species are found in all the islands, but the land ones are limited to the islands around Albermarle; they are not found in the extreme eastern or northern islands.

Marine Iguanas blending almost perfectly with San Cristóbal's black volcanic rocks. If we got too close, instead of running away, they spat at us.

Although he does not record the exact moment of revelation, it seems that it was while they were at Albermarle that he finally realised that the finches he had collected were similar to, yet different from, those of the other islands. He wrote in his journal that it appeared as if one species had been taken and modified for different ends. The seeds for his theory of evolution had just sprouted.

From Albermarle, they sailed to James Island, named after another of the Stuart kings of England. It is now called San Salvador, or sometimes Santiago. On James Island, Darwin and Mr Bynoe were left ashore, together with their servants and a tent, while *Beagle* went off to look for water. They found a group of people, who had been sent over from the settlement at Charles Island to dry and salt fish and tortoise meat. They went off to visit the two tortoise catchers, who were living in a small hovel about 6 miles inland, and at a height of about 2000 ft. Although, as on the other islands, the coastal strip was dry and barren, high up at the camp the damp from the clouds supported fairly lush vegetation.

While staying in the upper region Darwin and his group lived entirely on tortoise meat. He does not appear to have had any qualms about killing and eating these unique creatures, even though he had already noted that their numbers were dwindling. His favourite way of cooking them was to roast the breast plate with the meat attached, in a similar way to the gauchos cooking their *carne con cuero*. Cooked this way, he thought the tortoise meat was very good. He also discovered that young tortoises make an excellent soup, but otherwise he declared the meat to be indifferent.

Beagle returned with her water tanks filled for the long voyage which lay ahead. Their survey of the Galapagos was complete, and it was time to leave for their next destination, Tahiti. As they sailed away, Darwin little realised the repercussions that would be felt around the world from his stay in the Galapagos.

When we anchored in Wreck Bay, off the island of San Cristóbal – Darwin's Chatham Island – there were about half a dozen other yachts there, together with several little local fishing boats.

Since Darwin's visit, a small town and a large airport runway have been built, so the place no longer has quite the desolate aspect that he described. The arrival of the town has meant officialdom, and

Costumes and Intimidation had to be sought out and satisfied. Jeff came ashore with me, to help with the translating. Although my Spanish was improving, his was still much better.

We launched the inflatable and headed for shore. On the way in we saw that a couple of dinghies and several of the open fishing boats had big sea-lions lounging in them. We never saw one get in or out of a boat, but I made a mental note not to leave the dinghy in the water unattended. I did not fancy trying to persuade one of the beasts to get out if it chose to sunbathe in our dinghy.

Ashore we soon tracked down the Port Captain, who was very friendly and helped us to get the paperwork sorted out. Since we did not have an official visa from Ecuador, the rule was that we could only stay for three days. It was going to be a rushed visit. The Ecuadorian government has tightened up on visiting yachts after several incidents of crews abusing the hospitality of the islands. One group of yachties was caught with a row of marine iguanas roasting on the barbecue grill. Now, without a visa and an authorised guide, we were limited to three days, and we could only visit Wreck Bay, and Academy Bay on Santa Cruz. On my previous visit a few years before, things had been much less regulated, and we had wandered through the islands more or less at will. Those days are probably gone forever.

The next setback was fuel, or rather the lack thereof. We had had no reply from our agent in Britain about the availability of fuel. If we were to have any chance of keeping to the Boss's schedule across the Gulf of Panama, with its fickle winds, then fuel was going to be vital. We did not have enough to get all the way to Panama if there was no wind. The Port Captain told us that there was none in Wreck Bay, and the only place where there was any at all was at Baltra, a little island which houses the main airport and the naval base. He explained that the navy controlled all the fuel, and they were not allowed to sell it without permission from the mainland.

As soon as we got back to the boat, I fired off another telex to Britain, asking again that the Ecuadorian Embassy be approached, to authorise fuel for us. All we could do then was wait and hope that we would get permission before our three days ran out.

After lunch and a short nap, we all set off ashore. Lana and Nick went to see what fresh food was available, while Jeff and I went back to the Port Captain again. We showed him the copy of the telex we had sent, and explained that we were asking the Embassy in London to obtain permission for us to buy fuel. He was suitably impressed. He seemed to think the telex said that permission had been granted, and we did not point out his mistake. He made a few phone calls, and eventually said that we could buy 250 gallons of fuel at Baltra. I was hoping for 350, but any was better than none. He had been so helpful and friendly that we invited him to come to the boat for a drink after work. He was pleased to be asked and we agreed to pick him up later.

We walked back into town, to find that Lana and Nick had been picked up by two small boys and escorted to their mother's restaurant and bar. Mother turned out to be a very busy and businesslike woman called Cecelia. Her bar, thanks in no small part to the hustling of her sons, was the place where all the yachties ended up. She was also the main money changer, and the general organiser and procurer of things. In the bar, she had two thick books of photographs, drawings and comments from yacht crews who had visited over the past few years. Over a cold drink or two, we thumbed through the books, recognising many old friends from anchorages past.

To give the cook a well-deserved night off, we booked dinner with Cecelia for a little later, and then headed back to give the Port captain his guided tour of *Thalassi*. The first thing he spotted when he came on board was the radio. It turned out that he was a ham, and he was keen to try out *Thalassi*'s radio, which was bigger and more powerful than anything he had used before. I fired it up for him, and within a few minutes he was talking to some friends on the mainland. He was in ham heaven, and we had a firm friend.

After a beer or two, and several radio contacts, he settled down to tell us all about the Galapagos as he saw them. He was from the mainland, and sympathised with our desire to stay longer than three days. He could do nothing about it officially, but told us exactly where the patrol boat would be and when. He suggested that we could plan a visit to the outer islands around the schedule of the patrol boat, and avoid meeting it.

Although it was tempting, I did not feel we should risk it. The Boss already had a pretty low opinion of us, and it would be awfully hard to explain to him that his boat had been confiscated because we had made an illegal tour of the islands. When I explained this to the Port Captain, he seemed a little crestfallen. Then he had another idea. We could stay in Wreck Bay for our three days, and leave without clearing. We could then go to Academy Bay and clear in as if from Chile, and spend three days there. That seemed an altogether safer proposition.

We dropped the Port Captain back ashore, and went on to Cecelia's for an enjoyable dinner. We told her that we would like to drive round the island, and she promised to find us a taxi. What turned up next morning was not exactly a taxi, but it would do. What she had found for us was a rather rusty, old, green pick-up truck with three lawn-chairs in the back. Lana was ushered into the cab with the driver, while Nick, Jeff and I climbed into the back and settled down into the folding chairs.

Cecelia's two boys jumped aboard as well, and we set off out of town, up the twisting road that flanked the side of the highest hill. As we passed the cemetery, the two boys crossed themselves fervently. We realised why on the way down. Only one brake on the truck worked, the one on the after port wheel. On the descent, the driver managed to keep the truck down to a reasonable speed by leaving it in first gear with the engine turned off. Any attempts to stop resulted in the one wheel locking, but since its tyre was bald, this had little effect on our speed. But as the truck ground its way upwards, we were oblivious to this problem; otherwise we too might have crossed ourselves.

Eventually we reached the end of the road, but not the end of the journey. The driver and our guides were determined that we should go up to the rim of the crater, which was shrouded in clouds. They seemed to be suspended permanently over the peak, and provided plenty of moisture for plants to grow. This particular volcano had obviously been long dormant, as it was completely covered in grass.

We scrambled up the steep slope, our legs protesting – they were as yet unaccustomed to walking, after twelve days at sea. When we reached the rim, almost 3000 ft above sea level, we could look down through the mist into the crater itself. Far below, we could see a lake. Birds were circling beneath us, deep inside the crater.

At first the coolness of the clouds felt pleasant after the heat down on the shore, but quite soon the cold and dampness began to seep into us. Before too long we were ready to head back down to the warmth, and began the perilous ride back to town. Once we were back down on the level streets of the town, we eased our white-knuckled grips and paid the driver. We gave him an extra tip, hoping that he would spend at least some of it on his brakes.

We celebrated having cheated death once again by having lunch and a cold beer at Cecelia's. Suitably fortified, we then set off on foot to the eastern side of the island to look for the marine iguanas that Cecelia told us were there. The first part of the journey was easy. We just walked along the gigantic runway that had been carved across the tip of the island, for a mile or more. Once we left our smooth, paved path, however, the going became a little rougher and soon degenerated into sharp, jagged black lava rocks. We skirted along the shore searching for the iguanas.

We came to a family of sea-lions, playing in the surf. They did not

A friendly seal on the beach at San Cristóbal.

seem to be as fierce as their Falkland cousins – they did not roar at us, but simply retreated if they thought we were getting too close. After we had photographed them from every possible angle, we were about to call an end to our biological studies and retire once again to Cecelia's when Lana spotted an iguana. We must have walked within a few feet of it; its colour and jagged profile blended perfectly with the lava rocks it was sitting on. If it had not moved, we would probably have walked past it again.

As we walked slowly up to it, we realised that there were several of them. The longer we looked, the more we spotted. There were at least half a dozen sunbathing on one jumbled pile of rocks. The marine iguanas are between 3 and 4 ft long, with their tails forming

242

almost half their length. With their spiked plume, scaly skin and E.T. smile, they look positively prehistoric, like miniature dinosaurs. If they thought we were approaching too close, they spat at us with unnerving accuracy, but apart from this they did not do much except grin at us.

Once we had used up what film was left after the sea-lions, we headed back for town, and a last drink with Cecelia. As we were getting ready to leave, she asked us if we had any old clothes that we could give them. We thought we could find something, so offered to take them all out to the boat. She produced a very pretty daughter, whom she had wisely kept hidden from Nick and Jeff, and we all went back out to *Thalassi*. We managed to find them a few spare T-shirts, and Lana produced a skirt for the lovely daughter. They seemed well pleased with their haul, and we deposited them ashore, at the end of a long and hectic day.

The fuel question was still hanging over us, so we set off early the next morning for Baltra and the navy base. We reached the island just before dusk, and anchored off it for the night. It was still uncertain whether our friendly Port Captain had arranged the fuel for us, and we might yet be denied. I composed a fake telex and sent it to myself, saying that the Embassy in London had assured us of an ample supply of fuel. I thought that it might help if we ran into problems.

Early the next morning, we launched the dinghy, and Jeff and I went in to see how the land lay. To my immense relief they were expecting us. Our friend in Wreck Bay had organised it all for us, and we could come alongside and get the fuel. As soon as we had tied up alongside the small dock in front of the naval administration building, we were met by the Commandant of the base. It transpired that this was the changeover day from one to the next, and it was the retiring Commandant who had agreed we could get the fuel. Since he was leaving, it would not matter to him if they ran out in a week or two.

There was no pump or even a hose. A gang of conscripts wheeled down a 50-gallon drum on a rather shaky little cart. The new Commandant told us that we could buy only five drumfuls.

When the first drum was in place on the edge of the dock, Jeff and Nick got a syphon running, and the fuel trickled slowly into the tank. The two Commandants sat in the cockpit, beers in hand, supervising the proceedings. While Lana and I kept them entertained, and their glasses full, Jeff was chatting to the four young conscripts who had been delegated to shift the fuel. He was even more anxious than me to get extra fuel, and unbeknown to the rest of us, he arranged a trade – a carton of cigarettes and some of Nick's girlie magazines for an extra drum of fuel. All that remained to do was to get it past the Commandants. After the fourth drum was in, they all started saying loudly, Three down, two to go.' The new Commandant said he was sure we had four already. But everybody insisted it was only three, and when the retiring Commandant agreed with the men, he had to back down. So we got 300 gallons, and we were glad of every one of them.

When the last of the fuel was aboard, and the bill paid, we had an easy sail down to Academy Bay on the island of Santa Cruz, or as Darwin would have called it, Indefatigable. This is the second port of entry for the islands. It was obviously the more popular one, and there were about twenty other yachts anchored in the bay when we arrived. It is also the main port for the tourist boats which take people on escorted tours through the islands. Compared to Wreck Bay, it was positively jumping.

The anchorage at Academy Bay, on Santa Cruz island, home of the Darwin Institute.

244

The Galapagos

We got the anchor down and set, and were sitting in the cockpit looking around the anchorage when we were surprised to hear somebody calling *Thalassi* on the radio. It turned out to be the manager of the hotel at the northern end of the bay, the Hotel Galapagos. He had been watching us through his binoculars, and invited us all ashore to visit the hotel for a complimentary welcome drink. It was too late to deal with officialdom that evening, so we needed no second asking. We launched the dinghy, and motored over to their dock.

The hotel has a fabulous setting. With several stone terraces looking out over the bay, each with its own colony of iguanas frolicking in the surf in front of it, it is a magical place. Ken, the manager, showed us around with obvious pride, and organised a round of drinks for us. It was a shrewd move, and he soon recovered the cost, as we ended up staying for dinner.

Early next morning we set off to explore the town and take care of the formalities. We got our pass for three days, and walked up to visit the Darwin Institute. This is a multinational affair, and is concerned with all the wildlife of the islands, but especially the tortoises, it seems. They have a programme of collecting the eggs from the various islands, hatching them, and letting the tortoises grow to a size that renders them safe from predators before releasing them back on their own island. We saw tortoises of every size, from tiny newly hatched ones to monsters which weighed several hundred pounds. One group of big tortoises was in a pen that we could walk into, right in among them. As they walked, the bigger tortoises creaked. Lana could not decide whether they had creaky knees or whether it was their thick, scaly skin that squeaked. They did not seem to be too good at steering. One would set a course for some distant part of the pen, oblivious to the fact that it was on a collision course with another tortoise. They bumped each other with alarmingly loud crunches, but did not seem to suffer any damage.

As we told Ken that night, it was interesting enough but it still felt like a zoo. When we said we wanted to see wild tortoises, he organised an expedition for us the next day.

We made an early start, in another pick-up truck/taxi. At least this one had operable brakes, even if it did not have the lawn-chairs in the back. It was a trade-off that we were happy enough to make. Ken had told us that it was obligatory to go and see the lava tunnels first, before going on the tortoise hunt.

Our driver therefore deposited us at the end of one of the tunnels, where we paid a fee and, in return, each received the loan of a torch with very second-hand batteries. With no more ado or instruction, we were ushered off into the mouth of the tunnel and left to stumble our way through the darkness as one by one the batteries expired.

The tunnels were formed by rivers of lava that had cooled and solidified on the outside. The tunnel we were groping our way through was about a mile long, and by the time we reached daylight at the other end, we were down to one light, which was barely glimmering. We were a bit concerned that we were going to have to grope our way back through the tunnel to the beginning, when we spotted our driver. He had brought the trusty, rusty, pick-up round to collect us. We returned our lights, and continued onwards and upwards on our expedition.

Our next stop was a ranch with the unlikely name of Santa Rosa. It is in the south-west of the island, and high enough to be very lush. There were more trees here than we had seen for a long time. The plan now was to go on horseback into a nearby valley, where hopefully we could find some wild tortoises.

We sat in the shade, under a large tree, sipping cold drinks, while the horses were saddled for us. The equipment was, to put it kindly, basic. The bridles were made of rope and fencing wire, while the saddles were solid wood, carved from a gigantic log. The only concession to padding was an old sack as a saddle blanket which might have saved the horses from a little chafing, but did nothing for us. We sat directly on the rough wood.

Our guide, Roberto, set off at a good clip, and our horses ambled off in pursuit. Only Lana's seemed eager to keep up with our leader. Jeff's was the slowest, or perhaps the laziest. It kept falling so far behind, that eventually Roberto cut a large stick and told Jeff to keep hitting his horse.

Nick's horse was also strong-minded, and kept straying from the path. Its favourite trick was to walk under low branches to try and knock Nick off its back. When that failed, it took to walking close to every thorn bush it could find, scratching Nick's bare legs unmercifully. He threatened to turn it into kangaroo meat.

To begin with, the path lay through fairly open land, but as we progressed the trees became thicker, until after about an hour and a half, we reached virtually impenetrable jungle. Roberto leapt agilely to the ground and hitched his horse to a tree. He explained that from here on we were to go on foot. We slithered off our mounts a little less gracefully, and struggled to straighten our knees enough to walk. Roberto was hacking away with his machete, cutting a path through the jungle for us. He seemed oblivious to the fact that we could barely walk. The unaccustomed exercise and the wooden saddles had taken their toll.

The giant tortoises are being bred in the Institute, to ensure their survival. Once they are mature, they are released into the wild on the island their parents came from.

Fortunately the jungle was thick, so progress was slow enough for us to limp along with him. He led us down into the depths of the valley, which we assumed was a very overgrown crater. As we made our way ever deeper into the jungle, he told us about one group of tourists who had come into the valley without a guide. It took them a week to find their way out again. Hopefully Roberto knew where he was going and, more importantly, which way was back.

We had been hacking and stumbling our way along for about half an hour when we came upon a muddy track. Roberto became very excited. He bent down to pick up what was obviously animal drop-pings. He squeezed and shaped it like putty, then held it our for us to try. None of us was too keen, but we got the gist of what he was trying to show us. They were fresh, not yet hardened by the sun, so whatever had done them was close by. Motioning us to be quiet, he crouched down to follow the trail of droppings, and soon found us a tortoise, a genuine wild tortoise and quite a big one at that. While we crept up to peer at the beast, which was sitting placidly in a muddy puddle, Roberto cast around, and soon found us two more. We were well satisfied.

Having produced the tortoises for us, we thought Roberto would feel he had finished his job. Not a bit of it. Waving his machete wildly, he cut a path off in a new direction to show us what he called the *Láguna*. A lagoon it was not; it was a rather overgrown pond. Floating at one end was a group of what looked like very ordinary ducks. Roberto reached new paroxysms of excitement, pointing at the ducks. Why he was so excited, or exactly what sort of ducks we were looking at, we never did find out. We nodded and smiled gratefully at him for finding them for us, and then headed back to our horses.

We were pleased to find that all the horses were still there, even if our bodies were complaining as we climbed back on board; it was, we thought, better than walking back. By the time we got back to the ranch, however, I for one had changed my mind. I was of the firm opinion that I would be hurting less if I was carrying the horse than riding it.

There was a bit of a swell coming into the bay that night, and all the boats were rolling, but compared to the horses the motion was nothing. We all slept soundly.

We had only one day left, and that had to be given over to work. Jeff spent virtually the whole of it in the engine room, emerging only for meal-times and his cigarette breaks. Nick and I attacked the varnish work on deck while Lana did some last-minute food shopping, cleaning and stowing below, and made a Panamanian flag ready for our next landfall. We were going to take the short-cut back to Britain that Darwin had wished for by this stage. After the Galapagos, he became increasingly anxious to get back. The Boss's schedule might have suited him, but the Panama Canal was not even at the serious planning stage when he left the Galapagos. *Beagle* had to sail back the long way, across the Pacific.

Chapter 19

The Voyage Home

The *Beagle* was blessed with a fair wind as they left the Galapagos. She could have easily been becalmed for several days or even weeks, but the breeze quickly carried her down into the south-east trade winds, and they steadily ticked off 150 miles a day.

The sailing was almost perfect, with bright sunshine and deep blue water. The only clouds were the fluffy fair-weather trade-wind cumulus. They passed through the Tuamotus without stopping, but as they passed close to one of the atolls, sailing along close to the brilliant white, sandy beach, Darwin climbed up to the mast-head to look out across the enclosed lagoon.

Despite the idyllic conditions, however, he was feeling lethargic. He did little for the entire three weeks. He made only two entries in his journal during the passage, and did not even spend much time with his collections. He was still suffering from seasickness, but what was affecting him more was homesickness. He was growing more and more anxious to be back with his family.

Fitzroy also seemed to be anxious to get back, because they only stayed ten days in Tahiti. He had three tasks that had to be completed. The first and most time-consuming was to take the sun sights to check and rate the chronometers. Then there was the usual task of taking water on board. In Tahiti, which has good rainfall in the interior and many streams flowing down onto the coast, this was not difficult.

His third task was curious. Some two years previously a small ship, sailing under the British flag had been plundered in the Tuamotus. Since those islands came under the rule of the Queen of Tahiti, Fitzroy had been told to ask her for compensation, to the tune of some $3000. It turned out that the royal coffers were a little low at that time, but many of her subjects decided to chip in to pay the money. Fitzroy had a few pangs of guilt, that these people were paying for a crime committed by others, several hundred miles away. The local chiefs thanked him for his concern, but felt that since Pomarre was their Queen, they had to help her out of this embarrassment with the British Government. Somewhat to Fitzroy's surprise, the money was soon collected.

While all this was going on, Darwin managed a three-day expedition into the interior. He took along his servant to carry his gear, and two local guides who had been given the task of not only leading him, but also supplying the food. They were very much amused at the thought of carrying food up into the mountains when there was so much already there for the taking.

When it was time to camp for the night, they quickly built a little house using bamboo and banana leaves. Then one of them dived into the nearby stream and, using a small net, soon captured enough fish and fresh-water prawns for the evening meal. Darwin watched with fascination as they lit a fire by rubbing a sharpened stick in a groove cut in another piece of wood. He insisted on trying this for himself, and was inordinately proud when he finally got a little glowing ember.

While Darwin was practising the art of fire-making, the Tahitians got their own fire going, and then heaped rocks over it. As the wood burned down, they began to cook the evening meal on the hot rocks. The fish, prawns and some bananas, both ripe and green, were wrapped up tightly in banana leaves and placed on the hot rocks. The food cooked in a very short time, and the banquet was served on a cloth of banana leaves. For dessert, the Tahitians dug up a root from a kind of lily. It was as sweet as treacle, and made a delicious end to the meal. Darwin was well content.

By the time he got back down to the ship, the watering had been completed and Fitzroy had invited the Queen out to the ship with what turned out to be about 200 of her closest friends. He regretted that he was not able to fire a royal salute from the cannons, but having just spent six days rating the chronometers, he did not want to risk upsetting them with the shock of the guns. Instead they put on a firework display with signal rockets. The Tahitians were excited by the display; they had never seen anything quite like it before.

The next day *Beagle* sailed for New Zealand, another long passage of just over three weeks without a stop. The highlight of the passage was crossing the Dateline, and Darwin was quick to note that now, every mile they sailed brought them a mile nearer to Britain.

Crossing the Dateline gave him a psychological boost, but the gale a few days later brought him down again with a bump. He wrote in his journal that he was now earnestly wishing for the termination of the voyage. He was tired, not just from the regular bouts of seasickness, but also from the months and years of labour without any sustained periods of rest. He had even had enough of new sights; he was longing for things familiar.

They sailed into New Zealand's Bay of Islands four days before Christmas, but Darwin could find little good to say about it. The country around the bay where they were anchored was difficult for walking. There were few birds and almost no animals. He described the local Maoris as dirty and treacherous, and most of the British inhabitants, he said, were the very refuse of society. The only place he had anything good to say about was the settlement of Waimate, where the missionary inhabitants made him welcome.

Christmas itself made him very depressed. Counting the first Christmas, in Plymouth, this was his fifth on board the *Beagle*, and he was fervently hoping it would be his last. They sailed from New Zealand on 30 December. Despite the fact that it was midsummer the weather was unsettled, and there was a gale in prospect. Darwin wrote that he would rather face any gale then have to spend another hour in New Zealand.

A couple of weeks later, the *Beagle* reached Australia and dropped anchor in Sydney Harbour. There were many other large ships at anchor, and big warehouses lined the harbour. As he walked ashore that first evening, Darwin was astonished at how much had been achieved in the relatively few years that Australia had been settled by the British, compared to what had been achieved over centuries by the Spanish in South America. As he surveyed the booming town with patriotic pride, he congratulated himself on being born an Englishman. Over the next few days, however, as he explored inland, his enthusiasm was tempered a little. He saw the convict associations as lowering, and he felt that there was little culture, and few economic prospects.

From Sydney they crossed to Tasmania, and spent ten days anchored in Storm Bay. A little of Darwin's former enthusiasm returned, and during their stay he made several expeditions into the interior, mainly looking at things geological once more.

They made one last stop in Australia, spending a week at King George's Sound before leaving the continent for good. As they left, Darwin wrote in his journal that he did so without sorrow or regret. He had also written to Henslow in Cambridge, saying that he was tired of seeing new places unless they held some special scientific interest.

By coincidence, he found this interest at their next destination – the Cocos Keeling Islands. After two mostly rough weeks at sea, the palm-fringed tropical beaches of the atoll looked particularly appealing. This was his first chance to study an atoll closely, and he spent considerable time investigating the reef, seeking confirmation for his theory that the atoll had formed around a sinking mountain peak.

They completed the crossing of the Indian Ocean to arrive in Mauritius where, for the first time since leaving Valparaiso, they found a measure of European culture. Darwin went for an elephant ride, and passed what he called an idle and dissipated time.

It was as well that he had a good rest in Mauritius, because the three-week trip down to Cape Town was a fairly rough one, and he suffered worse than ever with the seasickness. He did not think much of South Africa – to his slightly jaundiced eye he had never seen a less interesting country. His mood was not improved when he received his mail and found that Professor Henslow had already started to publish some of his letters. Darwin had intended to wait until all his thoughts and notes were complete before making anything public.

The one bright spot in the visit seems to have been the social whirl of Cape Town. He enjoyed dining out on several occasions, and was stimulated by the long intellectual discussions he was able to have with people such as the Astronomer Royal, whom he met there.

After leaving Cape Town, they had a fairly gentle passage north, and Darwin was able to spend much of his time writing. He was mainly trying to consolidate his geological notes. Fitzroy too was busy writing. He had decided long before that he would write a book about the voyage, just as Lieutenant King had done on the *Beagle's* previous voyage. Fitzroy had asked Darwin if he might use parts of his journal to augment sections of his own book. Darwin agreed, and read out passages to Fitzroy. Even at this late stage in the voyage, he himself had no real intention of trying to write a book. He was hoping to publish some scientific papers, but not a book for the general public. It may well have been watching Fitzroy at work that encouraged him to do likewise.

They stopped at St Helena for six days, which was the time it took to take the sun sights and rate the chronometers again. During this time Darwin moved ashore, and took several long walks. Although his house was close to Napoleon's tomb, he chose to ignore this aspect of the island's history, as it depressed him. He was not even very interested in the flora, after discovering that of the 746 types of plants known on the island, only fifty-two are indigenous; all the rest have been introduced. Once more it was the geology that concerned him. He spent many hours wandering in the hills, looking at the rock formations. He was sure that the island had existed for many thousands of years, yet here again were signs of upheaval and suggestions that at some stage the land had been lower or the sea had been higher.

For once he was almost sad to be leaving. He had enjoyed St

Helena and found it interesting. He seemed to be getting a second wind now that the end of the voyage was almost in sight. When they reached Ascension Island, his spirits had another lift. When he received his mail from home, there was a letter from his sisters saying that their father had heard from Sedgewick at the University that it was his estimation that Charles should take a place among leading scientific men. This was heady stuff for somebody still not yet thirty years old.

His elation was short-lived. As they were preparing to sail, Fitzroy suddenly announced that they would return once more to Bahia, in Brazil, to check the chronometers against their outward trip. Darwin was torn. At times he looked forward to a last walk in the tropical forest he had enjoyed so much, but at others he felt heartily fed up with the whole journey and longed to get home. He wrote that he now loathed and abhorred the sea and all ships which sail on it.

The old sailors had a name for this phenomenon of increasing homesickness the closer one got to home. They called it channel fever – a longing to be up the English Channel. The *Beagle* was still several thousand miles from home, but there is no doubt that Darwin had a bad case of channel fever.

When they reached Bahia in early August, he took long walks in the jungle around Salvador, trying, as he put it, to fix the impression in his mind. He knew that he would not be back. Then as soon as the sights and the chronometer rating were complete, they set off north once more. An ill-timed gale sent them scurrying for shelter into Pernambuco, or Recife as it is now called. He cared for neither the place nor the inhabitants, and when they finally sailed, he remarked that he was glad to be away from it, from them, and from Brazil.

They crossed the Equator on 21 August, almost at the same spot as on their southward journey. Since all the crew were shellbacks, little was made of the event, and they beat northwards against the trade winds.

Just nine days later they reached Porto Praya in the Cape Verdes for the second time. Once more they stopped for the obligatory six days for the chronometers before heading onwards for the Azores, their last stop. They anchored off Terceira, once again for just six days. It was here that Darwin fulfilled one of his wishes. He found an active volcano; it was a very small one, but at least it was bubbling with hot mud and larva.

The *Beagle* made a brief stop at San Miguel, hoping for mail, but there was none so Fitzroy decided to sail on. Finally, to Darwin's unutterable relief, they started the last leg of the voyage, to the English Channel. They had a quick passage of seven days, but the

weather was bad for most of it. Poor Darwin finished the voyage at least as seasick as he had begun it. The ship drove up channel with close-reefed topsails set, a blustery south-westerly gale blowing, and driving rain – a typical autumn day.

Just before dusk, on Sunday 2 October 1836, the *Beagle* dropped her anchor in the shelter of Falmouth Harbour. Darwin was weak from seven days of seasickness. It was late, the gale was still blowing and rain was pouring down. Nevertheless, Darwin was ashore that night to catch the night mail-coach heading eastwards. He had spent almost five years aboard the *Beagle*, and he was not going to spend another night on board if he could help it. It took him almost forty-eight hours to get home to Shrewsbury; the traveller had finally returned.

When the weather in Falmouth abated, Fitzroy took the *Beagle* up channel and eventually reached Greenwich. When he completed the last of his calculations, using the eleven chronometers that were still running, he found that an error of thirty-three seconds had crept in during the five-year circumnavigation. Although he was perhaps a little disappointed, perfectionist that he was, it was really a remarkable achievement, given the equipment they had to work with.

Darwin never travelled far again. He settled down to write about his experiences and the rest, as they say, is history.

I think that if the Panama Canal had been in existence when the *Beagle* left the Galapagos, they would have almost certainly come back that way; Fitzroy seemed just as anxious as Darwin to finish the voyage. Although there had been talk of building a canal since 1534, when the King of Spain commissioned a survey, it was not until 1880 that anybody tried to build it. The French, who made this first attempt, struggled for twenty years before giving up. Finally, in 1913, the Americans achieved what at one stage had looked impossible, and the canal was opened. *Beagle* was almost eighty years too early to take the short cut back to England.

After leaving the Galapagos, the first couple of days saw us sailing along in uncharacteristically fair breezes. It seemed as though our struggle to find fuel was going to prove unnecessary. We need not have worried, however. On the third day, true to form, the wind vanished and a persistent drizzle set in. We hoisted the iron topsail and motored steadily onwards.

As we approached the mainland, the skies began to clear and finally the rain stopped. At around 3 a.m. on the fifth day, a welcome green smudge of land appeared on the radar screen. By dawn, we were feeling our way in through dozens of anchored ships.

We anchored off the Balboa Yacht Club to complete the formalities and wait for permission to go through the canal. While there we were visited by the former President of Panama, a gentleman by the name of Aristides Royo, the man with whom President Carter had reached agreement on the handover of the canal to the Panamanians in the year 2000. He had been told about us by one of the Boss's South American contacts.

He came out on the yacht club launch, and leaped on board. I came up into the cockpit to meet him and introduce myself. He shook hands, tucked two gigantic cigars into the top pocket of my shirt and sat himself down. I was still standing there, rather open mouthed, when he waved his arm imperiously in my direction, and said, 'You may sit.' I sat down, for once completely at a loss for words. He then proceeded to invite us to join his family for a picnic on Flamingo Island the next day. He explained that a simple meal like a paella would suffice. I was vaguely nodding and grinning vacantly at him when it finally dawned on me that he was inviting the whole family to come on *Thalassi* for the day, and that Lana would be expected to cook a modest little paella for about fifteen people. We could do without that; we had work to do and an almost impossible schedule to keep.

Fortunately Jeff had been eavesdropping, and came to the rescue. He came breezing into the cockpit and told me that he had found the problem with the main engine, and hoped to have it running in a couple of days. Regretfully I explained to the President that the boat was immovable until Jeff fixed the engine, and much as we would have liked to take them all out for a picnic, we would have to postpone it until some future visit. Perhaps he realised that he was being conned, because he left almost at once, without even taking the tour of the boat we offered.

Eventually all the formalities were done, and the required certificates and permissions granted. The following Tuesday, we headed off through the canal. We had the obligatory pilot on board, and to bring the crew numbers up to the required five (the canal regulations require four crew to handle the lines in the locks, in addition to the helmsman) we took a young Canadian called Paul from a cruising boat. The pilot does not participate; he just issues instructions. Paul was happy to come for the ride, and to take a look before taking his own boat through later.

Going up through the three sets of locks was quite painless. *Thalassi* was moored in the middle of the lock chambers, and as she rose we tightened the four mooring lines using the hydraulic winches. It was all much easier than when I had been through a few years before in a much smaller boat. Most yachts have to take two days going through the canal, spending the night at Gamboa, about halfway through. But on *Thalassi* we were able to make enough speed to get through in a single day.

There was a slight hold-up as we came down the locks at the northern end, at Gatun. We were put into the lock ahead of a Japanese car-transport ship. The ship had only inches to spare on either side, and it was guided into the lock by eight powerful electric locomotives, which in canal parlance are termed 'mules'. Just as the ship was squeezing into the lock, and being drawn ever closer to our stern, there was a tremendous bang, and one of the mules all but disappeared in a cloud of smoke. It took them a long time to organise another one and finally get the ship far enough into the lock to close the gates. Despite the delay, we still managed to go all the way through, and be tied up at the Cristóbal Yacht Club before dark.

The twin cities of Cristóbal and Colón have long had an unsavoury reputation. We were firmly warned not to leave the yacht club compound on foot, but to go everywhere by taxi. We took the advice and had no problems. Jeff managed to organise a truck to deliver fuel to us, Lana topped up the provisions and Nick was sent off to get enough cigarettes for the Atlantic crossing. We did not want any chance of him running out again at sea.

That evening there were some riots in town and somebody was shot, so we decided to move out early the next morning. We had received word that the Boss had changed his mind, and was too busy to come to Panama. Instead he would meet us in Antigua in a couple of weeks. We left at first light, and motored out through the break-waters into a stiff easterly breeze. The short, steep seas were very uncomfortable, and we were not making much headway, but I was determined to make our scheduled stop in the San Blas Islands, with or without the Boss to share it.

I had been there before, but none of the others had, and Lana especially had been looking forward to it. I felt it would do us all good to have a couple of days off after the hustle and bustle of Panama. Everybody had been working hard and deserved a short break.

All day the wind blew hard, at least twenty-five knots, and it stayed right on the nose. Progress was slow and uncomfortable. Finally, in the late afternoon, the islands came into sight. The San Blas group consists of literally hundreds of tiny, flat islands, each rising only a few feet above sea level. When making a landfall there, the first things one sees are trees, which appear to grow out of the sea. One has to be quite close before the land itself becomes visible.

Although the wind was stronger than we might have wished for, at least the visibility was good. The charts for the area are not very good, and I was a little nervous as we felt our way in through the reef. Some close friends of ours had lost their boat trying to fetch this same anchorage. A rain-squall had come at the wrong moment, visibility had fallen to almost nothing, and in an instant they were on the reef. With an anxious eye to windward, therefore, watching for squalls, we found the pass through the reef, and soon anchored in the lee of the main island, Porvenire.

Within moments of the anchor splashing down, we were surrounded by at least half a dozen dugout canoes, each full of women and children. They were hoping to sell us the *molas* which have become synonymous with these islands. They are squares of cloth sewn together in layers. A pattern is formed by cutting through the various layers to expose the different colours – a sort of reverse appliqué. All the edges of the cuts are hemmed with minute hand-sewn stitches. The smaller and neater the stitches, the better the *mola*. For the local women, they form the front and back of the blouses of their very colourful costumes.

They climbed on board, and soon had the deck covered in a bright array of *molas*. If they were disappointed to find only four of us on board, they did not show it, but proceeded with the hard sell. Lana, who loves to bargain, was in heaven, and in no time had amassed a good collection of *molas*.

The women of the San Blas are very striking. They are small, all under 5 ft, and their features look rather Asian. What fascinated Nick more than anything else was the fact that each woman had a gold ring through her nose. Once the selling frenzy was over, they climbed back into their canoes, and returned from whence they had come.

I went ashore to Porvenire to hunt out Costumes and Intimidation. Although the islands are technically part of Panama, they are semi-autonomous, and so I was required to clear in with them. I found the office easily enough, but it was empty. I cast around and eventually found somebody in uniform at a little bar. He granted us permission to stay as long as we wanted – formalities over. By this time it was almost dark, so we saved the explorations for the next day.

After breakfast, I decided we ought to get the work out of the way before we went off to play. The bottom of the boat needed scrubbing again, so Jeff, Nick and I put on scuba tanks and scrubbed while Lana baked bread and did some varnishing. *Thalassi* never seemed bigger than when scrubbing her bottom, but at least we were in clean, warm water. It took most of the morning to finish, so we agreed that lunch and a nap were in order; then the explorations could begin.

The first island we went to was called Nuala Naga. It is a very small island and almost completely covered with small, neat houses. The walls of the houses are made from bamboo, and the roofs thatched with palm fronds. As we peered in through the open doorways, we could see that in most cases the only furnishings were a couple of hammocks suspended over the beaten earth floor.

Lana thought that the whole village looked like a toy town. The houses were very small and packed together, yet everywhere was neat and tidy. There was no litter anywhere, and even the sandy paths between the houses looked as if they had recently been brushed. There were coconut trees squeezed in between the houses, but no signs of any gardens. All the fruits and vegetables are grown on the mainland, to which the men commute by canoe.

The next day we dinghied over to the neighbouring island, Whichub Huala. This was not quite as spotless and tidy as the other, but it was certainly much cleaner than an equivalent community in the West Indies. Once again there were *molas* being offered at every turn, as well as necklaces and beads. A young boy tried to sell us a toucan. The bird's beak was so brightly coloured that it almost looked as if it had been painted.

I had planned to leave after lunch, but a big rain squall came rattling through. When it was still overcast and squally at 4.30, our departure was officially postponed until the next morning. Although going out through the reef would be easier than coming in, I did not want to take a chance of making a premature end to the voyage.

From the San Blas, the logical route to Britain would have been to go north, pass west of Cuba, then ride the Gulf Stream north into the Atlantic. The second choice would be to pass between Cuba and Haiti, through the Windward Passage. Neither of these routes were for us, however. The Boss had said he would be waiting for us in Antigua. The fact that the island lay some 1200 miles dead to windward did not seem to enter his calculations at all.

We had a most miserable trip east. I did not want to get too close to the Colombian coast, as stories abounded of boats being attacked or confiscated in those waters. We stayed a minimum of 20 miles offshore, and battled strong headwinds and an adverse current. We motorsailed the whole time, slamming and crashing our way to windward.

The fuel was going more quickly than Jeff had expected, and it was obvious that we would not have enough to get to the West Indies in one hop. I decided to pull into Curaçao for fuel, and to let us dry out. The thrashing to windward had shown us deck leaks that we had not even suspected were there. The eighteen-hour respite in Curaçao did us all good. Then, once the fuel tanks were filled up again, we set off once more. This time conditions were a lot easier. Since Venezuela is a lot safer than Colombia, we were able to hug the coast, clear of the worst of the current. Progress was much improved, and morale was even beginning to rise a little, when we got a message from the Boss He had changed his mind once more, and would not now be joining us in Antigua. We could have taken the easy route after all. A few choice words were uttered over dinner that night.

We were so close to the Grenadines now that I decided to stick to our original plan. Besides, our mail had been sent to Antigua, and we were not going to miss our first post since leaving Chile. We made our landfall on Union Island in the Grenadines, and met up with our long-time friends Rick and Sue, who were working there. Nick and Jeff went off diving while Lana and I caught up on a few years' worth of Grenadines gossip.

From Union we had a good sail up to Antigua, making just a brief stop in St Lucia for Jeff to borrow a welding machine to fix something in the engine-room, and for me to see an old ham radio friend who was dying of cancer. Antigua was as busy as ever. We collected our mail and all went for a last tropical swim, before heading out across the Atlantic.

Our crossing to the Azores was quite painless, with very light winds for most of the way, so once more the Mercedes did sterling duty to help us stay on schedule. We arrived in Horta, Faial, thirteen days out from Antigua, and burned about the last gallon of fuel motoring across the harbour.

Like Darwin at this stage of the voyage, we were all getting channel fever; we were anxious to finish the trip. Lana and I had told the Boss that we would take the boat to Britain, but would then leave. He had organised a busy schedule of race-following, followed by a session in a boatyard putting in a new mast and we did not relish either prospect. In the meantime, we had work to do to ready her for the last leg of the trip.

Once the work was done, we took a last day off to enjoy Faial, our favourite island in the Azores. Lana and I decided to hire horses, and ride up to the volcanic crater at the top of the island. Jeff decided to come with us, but Nick opted out, saying that his rear end had barely recovered from the last horse ride in the Galapagos.

This time the horses were better equipped, and the ride up to the crater was very pretty, with hydrangeas and wild roses fringing the roads. Nevertheless, four hours in the saddle turned out to be a bit much, and we were all a bit bow-legged as we staggered back on board that evening.

It did not take long for the weather to turn cold as we sailed north. Blankets came out, and we took to wearing shoes and socks on night watch. Like the *Beagle* we had a quick passage. We too took a week, although we went a little further than the *Beagle*. We escaped the gale they had, but went barrelling up channel with a brisk south-westerly, under grey skies. We made such good speed over the last 100 miles or so that we actually sailed up the Lymington River one tide sooner than our schedule had dictated.

By coincidence, Darwin had arrived late on a Sunday night, as we did. But unlike him, we were not free to escape immediately. Clearing with Costumes and Intimidation took some time, especially when we showed them the Boss's guns and ammunition. They were a bit put out when I suggested that they would need a wheelbarrow to shift all the ammunition to their bonded store.

Lana and I stayed on board for a couple of days to clean the boat and make her ready to hand over to George, who would run her during the race-following period. He would then deliver her to Holland for the new mast. The Boss came down, and settled the outstanding bills. Much to our relief, we were all paid up to date.

Suddenly it was over. We finished the last of the packing, said our goodbyes, and retreated to our cottage in Ireland. It had been a good trip, but we were more than ready to stop, at least until the next adventure comes along.

After the hustle, bustle and civil unrest of Panama, the San Blas Islands seemed especially peaceful and tranquil.

Specifications

*T*halassi was designed by Ron Holland, and built in 1986 by the Belliure brothers in Calpe, Spain.

Her length overall was 83 ft 7 in, but she has since been extended to 90 ft. Her beam is 19 ft 6 ins, and her draught, with the centre-board up, is 9 ft, and 16 ft with it down.

She is built of glass-reinforced plastic, with additional Kevlar strengthening in the bows. Her total weight is some 80 tons.

Her engine is a 250-horsepower Mercedes, which can give her a maximum speed under power of 11 knots. A more economical cruising speed is between 7 and 9 knots, and she has a range under power of about 3000 miles. She has two electrical generators, one of 16kW and the other of 10kW. The working sail area is 3680 square feet, and all the sails are controlled by hydraulic furlers and winches, allowing one person to set or trim any sail alone.

Her electronic aids include a Furuno 48-mile radar, Magnavox satellite navigator, a Furuno Loran C. and an Anschutz gyro compass. The instruments for wind direction and strength, as well as boat speed and heading, have read-outs on deck for the helmsman, and they are repeated in each cabin as well, so that while lying in my bunk I could open one eye to see if the wind had changed, or if we were still on course.

For communication, she carries an 800W Skanti radio, with telex capability. This let us talk to the UK on an almost daily basis.

Best of all was the autopilot, made by a German boffin called Mr Seeger. It was wonderful, and freed us almost completely from the chore of having to steer. It was worth at least half a dozen more crew.

Thalassi's watermaker is able to make 30 gallons of fresh water an hour from sea-water, so we never had to take on fresh water from ashore. There was always enough water for showering, washing clothes and for running the dishwasher in the galley.

The galley cooker is electric, powered by either generator, and we had two freezers, a fridge and a large walk-in cooler for storing fresh food.

In Patagonia, we carried five anchors: two CQR plough-type

anchors, two collapsible fisherman-type Luke anchors, and a very large Danforth. Our main CQR anchor was on 100 metres of chain, but we had rope rodes, with a short length of chain for each of the other anchors. The rope allowed us to set them from the dinghy if needed – chain would have been too heavy for us to handle. The anchors were recovered using the hydraulic windlass, an easy job for one person.

We carried three boats for getting ashore or exploring. The main dinghy was an 18 ft semi-rigid inflatable, with a 50-horsepower outboard. We also had a 14 ft pulling boat, built of Kevlar. This could be rowed, sailed or powered by a 6-horsepower outboard. Finally we had a 10 ft inflatable which was called the cook's dinghy, although Lana much prefered to use the big one!

We normally sailed with one person on deck and another on standby within earshot. So even when there were only four of us sailing the boat, we usually had twelve hours a day off duty – an undreamed of luxury for the *Beagle's* crew.

Beagle

*B*eagle was a Cherokee class brig, of which over a hundred were built between 1808 and 1837. She was built at the Woolwich Naval Dockyard, and launched on 11 May 1820. She stayed in naval service until 1845, when she became a Coast Guard watch vessel. She served in that role for fifteen years before being broken up in 1870.

By definition, a brig only has two masts, yet all illustrations of the *Beagle* show her to have three. The small mizzen mast, with its fore and aft sail was fitted for her first survey voyage, to make her easier to steer and handle in confined waters. Although this third mast makes her a barque, Darwin always referred to her as a brig.

She was 98 ft long on deck, only 15 ft longer than *Thalassi*, yet she carried seventy-four crew. In fair weather she could set as many as twenty-four sails, and each of these had to be hoisted, set, furled and trimmed by hand.

Although she was fitted with a new patent anchor windlass to replace the capstan, it was still powered by hand, and recovering an anchor from a deep Patagonian anchorage would have been hard work indeed.

She carried seven boats on deck, a 28 ft yawl, a 25 ft cutter, three 25 ft whale-boats, a 21 ft gig and the smallest, the dinghy. None was powered, they had to be sailed or rowed, and they covered many hundreds of miles while surveying.

Beagle of course had no electricity; the only light was from oil lamps or candles. She also had no engine; she had to be sailed or, if becalmed, towed by rowers in the whale-boats.

There were no facilities for cold storage. Meat was preserved in brine, or in the newly invented Kilner jars – the forerunners of canned food.

Water was always rationed, and they never missed a chance to top up the tanks. The amount of water they could carry effectively limited the time they could be at sea.

Life on board, especially in the cold of the southern ocean, must have been rough indeed. We had it easy by comparison.

Thalassi sailing past the Romanche Glacier in the Beagle Channel – the blue of the ice almost matching the colour of her hull. This was the first big glacier we saw, and it was probably on the beach opposite this glacier, that Darwin and crew nearly perished when an icefall sent a wave across the channel which almost washed their boats away.

Index

Index

Index